ALL STAR ENGLISH™

AN INTEGRATED ESL CURRICULUM

2

Teacher's Guide

A Publication of the World Language Division

Director of Product Development: Judith M. Bittinger
Executive Editor: Elinor Chamas
Editorial Development: Laura M. Alavosus
Angela Castro
Karen Howse
Kathleen M. Smith
Text and Cover Design: Taurins Design Associates
Art Direction and Production: Taurins Design Associates
Production/Manufacturing Services: James W. Gibbons
Permissions: Gina Herlihy, Anita Palmer
Audio Program: Handy Music, Inc.

ISBN 0-201-88532-8

1 2 3 4 5 6 7 8 9 10 - CRK - 00 99 98 97 96

ALL STAR ENGLISH

ALL STAR ENGLISH is an integrated curriculum designed for middle and secondary school students. **ALL STAR** is focused on communicative competence—the ability to use language appropriately in a variety of contexts.

ALL STAR ENGLISH recognizes that it is not enough to be able to read, write and understand basic language. One must be able to use language to get things done. **ALL STAR ENGLISH** encourages students to do just that, empowering them

- ☆ to communicate effectively
- ☆ to think critically
- ☆ to pursue academic success
- ☆ to build self-esteem
- ☆ to value cultural diversity

ALL STAR ENGLISH PREPARES STUDENTS FOR SCHOOL SUCCESS

- ☆ **THEMES**—units of study relevant to the immediate interests of young adolescents

- ☆ **CONTENT**—continuous links to the English curriculum to help prepare students for transition into mainstream studies

- ☆ **LITERATURE**—fiction and non-fiction selections from around the world to encourage students to value diversity and celebrate their own cultures

- ☆ **ACADEMIC AND SOCIAL LANGUAGE**—the competencies needed to compete in school and in a literate culture

- ☆ **LEARNING STRATEGIES AND HIGHER ORDER THINKING SKILLS**—essential building blocks to mainstream success

- ☆ **COLLABORATIVE LEARNING**—projects and activities that encourage active participation, self-sufficiency, and self-esteem

STUDENT TEXTS AND LEARNING TOOLS

TWO BEGINNER TEXTS GET STUDENTS OFF TO A GREAT START.

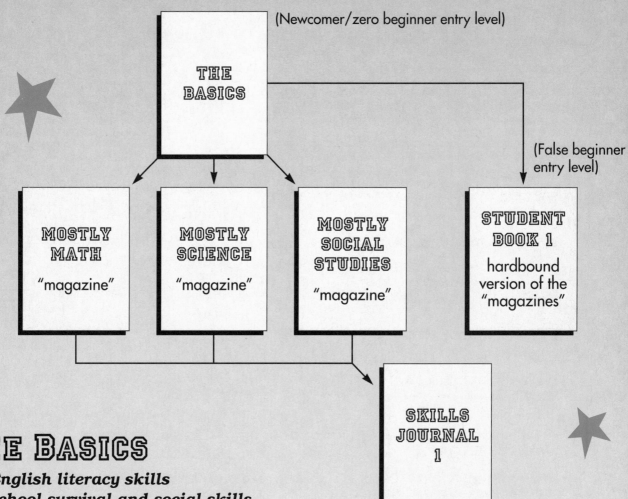

(Newcomer/zero beginner entry level)

THE BASICS

(False beginner entry level)

MOSTLY MATH "magazine"

MOSTLY SCIENCE "magazine"

MOSTLY SOCIAL STUDIES "magazine"

STUDENT BOOK 1 hardbound version of the "magazines"

SKILLS JOURNAL 1

THE BASICS

- *English literacy skills*
- *school survival and social skills*
- *fundamental grammar*
- *rapid vocabulary acquisition*
- *self-assessment*

STUDENT BOOK 1

- *content-based*
- *literature-based*
- *CALLA learning strategies*
- *links to mainstream curriculum*
- *collaborative learning*

UNIQUE LEARNING TOOLS POLISH SKILLS AND MAINTAIN INTEREST.

SKILLS JOURNAL

- *language practice and reinforcement of basic grammar*
- *guided and free writing responses to the reading experiences*
- *research activities*
- *self-assessment*

PROCESS WRITING PORTFOLIO PROGRAM

WRITING PROJECTS BOOK AND PORTFOLIO

- *topics and ideas expand upon specific ALL STAR selections*
- *brainstorming questions and activities for small group or individual creative thought*
- *simple to more complex writing assignments covering a wide variety of written genres*
- *editing exercises for polishing grammar and punctuation*

TEACHER HANDBOOK

- *the "how-to's" of establishing a systematic and satisfying writing program*
- *ways to motivate, monitor, and assess student progress*

BOOKBYTES CD-ROM

- *motivational tool for reading and responding to literature*
- *guided writing of book reviews, reports, and related activities*
- *extensive Booklists to encourage reading for pleasure and academic purposes*

STUDENT TEXTS AND LEARNING TOOLS

TWO COMPANION LEVELS BUILD ACADEMIC SKILLS AND CRITICAL THINKING.

STUDENT BOOKS

- *six unifying themes*
- *language development through content*
- *accelerated pace of purposeful reading, writing, and grammar activities*
- *multicultural literature*
- *recommended reading lists*
- *CALLA strategies*

SKILLS JOURNALS

- *language practice and reinforcement of basic grammar*
- *guided and free writing responses to the reading experiences*
- *research activities*
- *academic skill building*
- *self-assessment*

PROCESS WRITING PORTFOLIO PROGRAM

WRITING PROJECTS BOOK AND PORTFOLIO

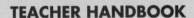

- *topics and ideas expand upon specific ALL STAR selections*
- *brainstorming questions and activities for small group or individual creative thought*
- *simple to more complex writing assignments covering a wide variety of written genres*
- *editing exercises for polishing grammar and punctuation*

TEACHER HANDBOOK

- *the "how-to's" of establishing a systematic and satisfying writing program*
- *ways to motivate, monitor, and assess student progress*

BOOKBYTES CD-ROM

- *motivational tool for reading and responding to literature*
- *guided writing of book reviews, reports, and related activities*
- *extensive Booklists to encourage reading for pleasure and information*

A Rich Array Of Language Development Through Content Activities Builds Understanding.

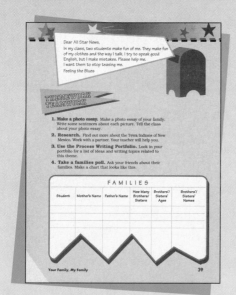

THEMEWORK/TEAMWORK

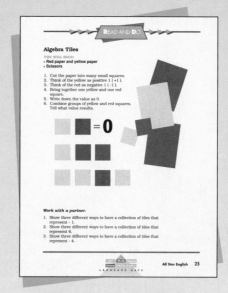

READ AND DO

CD ROM ADVENTURES

LANGUAGE POWER

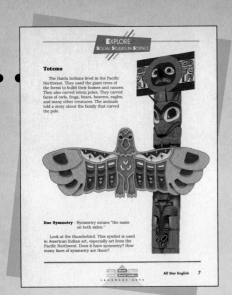

Totems

The Haida Indians lived in the Pacific Northwest. They used the giant trees of the forest to build their homes and canoes. They also carved totem poles. They carved faces of owls, frogs, bears, beavers, eagles, and many other creatures. The animals told a story about the family that carved the pole.

line Symmetry - Symmetry means "the same on both sides."

Look at the thunderbird. This symbol is used in American Indian art, especially art from the Pacific Northwest. Does it have symmetry? How many lines of symmetry are there?

All Star English   7

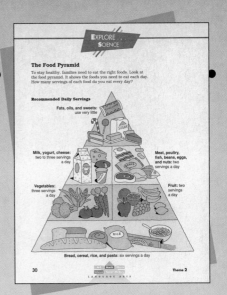

The Food Pyramid

To stay healthy, families need to eat the right foods. Look at the food pyramid. It shows the foods you need to eat each day. How many servings of each food do you eat every day?

Recommended Daily Servings

Fats, oils, and sweets: use very little

Milk, yogurt, cheese: two to three servings a day

Meat, poultry, fish, beans, eggs, and nuts: two servings a day

Vegetables: three servings a day

Fruit: two servings a day

Bread, cereal, rice, and pasta: six servings a day

30   Theme 2

← **EXPLORE** →
↓

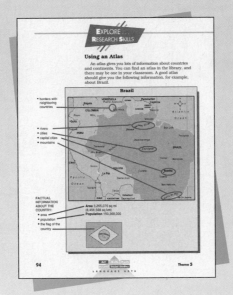

Using an Atlas

An atlas gives you lots of information about countries and continents. You can find an atlas in the library, and there may be one in your classroom. A good atlas should give you the following information, for example, about Brazil.

Brazil

- borders with neighboring countries
- rivers
- cities
- capital cities
- mountains

FACTUAL INFORMATION ABOUT THE COUNTRY:
- area
- population
- the flag of the country

Area 3,265,076 sq mi (8,456,508 sq km)
Population 150,368,000

94   Theme 5

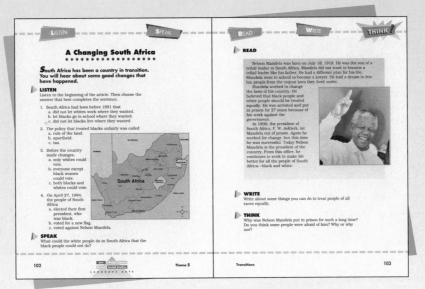

LISTEN   SPEAK   READ   WRITE   THINK

A Changing South Africa

South Africa has been a country in transition. You will hear about some good changes that have happened.

LISTEN
Listen to the beginning of the article. Then choose the answer that best completes the sentence.

1. South Africa had laws before 1991 that
   a. did not let whites work where they wanted.
   b. let blacks go to school where they wanted.
   c. did not let blacks live where they wanted.

2. The policy that treated blacks unfairly was called
   a. rule of the land.
   b. apartheid.
   c. tax.

3. Before the country made changes,
   a. only whites could vote.
   b. everyone except black women could vote.
   c. both blacks and whites could vote.

4. On April 27, 1994, the people of South Africa
   a. elected their first president, who was black.
   b. voted for a new flag.
   c. voted against Nelson Mandela.

SPEAK
What could the white people do in South Africa that the black people could not do?

102   Theme 5

READ

Nelson Mandela was born on July 18, 1918. He was the son of a tribal leader in South Africa. Mandela did not want to become a tribal leader like his father. He had a different plan for his life. Mandela went to school to become a lawyer. He had a dream to free his people from the unjust laws they lived under.

In 1990, the president of South Africa, F. W. deKlerk, let Mandela out of prison. Again he worked for change, but this time he was successful. Today Nelson Mandela is the president of the country. From this office, he continues to work to make life better for all the people of South Africa—black and white.

WRITE
Write about some things you can do to treat people of all races equally.

THINK
Why was Nelson Mandela put in prison for such a long time? Do you think some people were afraid of him? Why or why not?

Transitions   103

HOLISTIC ASSESSMENT

ix

MULTICULTURAL LITERATURE AND HIGH INTEREST MATERIAL MOTIVATE A LOVE OF READING.

PERSONAL RECOLLECTION

POETRY

FICTION

PHOTO ESSAYS

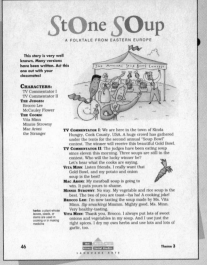

FOLKTALES

PLAYS

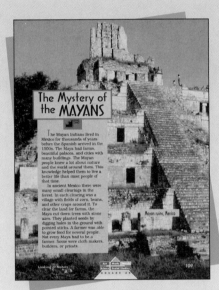

ARTICLES

ALL STAR NEWS
READING FOR INFORMATION AND FUN

ALL STAR TEACHING TOOLS

INNOVATIVE, TIME-SAVING TOOLS MAKE TEACHING EASY AND REWARDING.

TEACHER'S GUIDES

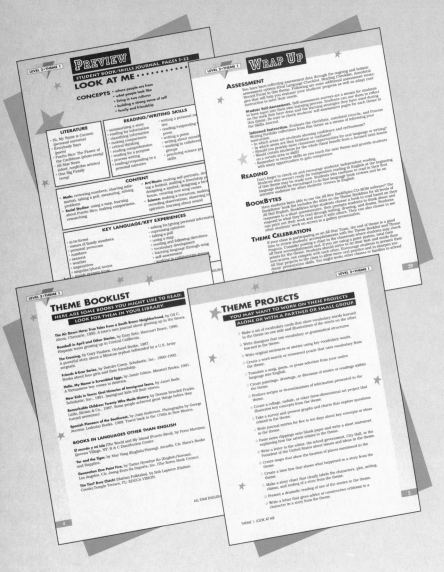

All Star Guides Provide

- *Theme Previews— clear, succinct outlines of theme content*

- *Theme Booklists— reproducible pages for students to promote independent reading for pleasure and information*

- *Theme Projects— reproducible pages for students to promote collaborative learning and independent research*

- *Theme Wrap Ups— assessment and celebration ideas for theme closure*

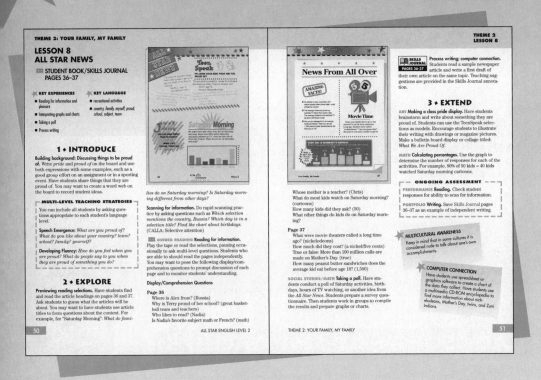

- *Three-step teaching plans—easy-to-follow, complete plans*
- *Multi-level teaching options—applications of the Natural Approach to include all students*
- *Ongoing assessment—reliable ways to monitor student progress*

AUDIO CASSETTE PROGRAM

- *professionally recorded*
- *high quality renderings of Student Book selections*
- *ideal for initial presentations, listening centers, individual practice*

PLACEMENT AND ASSESSMENT PACKAGES

- *easy-to-administer placement test*
- *observation checklists*
- *anecdotal records and charts*

THE ALL STAR ENGLISH TEAM OF EDUCATORS

Charles Skidmore is Assistant Headmaster for Curriculum at Brighton High School, Brighton Massachusetts. He is the recipient of the Golden Apple Award and the Harvard Prize Book, both awarded to outstanding teachers in the Boston Public Schools. He has authored many successful titles for secondary and adult ESL students.

Patricia Richard-Amato is Professor Emeritus at Cal State, Los Angeles. She has worked extensively with second language students from around the world, and has authored a number of successful titles for ESL teachers and students.

Anne Marie Drayton is an ESL teacher in the Boston Public Schools. She has extensive experience in developing curriculum for secondary and adult ESL students.

Wendy Abbott Hansen is a former teacher in the Minnesota Public Schools. She specializes in literature-based curriculum for middle school and secondary ESL students.

Carolyn Grigsby is a Mentor Teacher in the Jefferson School District, Daly City, CA. She has developed extensive material for ESL upper elementary and middle school ESL students.

THE AUTHORS AND EDITORS THANK ALL THE TEACHERS AND STUDENTS WHO CONTRIBUTED TO THE DEVELOPMENT OF ALL STAR ENGLISH. SPECIAL ACKNOWLEDGMENT TO:

REVIEWERS/ADVISORS/FIELD TEST TEACHERS

Beverly J. Adams, Tehipite Middle School, Fresno, CA

Elvira Perez-Ayala, San Antonio Independent School District, San Antonio, TX

Victoria Delgado, Supervisor of Bilingual Education, CSD #32, Brooklyn, NY

Debra Ettenberg, Assistant Director of Instruction, Planning and Technology, BOCES, Commack, NY

Faye Flores, Hastings High, Alief Independent School District, Alief, TX

Jo Kozicki Fritschel, San Diego City Schools, San Diego, CA

Beth Harris, ESL/Bilingual Coordinator, Alief Independent School District, Alief, TX

Ana Hernandez, Master Teacher, Consultant, Hawthorne, CA

Virginia Jama, New York City Board of Education, New York City, NY

Linda New Levine, ESL Consultant, Lake Katonah, NY

Linda Lewis-White, Thornton Elementary School, Arlington, TX

John Mundahl, Resource Teacher, Minneapolis Public Schools, Minneapolis, MN

Angie Sagastume, San Francisco Unified School District, San Francisco, CA

Melanie Uzzell, Houston Independent School District, Houston, TX

Lavonne Walker, Medford School District, Medford, OR

Phyllis Ziegler, Director of ESL, New York City Board of Education, New York City, NY

FIELD TEST STUDENT REVIEWERS

Erick Almanza
Ruben Aguirre
Bertha Arciga
Janette Baza
Voeun Bun
Alberto Camarenas
Koua Cha
Chanh Chanthirong
Antonio Fernandez
Gerardo Hernandez

Luis Leonardo
Tony Douang Kham
Daniel Murillo
Nung Noum
Vanessa Ramos
Amalia Resendez
Daniel Ruiz
Erika Ruiz
Alex Sancedo

Dia Vang
Mai Kaying Vang
May Vang
Mee Vang
Gregorio Villqueal
Lee Xiong
Pao Xiong
Xiong Xiong
Koua Yang

CONTENTS

PREVIEW

STUDENT BOOK/SKILLS JOURNAL, PAGES 3–22

LOOK AT ME • • • • • • • • • • • • • •

CONCEPTS
- where people are from
- what people look like
- living in two cultures
- building a strong sense of self
- family and friendship

LITERATURE

- Hi, My Name is Carmen *(personal narrative)*
- Everybody Says *(poem)*
- Puerto Rico: The Flower of the Caribbean *(photo essay)*
- All Star News *(short, nonfiction articles)*
- One Big Family *(song)*

READING/WRITING SKILLS

- summarizing a story
- reading for information
- classifying information
- making comparisons
- critical thinking
- reading comprehension
- reading for a purpose
- process writing
- reading/responding to a personal narrative
- writing a personal narrative
- reading/responding to a poem
- writing a poem
- writing about oneself
- working in collaborative groups
- practicing science process skills

CONTENT

- **Math:** reviewing numbers, charting information, taking a poll, measuring, solving problems
- **Social Studies:** using a map, learning about Puerto Rico, making comparisons, researching
- **Art/Music:** making self-portraits, describing a festival, making a friendship poster, designing a symbol, designing a bird house, creating new song verses
- **Science:** making a terrarium, making and recording observations, observing transpiration, learning about sound

KEY LANGUAGE/KEY EXPERIENCES

- *to be* forms
- names of family members
- personal pronouns
- numbers
- seasons
- weather
- imperatives
- singular/plural nouns
- simple present tense
- introducing oneself/classmates
- asking for/giving personal information
- expressing opinions
- taking a poll
- using a map
- reading and following directions
- vocabulary development
- learning language through song
- self-assessment
- working in collaborative groups
- practicing science process skills

THEME BOOKLIST/ THEME PROJECTS

As this new theme begins, photocopy the Theme Booklist/Theme Projects pages (following spread) for students. Encourage students to read as many books as they like from the Booklist, and to complete any of the assignments on the Project list as homework for this theme.

AWARDING POINTS FOR ALL STAR TEAMS

This is a good opportunity to motivate students through an All Star Team approach. Consider assigning point values to each project, including reading books from the booklist. Explain to students that they will accumulate points for each book they read or project they complete during the theme. Students will try to top their own scores as they work through each theme, competing against themselves, not each other. Remind students that they will have the opportunity to present their *All Star* projects to the class at the end of the theme.

BOOKBYTES

If you have a computer with a CD-ROM drive available, introduce students to the *All Star BookBytes* software which is correlated to the Theme Booklists throughout *All Star English*. *BookBytes* categorizes the books by genre and helps students choose a book to read based on their answers to a short questionnaire. It then prompts students to think about and respond to what they've read through writing, drawing, and drama activities. Students can print out their work and share it with others or view work on-screen in a gallery presentation.

THEME BOOKLIST

HERE ARE SOME BOOKS YOU MIGHT LIKE TO READ.
LOOK FOR THEM IN YOUR LIBRARY.

The Air Down Here: True Tales from a South Bronx Neighborhood, by Gil C. Alicea. Chronicle, 1995. A teen's own journal about growing up in the Bronx.

Baseball in April and Other Stories, by Gary Soto. Harcourt Brace, 1990. Hispanic teens growing up in Central California.

The Crossing, by Gary Paulsen. Orchard Books, 1987.
A powerful story about a Mexican orphan befriended by a U.S. Army sergeant.

Friends 4-Ever Series, by Deirdre Corey. Scholastic, Inc., 1990–1992. Books about four girls and their friendship.

Hello, My Name is Scrambled Eggs, by Jamie Gilson. Minstrel Books, 1991. A Vietnamese boy comes to America.

New Kids in Town: Oral Histories of Immigrant Teens, by Janet Bode. Scholastic, Inc., 1991. Immigrant kids tell their stories.

Remarkable Children: Twenty Who Made History, by Dennis Brindell Fradin. Little, Brown & Co., 1987. Some people achieved great things before they turned seventeen!

Spanish Pioneers of the Southwest, by Joan Anderson. Photographs by George Ancona. Lodestar Books, 1989. Travel back to the 1700s in New Mexico.

BOOKS IN LANGUAGES OTHER THAN ENGLISH

El mundo y mi isla (The World and My Island [Puerto Rico]), by Perez Martínez. Queens Village, NY: R & C Distribution Center.

Yer and the Tiger, by May Yang (English/Hmong). Arcadia, CA: Shen's Books and Supplies.

Generation One Point Five, by Tanya Hyonhye Ko (English/Korean). Los Angeles, CA: Jeong-Eum-Sa Imports, Inc. (The Korea Book Center).

Tim Tim? Bwa Chèch! (Haitian Folktales), by Bob Lapierre (Haitian Creole).Temple Terrace, FL: EDUCA VISION.

THEME PROJECTS

YOU MAY WANT TO WORK ON THESE PROJECTS ALONE OR WITH A PARTNER OR SMALL GROUP.

☆ Make a set of vocabulary cards that show vocabulary words learned in the theme on one side and illustrations of the words on the other.

☆ Write dialogues that use vocabulary or grammatical structures learned in the theme.

☆ Write original sentences or stories using key vocabulary words.

☆ Create a word search or crossword puzzle that uses vocabulary from the theme.

☆ Translate a song, poem, or prose selection from your native language into English.

☆ Create paintings, drawings, or dioramas of stories or readings within the theme.

☆ Produce scripts or dramatizations of information presented in the theme.

☆ Create a collage, mobile, or other three-dimensional art project that illustrates key concepts from the theme.

☆ Take a survey and present graphs and charts that explore questions related to the theme.

☆ Write journal entries for five to ten days about key concepts or ideas in the theme.

☆ Paste news clippings onto blank paper and write a short statement explaining how the article relates to the theme.

☆ Write a letter to the editor, the school government, City Hall, or the President of the United States about issues and ideas in the theme.

☆ Create maps that show the location of places mentioned in the theme.

☆ Create a time line that shows what happened in a story from the theme.

☆ Make a story chart that clearly labels the characters, plot, setting, climax, and ending of a story from the theme.

☆ Present a dramatic reading of one of the stories in the theme.

☆ Write a letter that gives advice or constructive criticism to a character in a story from the theme.

LESSON 1
THEME OPENER

STUDENT BOOK/SKILLS JOURNAL PAGE 3

 KEY EXPERIENCES

- Introducing oneself/classmates
- Previewing theme content and titles
- Playing a name matching game
- Discovering the library
- Self-assessment

KEY LANGUAGE

- *Hi. I'm ... What's your name?*
- *My name is ...*
- *His/her name is ...*
- *to be* forms

MATERIALS

- magazines or newspapers with pictures of friends

1 • INTRODUCE

Theme 1, Look at Me, focuses on students' abilities to communicate personal information. Students will ask and answer questions about family, names, addresses, and phone numbers. They will learn about Puerto Rico and discuss their own places of origin.

Building background: Introductions. Introduce yourself to the class; greet students and ask for their first and last names. Have students write their names on name tags or on index cards and decorate them if they wish. Students can practice introducing themselves and classmates.

MULTI-LEVEL TEACHING STRATEGIES

You can include all students by asking questions appropriate to each student's language level.

Speech Emergence: *Is your first name Olga or Elena? Please say your last name for me.* Point to one of the students. *What is his name?*

Developing Fluency: *Spell your name for me.*

2 • EXPLORE

Activating prior knowledge. Open to page 3. Read the unit title "Look at Me" aloud. To prompt discussion, ask multi-level questions such as *How many children do you see? Are there more boys or more girls? How old are they? Do they look like you?*

Reading Corner. Have students read the titles, authors, and descriptions of the three books listed under Reading Corner. These are just a few selections from the Theme Booklist, chosen to help motivate students to want to read. Have the books available for students to look at. Prompt discussion about which book each student would like to read and why. Allow students to sign up for turns with the books. Use this experience to get your students excited about reading.

Previewing unit content. Guide students as they look through the unit, inviting them to comment on titles, photos, and art. Call on volunteers to read the selection titles aloud.

 **Activating prior knowledge; self-assessment.** Students complete chart before and after lesson. Teaching suggestions are provided in the Skills Journal annotation.

3 • EXTEND

Playing a name matching game. Split the class into four equal groups. Students in each group mix up their name tags or cards. Two groups work cooperatively to match cards or tags to students by asking each other questions. (CALLA: Cooperation)

Discovering the library. Lead students on a tour of your school or local library. With students, gather the books recommended for this theme in the Theme Booklist. Students will enjoy participating in this search and, in so doing, will practice basic library and research skills. In the classroom, plan to read aloud to students each day. You may wish to record the books on tape and let students read the books as they listen to the tapes. Encourage students to read independently whenever possible.

THEME 1

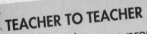

Reading Corner

Try these terrific books!

New Kids in Town
by Janet Bode
Immigrant kids tell their stories.

Hello, My Name is Scrambled Eggs
by Jamie Gilson
A Vietnamese boy comes to America.

Friends 4-Ever
by Deirdre Corey
Books about four girls and their friendship.

3

◆ TEACHER'S NOTES ◆

BOOKBYTES

Have students use the BookBytes software as motivation for reading and writing about what they've read.

TEACHER TO TEACHER

If other teachers can pronounce your students' names, students in other classes will have a model to follow. After you have had a chance to meet with your class and get the names yourself, you can provide assistance by passing along a list with phonetic clues.

MULTICULTURAL AWARENESS

Keep in mind that in some cultures people are addressed by last name; also, in some cultures family name precedes first name.

LESSON 2
HI, MY NAME IS CARMEN

 STUDENT BOOK/SKILLS JOURNAL PAGES 4–6

⭐ **KEY EXPERIENCES**

- Reading/responding to a personal narrative
- Writing a personal narrative
- Using a map

⭐ **MATERIALS**

- map/photographs showing Puerto Rico
- travel brochures

⭐ **KEY LANGUAGE**

- *My name is ...*
- *I'm from ...*
- *spare time, basement, artist, astronaut, allowance, workshop*
- *to be* forms
- names of family members

Hi, My Name is Carmen

Hi, my name is Carmen Ortiz. I'm from Puerto Rico, but I live in New York now. I live with my parents and my brother, José. I am 13 years old. José is 15 years old. We both have brown hair and brown eyes like our parents.

My father is a truck driver. In his spare time, he likes to make things out of wood. He has a workshop in the basement. My mother is an artist. She paints beautiful pictures. People buy her paintings.

4   Theme 1

1 ◆ INTRODUCE

Building background: Discussing Puerto Rico. Tell students they are going to read about a girl from Puerto Rico. Have a volunteer find Puerto Rico on a map. Find out what students already know about this island and its people. If possible, use photographs and travel brochures to introduce new information. List vocabulary generated during the discussion on the board.

MULTI-LEVEL TEACHING STRATEGIES

You can include all students by asking questions appropriate to each student's language level.

Speech Emergence: *Is Puerto Rico part of the U.S.? What languages do people speak in Puerto Rico?*

Developing Fluency: *Where is Puerto Rico? What do you think the weather is like there?*

Making a family word web. With students, brainstorm a list of words for family members. Encourage students to include alternates such as *mother/mom* or *father/dad* as well as the words they use in their own languages.

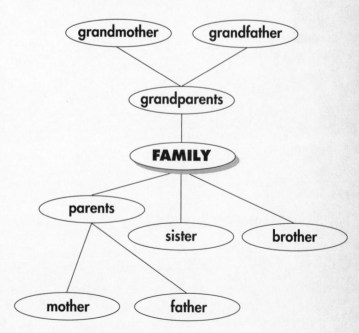

My favorite color is red, and my favorite thing to wear is my red sweater. I love to read. I go to the library every week because I want to know everything about the world. I want to go to college. I want to be a math teacher or an astronaut.

My best friend is Carolina Hernandez. She is from Mexico. We like to go to the mall on weekends. We like to windowshop, but sometimes we buy things.

Carolina loves music. She buys CDs with her allowance. She wants to be a musician. I'm saving my money for college, but sometimes I buy earrings.

USA

Mexico City

Look at Me   5

2 ◆ EXPLORE

Activating prior knowledge. Open to page 4 and invite a volunteer to read the title, "Hi, My Name Is Carmen," aloud. Then have students look through the photo essay, commenting on the pictures. To prompt discussion, ask multi-level questions.

GUIDED READING Reading a personal narrative. Read the story aloud or play the tape once through as students follow along in their books. Reread the story, pausing at the end of each page to discuss. Students who are able to should read independently. You may want to pose the following display/comprehension questions to prompt discussion of each page and monitor students' understanding.

Display/Comprehension Questions

Page 4
Is the girl's first name Carmen or Ortiz? (Carmen)
How many people are in Carmen's family? (four including Carmen)

What is her father's job? (truck driver)
Is her mother an artist or a teacher? (artist)
Do people buy her mother's paintings? (yes)

Page 5
Does Carmen like blue or red better? (red)
What's her favorite pastime? (reading)
How often does Carmen go to the library? (every week)
What does Carmen want to be? (math teacher or astronaut)
Carmen and Carolina are both from places where Spanish is spoken. True or false. (true—background knowledge)
What does Carmen's friend love? (music)
What is an allowance? (Answers will vary.)
Does she buy tapes or CDs? (CDs)

Page 6
What does Carmen miss about Puerto Rico? (friends, food, music, dancing)
Show me what a smile is. Now find the words *smiles* and *smile* on the page.
Why is Carmen happy to be in New York?

Discussing a personal narrative. Discuss what makes this piece a personal narrative. Help students look for clues in the title and in the story itself. Ask multi-level questions such as *How do you know Carmen is writing about herself? Find the word "my" in the title. Now count the words "my" in the story. What other words tell you that Carmen is writing about herself?*

Your Turn. With the class, read the discussion questions listed under "Your Turn." You may want to expand upon the text questions with the following Reference Questions to help students express personal information and opinions.

Reference Questions
What do your mother and father do?
What are your favorite things to do?
Who is your best friend?
What do you like to do together?
What job do you want when you are older?
What is your home country?
What do you miss about it?
Would you want to be friends with Carmen or

Carolina? Why or why not?
How much do you think Carolina gets for an allowance?

 **SKILLS JOURNAL PAGES 4-6** **Page 4: Data collection.** Students compile personal information and information from the reading. **Page 5: Practicing key vocabulary.** Students complete cloze paragraphs. **Page 6: Using adjectives.** Students describe cartoon characters using words from a data bank. Teaching suggestions are provided in the Skills Journal annotations.

3 ◆ EXTEND

SOCIAL STUDIES Using a map. Students can work in pairs or small groups to trace possible routes from Puerto Rico to New York. Ask students to develop a list of possible entry points into the mainland U.S. and means of transportation. Circulate and assist with vocabulary as needed. Later, have students share their ideas with the class. (CALLA: Imagery)

Writing a personal narrative. Students can use the story as a model for their own personal narratives. Suggest that students include drawings or photographs with their narratives.

Grammar in context. Many students will benefit from rewriting the narrative in the third person. Point out the *-s/-es* endings of all the verbs. Further extend this important grammatical point with a board chart that displays other common verbs under pronoun headings:

I/You	He/She/It	We/They
smile	smiles	smile
listen	listens	listen

Home-School Connection: Sharing words for family. Refer to the word web from Introduce. Encourage the students to expand the web by contributing as many words as they can think of for family members in their own languages. Be sure to label each word with the name of the language and/or culture

*S*ome days, I really miss Puerto Rico, I miss my friends. I miss the food, the music, and the dancing. Other days, I am happy to be in New York. My family is here. My new friends are here. Carolina says, "Carmen, you are my best friend." And then she smiles. I smile, too.

 **YOUR TURN** Talk about yourself. Tell a partner about your family. What are your favorite things? What do you like about the United States?

6   Theme 1

group. Invite students to select five words to share with their families and practice at home.

PROCESS WRITING PORTFOLIO See the list of ideas and writing topics related to this theme.

----- **ONGOING ASSESSMENT** -----

PERFORMANCE Oral language. Ask individual students to summarize what they learned about Carmen. As needed, guide students with multi-level questions.

✦ TEACHER'S NOTES ✦

PREDICTABLE PROBLEMS

The word *island* will probably come up during discussion. Make sure students understand that the s in *island* is silent. Can students cite other words that contain silent letters?

MULTICULTURAL AWARENESS

Explore the music of Puerto Rico: the salsa, bomba y plena. Encourage students to bring in favorite songs from their cultures. Compare and contrast. Play recordings of Pablo Casals and other classical musicians.

THEME 1: LOOK AT ME

LESSON 3
EVERYBODY SAYS

 **STUDENT BOOK/SKILLS JOURNAL PAGE 7**

⭐ **KEY EXPERIENCES**
- Reading/responding to a poem
- Writing a poem
- Making comparisons
- Making self-portraits

⭐ **KEY LANGUAGE**
- *look like,*
- *the image of*

⭐ **MATERIALS**
- pictures of families

EVERYBODY SAYS
DOROTHY ALDIS

Everybody says
I look just like my mother.
Everybody says
I'm the image of Aunt Bee.
Everybody says
My nose is like my father's
But I want to look like ME!

YOUR TURN Do you look like anyone in your family? Talk about this with a partner.

Look at Me

Art Math Music
Science Social Studies
LANGUAGE ARTS

7

1 ◆ INTRODUCE

Building background: Describing people. Show pictures of family groups. Ask students to describe the people's hair color, eye color, height, weight, nose, skin, and expressions. Invite students to point out similarities and differences among the people. Students can guess the family relationships in the pictures.

MULTI-LEVEL TEACHING STRATEGIES

You can include all students by asking questions appropriate to each student's language level.

Speech Emergence: *Is her hair long? Who is happy? Do they look the same or different? What color are her eyes?*

Developing Fluency: *What does she look like? Tell me about his face. How are they the same? How are they different?*

Making comparisons. Use student ideas to create a Venn diagram to show similarities and differences among the people in the photos. (CALLA: Grouping)

2 ◆ EXPLORE

Activating prior knowledge. Ask students to look at the title of the poem and the picture on page 7. To prompt discussion, ask multi-level questions such as *Do you look like someone in your family? Who do you want to look like?*

 **GUIDED READING Reading a poem.** Read or play the tape for the poem as students follow along in their books. Read the poem again chorally. Ask questions to check understanding: *Who does she look like? Does she like to be compared to others in her family? Why? Who does she want to look like?*

Independent reading. Have students read the poem silently. Then have volunteers read the poem aloud.

 **SKILLS JOURNAL PAGE 7** **Discussing a poem.** Encourage students to discuss how the poem makes them feel. Ask if they like the poem and have them explain why or why not.

What do they like best about the poem? How do they think the author of the poem feels? Do they feel the same way?

Home-School connection; creative writing. Students complete a cloze poem. Teaching suggestions are provided in the Skills Journal annotation.

3 ♦ EXTEND

Writing a poem. Encourage students to discuss other similarities between people. Write student ideas on the board: *I walk just like..., I act just like..., I talk just like..., I sound just like..., Tuan looks just like....* Students can work individually to create a poem about themselves or each student can contribute one line to create a class poem.

ART Making self-portraits. Have students create self-portraits to illustrate their poems. Students might use pencil, charcoal, cut paper, or markers on a variety of papers, or they might create photo collages by cutting up magazines and using illustrations that describe their features or interests. Encourage individuality.

- - - ONGOING ASSESSMENT - - -

PERFORMANCE Oral language. Have students read the poem they wrote on Skills Journal page 7.

PORTFOLIO Writing. Save Skills Journal page 7 as an example of independent writing.

★ **PREDICTABLE PROBLEM**
Students may be confused with the two meanings of *like*. *What do you like? Who do you look like?* Help students distinguish between the two meanings. Present *look like* as a useful expression.

★ **LANGUAGE NOTE**
As needed, explain that *just* in this case means *exactly*.

LESSON 4
LANGUAGE POWER

STUDENT BOOK/SKILLS JOURNAL
PAGES 8–9

★ KEY EXPERIENCES

- Talking about ID cards
- Asking for and giving personal information
- Reviewing numbers
- Making an ID card
- Charting information
- Making a class directory

★ KEY LANGUAGE

- *to be* forms
- personal pronouns
- numbers

★ MATERIALS

- index cards

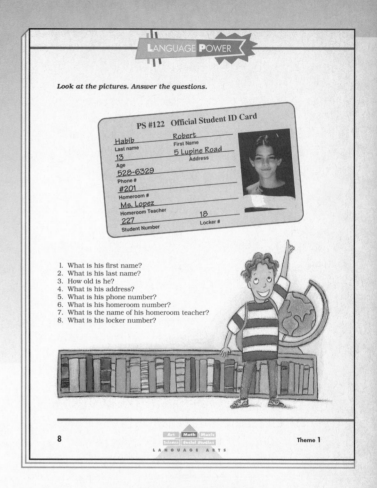

1 ◆ INTRODUCE

Building background: Personal information. Display for the students your driver's license and other ID cards, such as a library card or Social Security card. Point to information on one of your ID cards as you say: *My first name is .... My last name is.... My address is ....* Ask students what information the cards tell about you: *What is my first name? What is my last name? What is my address?* (CALLA: Activating prior knowledge)

┌ MULTI-LEVEL TEACHING STRATEGIES ┐

You can include all students by asking questions appropriate to each student's language level.

Speech Emergence: *What is your last name? How old are you?*

Developing Fluency: *What is your address? What is the name of your homeroom teacher? Write your name and address for me.*

Reviewing numbers and letters. Have students volunteer to write their names, addresses, and phone numbers on the board. Ask the class to read aloud the information in order to review numbers. Ask volunteers to identify the beginning letters of the students' names.

2 ◆ EXPLORE

Activating prior knowledge. Open to pages 8–9. To prompt discussion, ask multi-level questions such as *What do you see in the pictures? Do the ID cards include the students' names? What else do the ID cards tell about the students?*

Exploring key vocabulary. As needed, point out that "ID" is short for "identification." Explain that "PS" is used in New York City as the abbreviation for "public school" and that this is school number 122. Invite volunteers to explain *homeroom* and *locker*.

GUIDED READING Reading questions. Ask students to follow along as you read through all the questions. Then model asking and answering the first question. Read or have volunteers read the remaining questions and ask for students to volunteer responses.

Grammar in context. Stress the use of *he/his, she/her* and the singular *is*. Practice and contrast third person *they/are* usage by posing questions

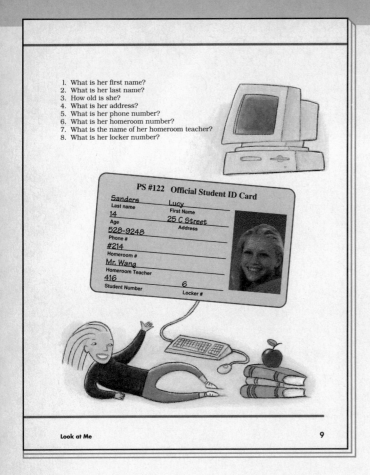

1. What is her first name?
2. What is her last name?
3. How old is she?
4. What is her address?
5. What is her phone number?
6. What is her homeroom number?
7. What is the name of her homeroom teacher?
8. What is her locker number?

PS #122   **Official Student ID Card**

Last name *Sanders*   First Name *Lucy*
Age *14*   *25 C Street*
Phone # *528-9248*   Address
Homeroom # *#214*
Homeroom Teacher *Mr. Wang*
Student Number *416*   Locker # *6*

Look at Me   9

Page 8: Vocabulary development. Students complete their school schedules. **Page 9: Writing.** Students list class and school rules. Teaching suggestions are provided in the Skills Journal annotations.

3 ◆ EXTEND

MATH Charting information. As a whole class activity, encourage students to make a chart that classifies information from their ID cards. For example, students might record the different ages and how many students of each age are represented in the class, how many different first names there are, how many different homeroom teachers. (CALLA: Grouping)

Making a class directory. Invite students to compile a class directory of students' names, addresses, and phone numbers. Encourage students to plan the tasks required to make the directory and then to divide the tasks among themselves. Review or teach alphabetizing as needed. (CALLA: Cooperation)

ONGOING ASSESSMENT

PERFORMANCE Oral language. Circulate to observe the students' proficiency at exchanging personal information as they ask and answer questions about their ID cards.

about information in common such as *What are their ID numbers? What is the name of their school? Where do they go to school? Are they in the same homeroom? Are they the same age?* You may also pose questions about your own class to practice third person *we/are.*

Pronunciation: Usage of numbers. As you read the numbers with students, help them understand the different conventions for saying the numbers for age (*thirteen,* not *one three*), telephone (*five two eight six three two nine*), room (*two oh one* or *two hundred one*), locker (*eighteen*). Practice other examples.

Pair work. Have students work in pairs and use the questions on pages 8–9 to practice asking for and giving personal information.

Making an ID card. Pass out index cards. Have students make their own personal ID cards, using the ID cards illustrated on pages 8–9 as models. Have students exchange cards and work in small groups to ask and answer questions about others.

★ **MULTICULTURAL AWARENESS**
Keep in mind that in some cultures people are addressed by last name; also, in some cultures family name precedes first name.

LESSON 5
EXPLORE. . . SCIENCE

STUDENT BOOK/SKILLS JOURNAL
PAGES 10–11

★ KEY EXPERIENCES

- Reading/following written directions

- Discussing rain forests

- Building a rain forest model

- Making and recording observations

- Reading for information

- Using a chart

★ KEY LANGUAGE

- *gravel, jar, pebbles, plants, rain forest, soil, water*

★ MATERIALS

- pictures of rain forests

- large glass jars with lids

- gravel or pebbles

- small plants, such as ferns, ivies, moss

- soil

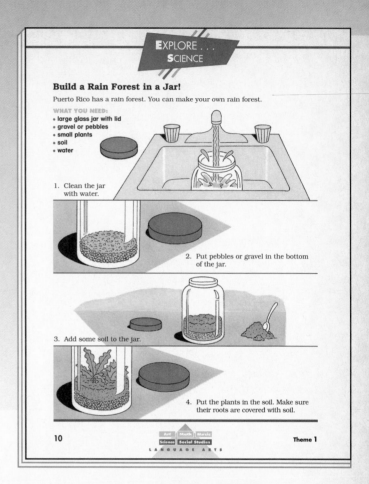

1 ◆ INTRODUCE

Building background: Discussing rain forests. Display pictures of jungles and other rain forests. Explain that a rain forest is a large, very thick growth of trees and plants that usually have large, broad leaves. Help students observe that they are called rain forests because they grow in areas with a great deal of rain.

⌐ MULTI-LEVEL TEACHING STRATEGIES ¬

You can include all students by asking questions appropriate to each student's language level.

Speech Emergence: *What is a forest? Why is the forest in the picture called a rain forest?*

Developing Fluency: *What kinds of plants grow in rain forests? In what parts of the world are rain forests?*

2 ◆ EXPLORE

Activating prior knowledge. Open to pages 10–11. Read aloud the title, "Build a rain forest in a jar!" To prompt discussion, ask multi-level questions such as *What do the pictures show? What do you think we are going to do?* (CALLA: Predicting)

Exploring key vocabulary. Show students the materials needed for the activity and have volunteers identify the items. Have students read aloud with you the list of materials. Ask volunteers to name the plants that are pictured. Have students tell what pebbles and gravel are and give other words that mean the same as or almost the same as *soil* (*dirt, ground, land*).

GUIDED READING Reading directions. Read the directions for the activity while students follow along. Have students reread independently. Then ask multi-level questions such as *What do you put in the jar first? Then what do you put in? How large do you think the plants will grow?*

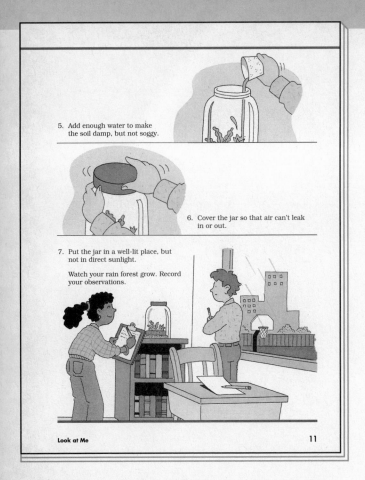

5. Add enough water to make the soil damp, but not soggy.

6. Cover the jar so that air can't leak in or out.

7. Put the jar in a well-lit place, but not in direct sunlight.

Watch your rain forest grow. Record your observations.

Look at Me   11

Building the rain forest model. In small groups, students build model rain forests. Circulate and help them. If students are having difficulty, demonstrate or have a volunteer do so. Caution students to add enough water to moisten the soil thoroughly, but not so much as to make it swampy.

Reading for information; using a chart. Students write information from the reading in a chart. Teaching suggestions are provided in the Skills Journal annotations.

3 ◆ EXTEND

SCIENCE Making and recording observations. Have students make a chart on which they can record the growth of the plants in their rain forest jars. Suggest that students measure the size of the plants when they complete the planting and then measure the growth every week. Also have students observe the condition of the plants when they are first planted to see if the leaves are

upright or drooping and wilting. Have students compare the condition of the plants each day. Do they remain upright or do they begin to wilt? Ask, *What causes plants to droop or wilt?* (CALLA: Grouping)

SCIENCE Observing transpiration. Briefly discuss the water cycle. Explain how water is absorbed by the roots of a plant. The water that is not used by the plant goes into the air as water vapor. Have students observe the water drops that accumulate on the sides of their rain forest jars. Ask, *Where did this water come from?* (from the plants releasing water through their leaves into the air) Write student responses on the board. (CALLA: Induction)

If water does not collect on the sides of the rain forest jar and the plants begin to wilt or droop, have students add more water and check to be sure that the lid seal is tight.

SOCIAL STUDIES Map skills. The climate of Puerto Rico, with its heat and rainfall, is conducive to rain forests. Have students locate on a map other regions where rain forests are common. Make sure to point out the temperate rain forests of Washington state and of British Columbia, Canada, as well.

 **PROCESS WRITING PORTFOLIO** See the list of ideas and writing topics related to this theme.

LESSON 6
PUERTO RICO: THE FLOWER OF THE CARIBBEAN

📷 **STUDENT BOOK/SKILLS JOURNAL PAGE 12–15**

⭐ **KEY EXPERIENCES**

- Reading nonfiction for information
- Summarizing/classifying information
- Writing factual articles
- Making comparisons

⭐ **KEY LANGUAGE**

- *There is/there are...*
- *baseball, sport*
- *both, many, most, some*
- *seasons, weather, land features*
- *numbers review*
- *singular/plural nouns*

⭐ **MATERIALS**

- map, globe
- travel brochures
- photographs showing Puerto Rico

1 ♦ INTRODUCE

Building background: Talking about Puerto Rico.
Recap any discussion from Lesson 2. You may want to bring in pictures, travel brochures, and books about Puerto Rico. Find out what students know about the island. Make a chart and list student ideas, leaving question marks in spots where students can't yet fill in information. Add to the chart as students learn more. Help students locate Puerto Rico on a world map or globe. Encourage students to find their parents' or their own countries of origin on the map or globe, too.

┌ **MULTI-LEVEL TEACHING STRATEGIES** ┐

You can include all students by asking questions appropriate to each student's language level.

Speech Emergence: *Is it hot or cold in Puerto Rico? What sea is around Puerto Rico?*

Developing Fluency: *What do you know about Puerto Rico? What is the weather like in Puerto Rico? What language(s) do people speak in Puerto Rico?*

2 ♦ EXPLORE

Activating prior knowledge. Open to page 12. Ask a volunteer to read the title, "Puerto Rico: The Flower of the Caribbean," aloud. Then have students look through the story, commenting on the photos. To prompt discussion, ask multi-level questions such as *Have you ever been to Puerto Rico? Do you think it is hot or cold there? What else do you know about Puerto Rico?*

Puerto Rico is an island in the Caribbean Sea. Its nearest neighbors are Haiti and the Dominican Republic to the west and the Virgin Islands to the east. There are mountains, valleys, and plains. There is a beautiful rain forest. There are miles and miles of beaches in Puerto Rico. People like to go to the beach to swim or sit in the sun. The weather is warm all year, but rains come in the summer and fall. The dry season is December to March.

Look at Me   13

GUIDED READING Reading nonfiction. Read the article aloud or play the tape once through as students follow along in their books. Reread the article, pausing at the end of each paragraph to discuss. Students who are able to should read independently. You may want to pose the following display/comprehension questions to prompt discussion of each page and monitor students' understanding.

Display/Comprehension Questions

Pages 12-13

What places are near Puerto Rico? (Dominican Republic, Haiti, Cuba)
Are there mountains on Puerto Rico? (yes)
What can people do at the beach? (swim, sit in the sun)
In what seasons does it rain? (summer and fall)
When is the dry season? (December to March)

Page 14

Who discovered Puerto Rico? (Columbus)
In what year did he discover Puerto Rico? (1493)

What country claimed the island? (Spain)
Is Puerto Rico still part of Spain? (no)
Is Puerto Rico a state or territory of the United States? (territory)
What languages do people speak there? (Spanish and English)
Why do you think people speak these two languages?
How many people live in Puerto Rico? (3.8 million)
What is the capital city? (San Juan)

Page 15

What does Puerto Rico want to do in 2004? (host the Summer Olympic games)
Name a sport that is popular in Puerto Rico. (baseball)
Are there many festivals in Puerto Rico? (yes)
What can people do at the festivals? (buy crafts, listen to music, dance, eat food)

Summarizing information. Go back to the chart at the beginning of the lesson. See if students can fill in any question marks or add additional information about Puerto Rico that they learned from the article. Then call on individual students to contribute information to a class summary.

Your Turn. With the class, read the instructions under "Your Turn." Have students work with partners as they talk about their home countries. Depending on the level of the class, you may want to follow up by having students describe their partner's home country for the class.

SKILLS JOURNAL PAGES 12-15 **Page 12: Learning language through song.** Students listen to a song, then sing along. **Page 13: Using a chart.** Students use information from a chart to distinguish true and false statements. **Page 14: Vocabulary development.** Students learn geography words. **Page 15: Solving a puzzle.** Students decode messages and create their own secret codes and messages. Teaching suggestions are provided in the Skills Journal annotations.

3 ◆ EXTEND

SOCIAL STUDIES Learning about Puerto Rico.
Students can work in small groups to find out more information about Puerto Rico. Suggest that students continue to add to the class chart. Later, students can use the chart information to write a report. (CALLA: Resourcing)

SOCIAL STUDIES Making comparisons. Make a chart on the board. With students, brainstorm a list of categories to consider as they compare Puerto Rico with another country of their choosing. Students can refer to the article to fill in information about Puerto Rico. Encourage students to use a variety of other resources to complete the chart with information about other countries. Resources might include recalling their own experiences, asking friends and parents, looking on maps and in atlases, and looking in books and encyclopedias.

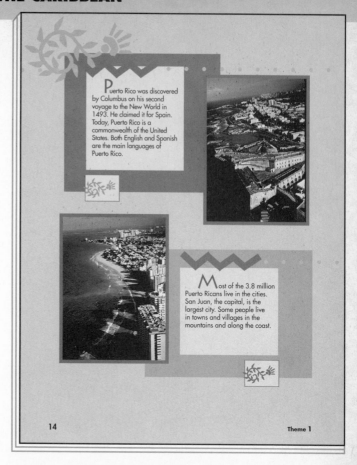

	Puerto Rico	another country
weather		
seasons		
land		
languages		
favorite sports		
largest city		
population		
festivals		

ART/MUSIC Describing a festival. Students can create illustrations to use as graphic aids in explaining festivals that are important in their own or another cultural group. Explore the music forms associated with festivals such as the *salsa, bomba y plena* in Puerto Rico. Encourage students to bring in favorite songs from their cultures. Help students prepare a class presentation describing the art and music of their cultures' festivals.

PROCESS WRITING PORTFOLIO See the list of ideas and writing topics related to this theme.

ONGOING ASSESSMENT

PERFORMANCE Reading. Check student responses for ability to read for information.

PREDICTABLE PROBLEM
Students may not be familiar with the difference between a state and a territory. Point out that Puerto Ricans are citizens of the United States and have the right to vote in national elections.

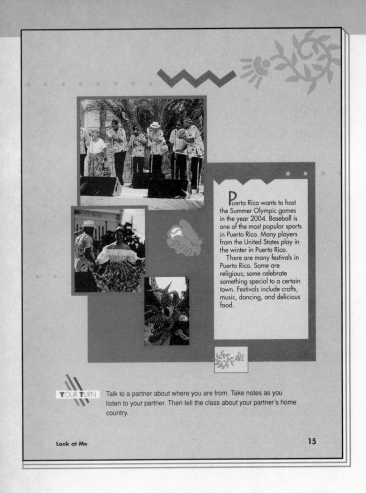

Puerto Rico wants to host the Summer Olympic games in the year 2004. Baseball is one of the most popular sports in Puerto Rico. Many players from the United States play in the winter in Puerto Rico.

There are many festivals in Puerto Rico. Some are religious; some celebrate something special to a certain town. Festivals include crafts, music, dancing, and delicious food.

YOUR TURN   Talk to a partner about where you are from. Take notes as you listen to your partner. Then tell the class about your partner's home country.

Look at Me   15

◆ TEACHER'S NOTES ◆

LESSON 7
ALL STAR NEWS

📻 **STUDENT BOOK/SKILLS JOURNAL PAGES 16–17**

⭐ **KEY EXPERIENCES**

■ Reading for information and pleasure

■ Taking a poll

■ Making a friendship poster

■ Process writing

⭐ **KEY LANGUAGE**

■ *friendship, friend, teen*

■ *freedom, lighthouse*

⭐ **MATERIALS**

■ magazine pictures, construction paper

■ measuring tapes, rulers, yard-sticks

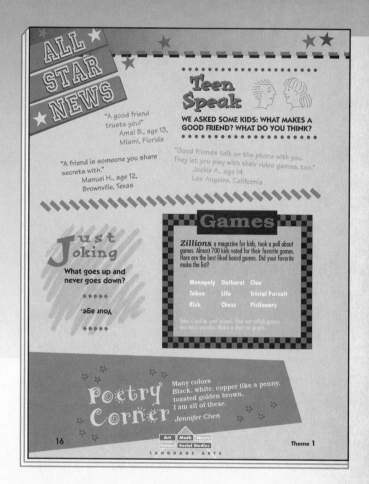

1 ◆ INTRODUCE

Building background: Talking about friendship. Write the word *friendship* on the board. Ask students if they recognize any part of the word and know what this word means. Display pictures of friends doing different things together as prompts for discussion. Encourage students to share favorite activities with friends and qualities they look for in a friend.

┌─ **MULTI-LEVEL TEACHING STRATEGIES** ─┐

You can include all students by asking questions appropriate to each student's language level.

Speech Emergence: *What do you do with your friend? Where do you go? When can you see your friends?*

Developing Fluency: *How did you meet your friend? What does it mean to be a friend? Why do you like your friend?*

└─────────────────────────────────────┘

2 ◆ EXPLORE

Reading comprehension. Tell students not to worry if they don't understand or remember everything the first time they read the *News.* Give students many chances to read silently (with or without the tape). Adjust your comprehension questions to the level of each student for informal assessment of understanding. Encourage students to decipher any unfamiliar words from context.

Previewing reading selections. Have students find and read the article headings on pages 16 and 17. Ask students to guess what the articles will be about. You may want to have students use article titles to form questions about the content. (CALLA: Predicting)

📻 **GUIDED READING Reading for information.** Play the tape or read the selections, pausing occasionally to ask multi-level questions. Students who are able to should read the pages independently. You may want to pose the following display/comprehension questions to prompt discussion of each page and monitor students' understanding.

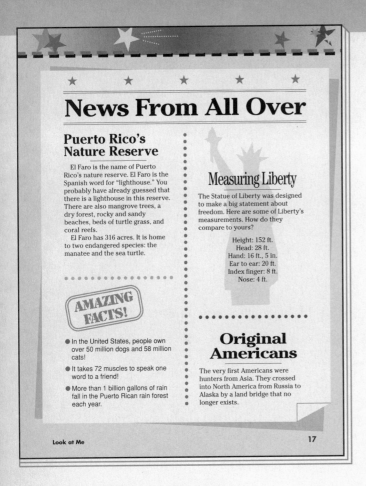

News From All Over

Puerto Rico's Nature Reserve

El Faro is the name of Puerto Rico's nature reserve. El Faro is the Spanish word for "lighthouse." You probably have already guessed that there is a lighthouse in this reserve. There are also mangrove trees, a dry forest, rocky and sandy beaches, beds of turtle grass, and coral reefs.

El Faro has 316 acres. It is home to two endangered species: the manatee and the sea turtle.

AMAZING FACTS!

- In the United States, people own over 50 million dogs and 58 million cats!
- It takes 72 muscles to speak one word to a friend!
- More than 1 billion gallons of rain fall in the Puerto Rican rain forest each year.

Measuring Liberty

The Statue of Liberty was designed to make a big statement about freedom. Here are some of Liberty's measurements. How do they compare to yours?

Height: 152 ft.
Head: 28 ft.
Hand: 16 ft., 5 in.
Ear to ear: 20 ft.
Index finger: 8 ft.
Nose: 4 ft.

Original Americans

The very first Americans were hunters from Asia. They crossed into North America from Russia to Alaska by a land bridge that no longer exists.

Look at Me   17

Display/Comprehension Questions

Page 16

How many kids voted in the poll about games? (700)

What colors are named in the poem? (black, white, copper, golden brown)

Page 17

What is El Faro? (a nature reserve in Puerto Rico)

How tall is the Statue of Liberty? (152 ft.)

How many muscles do you use to speak? (72)

How much rain falls in the Puerto Rican rain forest? (1 billion gallons)

Are there more cats or more dogs in the United States? (cats)

Where did the first Americans come from? (Asia)

SKILLS JOURNAL
PAGES 16-17

Process writing. Students read a school newspaper article, then write their own. Teaching suggestions are provided in the Skills Journal annotation.

3 ♦ EXTEND

MATH Taking a poll. Have students prepare and conduct a poll of games students in your school enjoy. Students can prepare questions or survey questionnaires to give to other students. Then the class works in groups to compile the results and prepare charts or graphs.

ART Making a friendship poster. Have students make posters with their own definitions of a good friend. Make a "What Makes a Good Friend" bulletin board display, using student posters or pictures from magazines and student definitions.

MATH Measuring/Solving problems. Invite students to measure themselves and objects in the classroom. Also use pages 16 and 17 to create math problems or have students write the problems. For example: How many gallons of rain fall in the Puerto Rican rain forest each month? Can the Statue of Liberty's head fit in this classroom? Are you taller or shorter than the statue's nose?

POETRY Creative Writing. Students use the poem as a model for their own poems to describe themselves and others. Brainstorm positive color words and descriptive adjectives and be sensitive to stereotypes.

ONGOING ASSESSMENT

PERFORMANCE Reading comprehension. Check student responses for ability to read for specific information.

PORTFOLIO Writing. Save Skills Journal pages 16–17 as an example of independent writing.

COMPUTER CONNECTION

Students can use a spreadsheet software program to create a chart of the data they collect about favorite games. Students also can use a multimedia CD-ROM encyclopedia to find pictures of some of the animals and objects mentioned in the article "Puerto Rico's Nature Reserve."

LESSON 8
ALL STAR NEWS

STUDENT BOOK/SKILLS JOURNAL
PAGES 18–19

★ KEY EXPERIENCES

■ Reading for information and pleasure

■ Reading and following written directions

■ Responding to a letter

■ Working in collaborative groups:

• posters

• photo essays

• polling and charting

■ Practicing science process skills

★ KEY LANGUAGE

■ *owner, different, decorated*

★ MATERIALS

■ sticks, 12" and 6" (one set per student); twine; assorted decorating objects such as feathers, buttons, and braid; paints and/or colored markers; poster paper; magazines and newspapers; scissors; paste

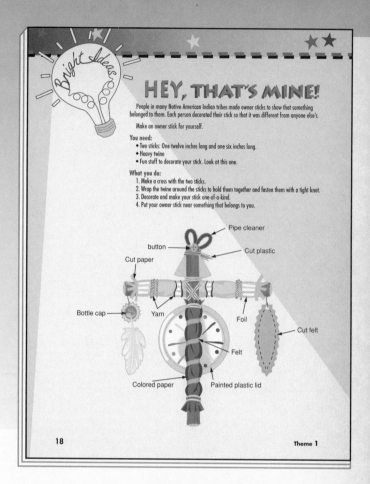

1 ◆ INTRODUCE

Building background: Talking about ownership. Write *owner* on the board and ask volunteers to explain its meaning. Ask, *How can you show that you own something?* Elicit that people often show ownership by saying "That's mine," or by putting tags with their names or special marks on objects.

Exploring key vocabulary. Introduce the possessive pronouns and the word *different*. Elicit that *different* means "not the same as."

MULTI-LEVEL TEACHING STRATEGIES

You can include all students by asking questions appropriate to each student's language level.

Speech Emergence. Point to a student's book bag. *How can you show that this is your bag?*

Developing Fluency. Write *decorated* on the board and ask, *What do you think this word means?*

2 ◆ EXPLORE

Activating prior knowledge. Open to page 18. To prompt discussion, ask multi-level questions such as *What do you think the object in the photo is? Have you ever seen anything like this before? What do you think it is used for?* (CALLA: Making inferences)

GUIDED READING Reading directions. Give students time to look over page 18. Read aloud the title, "Hey, That's Mine!" and the directions for making an owner stick, or ask volunteers to do so. Ask multi-level questions such as, *What is an owner stick? How can an owner stick be used to mark something as yours?*

Bright Ideas. Allow students to make owner sticks. Encourage them to search for unique objects that will make their sticks one-of-a-kind. Have them explain why they chose certain objects to decorate their sticks.

Mailbox. Direct students to the Mailbox on page 19. Read aloud or ask a volunteer to read the letter

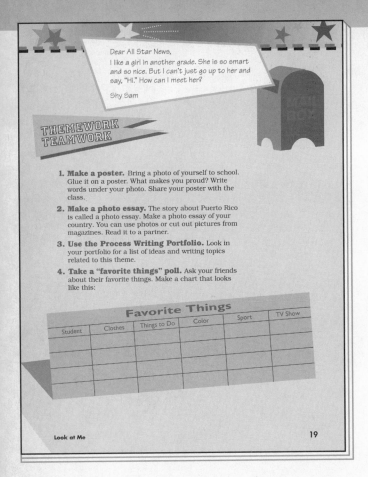

Dear All Star News,
I like a girl in another grade. She is so smart and so nice. But I can't just go up to her and say, "Hi." How can I meet her?

Shy Sam

THEMEWORK TEAMWORK

1. **Make a poster.** Bring a photo of yourself to school. Glue it on a poster. What makes you proud? Write words under your photo. Share your poster with the class.

2. **Make a photo essay.** The story about Puerto Rico is called a photo essay. Make a photo essay of your country. You can use photos or cut out pictures from magazines. Read it to a partner.

3. **Use the Process Writing Portfolio.** Look in your portfolio for a list of ideas and writing topics related to this theme.

4. **Take a "favorite things" poll.** Ask your friends about their favorite things. Make a chart that looks like this:

Favorite Things

Student	Clothes	Things to Do	Color	Sport	TV Show

Look at Me   19

3 ♦ EXTEND

SOCIAL STUDIES Researching owner sticks. In pairs or small groups, have students research and write reports on owner sticks and the Native American Indian Tribes that used them.

ART Designing a symbol. Ask students to design a special symbol to mark possessions as theirs. Encourage them to try to design a symbol that is both unique and personal so that others will recognize who the object belongs to. After students have completed their designs, have classmates see if they can guess the owner of each mark. (CALLA: Imagery)

PROCESS WRITING PORTFOLIO See the list of ideas and writing topics related to this theme.

ONGOING ASSESSMENT

PERFORMANCE Oral language. Evaluate students' oral reports or discussions of their Themework/Teamwork projects.

PORTFOLIO Writing. Save Skills Journal page 18 as an example of independent writing.

★ **PREDICTABLE PROBLEM**
Many students over generalize the final s from *yours, ours, theirs* to include *mine* as *mines*. Remind students that the correct form is *mine*.

from Shy Sam. Ask multi-level questions such as, *Why does he sign the letter "Shy Sam?" Have you ever felt this way about meeting someone? What did you do? What do you think Sam should do to meet the girl?* Have students split into small groups to discuss Sam's problem and what he might do to meet the girl. Have them share their solutions with the class. Students write a letter to Shy Sam on page 18 of their Skills Journals.

Themework/Teamwork. Have students look over the activities. Then read and discuss all the projects. Students can work in pairs or collaborative groups. They can choose one or more of the activities to explore. Allow time for all students to share and explain their projects.

SKILLS JOURNAL PAGES 18-19 **Page 18: Expressing opinions; letter-writing.** Students write letters offering advice to "Shy Sam." **Page 19: Science process skills.** Students read a cartoon science experiment, then try it themselves. Teaching suggestions are provided in the Skills Journal annotations.

LESSON 9
HOLISTIC ASSESSMENT

STUDENT BOOK/SKILLS JOURNAL PAGES 20–21

★ KEY EXPERIENCES

- Demonstrating comprehension
- Summarizing a story
- Thinking critically
- Self-assessment
- Writing about oneself

★ KEY LANGUAGE

- *carpenter, dog house, bird house*

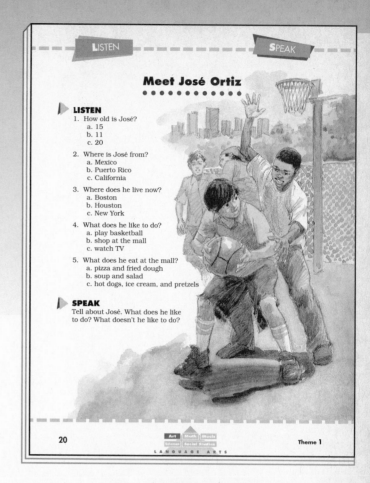

1 ◆ INTRODUCE

These two pages offer a variety of assessment opportunities. The content expands upon the information in the photo essay, "Hi, My Name is Carmen," on pages 4–6. The left-hand page consists of listening and speaking activities that follow a taped presentation. In the speaking activity, students are asked to summarize what they have heard. The right-hand page consists of writing and critical thinking activities. These follow a reading passage that completes the listening component. You can use the activities to assess listening, speaking, reading, writing, and critical thinking skills. Have students work as a class or in small groups as you circulate and record observations on the **Anecdotal Record Form,** the **Reading Checklist,** and the **Writing Checklist** in the *All Star Assessment Package.*

Observing and recording student performance. Note the level of participation and the particular abilities of each student. How much do students understand? How well can they express themselves orally? What language structures do they use? What new words and concepts do they use? How actively do they participate? Use the **Anecdotal Record Form** in the *All Star Assessment Package* to record your observations and note areas for further development. Place in students' **portfolios.** Also review students' self-assessment pages in the **Skills Journal.**

2 ◆ EXPLORE

Activating prior knowledge. Ask students to tell you what they remember about Carmen Ortiz and her family. You may want to have students reread pages 4–6.

Listening. Read or play the tape for the first part of "Meet José Ortiz." You will find the tapescript in the Appendix. Have students work independently to answer the listening questions. Read or play the tape again for students to check their work.

Speaking. Discuss what students have heard up to this point. Ask multi-level questions such as *How old is José? Whose brother is he? Does he like the same things as Carmen?* If some students are struggling, play the tape again and summarize the story once yourself. Ask questions again. When you are satisfied with this stage, go on to the next.

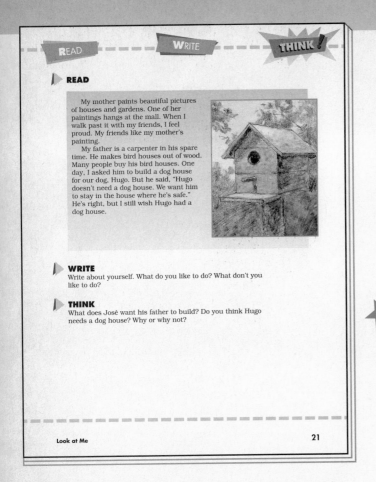

READ   WRITE   THINK!

READ

My mother paints beautiful pictures of houses and gardens. One of her paintings hangs at the mall. When I walk past it with my friends, I feel proud. My friends like my mother's painting.

My father is a carpenter in his spare time. He makes bird houses out of wood. Many people buy his bird houses. One day, I asked him to build a dog house for our dog, Hugo. But he said, "Hugo doesn't need a dog house. We want him to stay in the house where he's safe." He's right, but I still wish Hugo had a dog house.

WRITE
Write about yourself. What do you like to do? What don't you like to do?

THINK
What does José want his father to build? Do you think Hugo needs a dog house? Why or why not?

Look at Me   21

3 ◆ EXTEND

ART Designing a bird house. Have students design a bird house; those who have dogs may prefer to design a dog house. Encourage students to draw plans for their designs, including dimensions and a list of materials needed.

Home-School Connection. Have students take home copies of Skills Journal pages 20–21 to show family members their progress. Be sure to put these pages in students' assessment portfolios.

PREDICTABLE PROBLEM

Some students may be confused by the uses of the word *dog* in *hot dog* and in *dog house.* Make sure students understand that a hot dog has nothing to do with the animal.

 Reading. Read the story on page 21 or play the tape as the students listen and follow along in their books. Ask multi-level questions to monitor understanding. Then have the students do partner reading, alternating paragraphs.

Writing. Encourage students to tell you what they have heard and read. Do not look for word-for-word retelling, even from your best students. Have them relate their own pastimes as a pre-writing activity. Then have them do a "Quick Write" activity (if you are using the Skills Journal, see page 20).

Thinking. Ask students questions such as *Do you think José's father will build a dog house? What do you think José's mother might make for José?*

SKILLS JOURNAL PAGES 20-21 **Page 20: Assessment; reinforcing vocabulary.** Students circle words that do not belong in vocabulary groups. **Page 21: Self-assessment; Home-School connection.** Students check off things they have learned to do and words they have learned. Teaching suggestions are provided in the Skills Journal annotations.

THEME 1: LOOK AT ME

LESSON 10
ONE BIG FAMILY

🖥 STUDENT BOOK/SKILLS JOURNAL PAGE 22

★ KEY EXPERIENCES

- Reviewing the theme
- Singing a song
- Creating new song verses
- Making a dictionary

★ KEY LANGUAGE

- *everyone, hello*
- present tense

1 ◆ INTRODUCE

Reviewing the theme. Engage students in a discussion and review of some of the things they learned in this theme.

MULTI-LEVEL TEACHING STRATEGIES

You can include all students by asking questions appropriate to each student's language level.

Speech Emergence: *Where do Carmen and José Ortiz come from? Where is Puerto Rico? What is the weather like there? Where do you come from?*

Developing Fluency: *How would you describe yourself? Why do you think this theme is called* Look at Me?

2 ◆ EXPLORE

Activating prior knowledge. Open to page 22. To prompt discussion, ask multi-level questions such as *What is the title of this song? What is the Spanish word for* hello? *What is the word for* hello *in your first language?*

🖥 Guided listening/reading. Read through the song several times with the students. Then play the tape of the song several times, inviting students to sing along as soon as they are ready.

📖 SKILLS JOURNAL PAGE 22

Creating original song verses; appreciating multicultural diversity.
Students share how to say hello and good-bye in different languages. Teaching suggestions are provided in the Skills Journal annotation.

3 ◆ EXTEND

Creating new verses for the song. Ask students to take turns stating their first language and telling the word for *hello* in that language. Then have all students join with them in adding a new verse for the song, using the name of their language and its word for *hello.*

Making a "hello" dictionary. Invite students to research and list the word for *hello* in as many languages as they can. Have them compare their lists. (CALLA: Selective Attention; Resourcing)

WRAP UP

ASSESSMENT

You have been collecting assessment data through the ongoing and holistic assessment options (Oral Language Checklist, Reading Checklist, Anecdotal Record Form) in this theme. Following are some additional assessment strategies that will help you evaluate your students' progress as well as adapt your instruction to meet their needs.

Student Self-Assessment. Self-assessment surveys are a means for students to have input into their own learning process. Students can use them to reflect on the work they have done and the learning strategies they have used during this theme. Be sure to check students' self-assessment pages for each theme in the Skills Journal.

Informed Instruction. Evaluate the checklists, anecdotal records, and Process Writing Portfolio collections from this theme as a means of informing your instruction.
- In which areas are students showing confidence and enthusiasm?
- In which areas are they hesitant or confused?
- Should you provide more classroom opportunities for oral language or writing?
- Would certain students (or the whole class) benefit from a focused mini-lesson on a certain area or skill?
- Remember to recycle skills as you teach the next theme and provide students with many opportunities to gain competence.

READING

Don't forget to check on and encourage students' independent reading. Students who weren't ready for independent reading in English at the beginning of this theme may be ready now. Students who continue to read in their first language should be encouraged to do first language book reviews and be an attentive audience for other students' reviews in English.

BOOKBYTES

Have students been able to use the *All Star BookBytes* CD-ROM software? The BookBytes' book list includes the titles on the Theme Booklists for all levels of *All Star English.* BookBytes helps students choose a book to read based on their responses to a short questionnaire, then prompts students to think about and respond to what they've read through writing, drawing, and drama. Students can print out their work and share it with others. They can also choose to see other students' work on-screen in a gallery presentation.

THEME CELEBRATION

If your class is participating as an All Star Team, the end of theme is a good time to review students' accomplishments with the Theme Booklist and Theme Projects. Consider posting a chart in the classroom where students may check off their accomplishments and, if you are using a point system, total their points for the theme. Students should strive to do their best and outdo their *own* scores, not compete with each other. Encourage students to present their All Star projects to the class to allow more oral practice and to sharpen students' presentation skills. You might invite other classes or families to attend the presentations.

PREVIEW

STUDENT BOOK/SKILLS JOURNAL, PAGES 23-42

YOUR FAMILY, MY FAMILY • •

CONCEPTS
- appreciating multicultural diversity
- Native American cultures
- healthy eating
- family activities
- birthdays
- friends

LITERATURE

- In My Mother's House *(poem excerpt)*
- My Bird Day *(poem)*
- The Dance *(poem)*
- All Star News *(short nonfiction articles)*
- Birthday *(song)*

READING/WRITING SKILLS

- summarizing a story
- critical thinking
- reading comprehension
- reading/responding to free verse
- understanding figurative language
- reading for information
- reading/responding to a photo essay
- reading/responding to a poem
- writing a poem
- process writing
- responding to a letter

CONTENT

- **Math:** comparing geometric shapes, taking a poll, calculating percentages, measuring
- **Social Studies:** describing one's family, making a chart, discussing New Mexico, making comparisons, researching, describing a family activity/celebration
- **Art/Music:** making a family tree, following written directions, designing a kite, making a display, designing letterhead, singing birthday songs
- **Science:** planning a meal, keeping a food diary, discussing health, drawing conclusions from an experiment

KEY LANGUAGE/KEY EXPERIENCES

- family members
- simple present tense
- prepositions of place
- rooms of the house
- present progressive
- self-assessment
- following oral/written directions
- distinguishing true/false statements
- interpreting a graph
- practicing math skills
- working in collaborative groups
- vocabulary development
- expressing opinions
- describing quantity
- practicing science process skills

THEME BOOKLIST/ THEME PROJECTS

As this new theme begins, photocopy the Theme Booklist/Theme Projects pages (following spread) for students. Encourage students to read as many books as they like from the Booklist, and to complete any of the assignments on the Project list as homework for this theme.

AWARDING POINTS FOR ALL STAR TEAMS

This is a good opportunity to motivate students through an All Star Team approach. Consider assigning point values to each project, including reading books from the booklist. Explain to students that they will accumulate points for each book they read or project they complete during the theme. Students will try to top their own scores as they work through each theme, competing against themselves, not each other. Remind students that they will have the opportunity to present their *All Star* projects to the class at the end of the theme.

BOOKBYTES

If you have a computer with a CD-ROM drive available, introduce students to the *All Star BookBytes* software which is correlated to the Theme Booklists throughout *All Star English. BookBytes* categorizes the books by genre and helps students choose a book to read based on their answers to a short questionnaire. It then prompts students to think about and respond to what they've read through writing, drawing, and drama activities. Students can print out their work and share it with others or view work on-screen in a gallery presentation.

THEME BOOKLIST

HERE ARE SOME BOOKS YOU MIGHT LIKE TO READ.
LOOK FOR THEM IN YOUR LIBRARY.

Arrow to the Sun: A Pueblo Indian Tale, by Gerald McDermott. Viking, 1974. A beautifully illustrated creation tale.

Ceremony of the Panther, by Luke Wallin. Bradbury Press, 1987. A boy moves to an Indian reservation and makes a new friend—Thomas Three Feathers.

El Güero: A True Adventure Story, by Elizabeth Borton de Treviño. Farrar, Straus and Giroux, 1989. A boy's adventure in Baja, California in the 1980s.

The Emperor and the Kite, by Jane Yolan. Philomel, 1967. A Chinese girl helps her father escape from a tower.

Journey to the Bright Kingdom, by Elizabeth Winthrop. Holiday House, 1979. An expanded Japanese folktale about family love.

Poems for Father, selected by Myra C. Livingston. Holiday House, 1989. Special thoughts for fathers. Also, *Poems for Mother*, 1988.

Racing the Sun, by Paul Pitts. Avon/Camelot Books, 1988. A boy's grandfather teachers him about the Navajo culture.

Shelters: From Teepee to Igloo, by Harvey Weiss. Thomas Crowell, 1988. Homes around the world.

Sweetgrass, by Jan Hudson. Philomel Books, 1989. The story of a Blackfoot girl living in western Canada.

The Two-Thousand-Pound Goldfish, by Betty Byars. Scholastic, Inc., 1991. What do you do if your mother is wanted by the FBI?

Year Walk, by Ann Nolan Clark. Viking, 1975. A Basque boy moves to Idaho and helps his grandfather herd sheep across the frontier.

BOOKS IN LANGUAGES OTHER THAN ENGLISH

Tamales de elote/Green Corn Tamales (bilingual), by Gina Macaluso Rodríguez. Tucson, AZ: Hispanic Books Distributors.

Mi tío Teo (My Uncle Theo), by Pilar Mateos. Barcelona, España: ediciones sm.

Grandmother's Path, Grandfather's Way, by Lue Vang and Judy Lewis (English/Hmong). Covina, CA: Multicultural Distribution Center.

Four Champa Trees, by Alice Lucas and Yon-Shan Tang (English/Lao). Arcadia, CA: Shen's Books and Supplies.

★ THEME PROJECTS

YOU MAY WANT TO WORK ON THESE PROJECTS
ALONE OR WITH A PARTNER OR SMALL GROUP.

☆ Make a set of vocabulary cards that show vocabulary words learned in the theme on one side and illustrations of the words on the other.

☆ Write dialogues that use vocabulary or grammatical structures learned in the theme.

☆ Write original sentences or stories using key vocabulary words.

☆ Create a word search or crossword puzzle that uses vocabulary from the theme.

☆ Translate a song, poem, or prose selection from your native language into English.

☆ Create paintings, drawings, or dioramas of stories or readings within the theme.

☆ Produce scripts or dramatizations of information presented in the theme.

☆ Create a collage, mobile, or other three-dimensional art project that illustrates key concepts from the theme.

☆ Take a survey and present graphs and charts that explore questions related to the theme.

☆ Write journal entries for five to ten days about key concepts or ideas in the theme.

☆ Paste news clippings onto blank paper and write a short statement explaining how the article relates to the theme.

☆ Write a letter to the editor, the school government, City Hall, or the President of the United States about issues and ideas in the theme.

☆ Create maps that show the location of places mentioned in the theme.

☆ Create a time line that shows what happened in a story from the theme.

☆ Make a story chart that clearly labels the characters, plot, setting, climax, and ending of a story from the theme.

☆ Present a dramatic reading of one of the stories in the theme.

☆ Write a letter that gives advice or constructive criticism to a character in a story from the theme.

LESSON 1
THEME OPENER

STUDENT BOOK/ SKILLS JOURNAL PAGE 23

 KEY EXPERIENCES
- Discussing families
- Previewing theme content and titles
- Making a family tree or chart
- Self-assessment

KEY LANGUAGE
- family members
- family activities

MATERIALS
- drawing paper
- colored markers
- example of a family tree

1 • INTRODUCE

Theme 2, Your Family, My Family, presents family relations and activities. Students will read and talk about home and family celebrations. They will learn prepositions of place and study the food pyramid.

Building background: Discussing families. Open to page 23 and direct students' attention to the photo. Read the theme title aloud and ask students what they think they will find in this theme. Encourage students to tell about their families by modeling a description of your family. For example, *There are four people in my family, myself, my mother, my father, and my brother. I also have two grandparents....*

MULTI-LEVEL TEACHING STRATEGIES

You can include all students by asking questions appropriate to each student's language level.

Speech Emergence: *How many people are in your family? What family members live with you?*

Developing Fluency: *Tell me what you see in the picture. Who do you think these people are?*

Exploring key vocabulary. As students tell about their families, write on the board the family members mentioned. Make sure the list includes at least the following: *grandmother, grandfather, mother, father, brother, sister, aunt, uncle, cousin.* Ask multi-level questions that prompt definitions of these terms: *What do you call your mother and father's parents? What do you call your aunt and uncle's children?*

2 • EXPLORE

Activating prior knowledge. Guide students as they look through the unit, inviting them to comment on titles, photos, and art. Call on volunteers to read the selection titles aloud. To prompt discussion, ask multi-level questions such as *Do you know what pueblos are? What do you think this part of the theme will be about?* (CALLA: Predicting)

Reading Corner. Have students read the titles, authors, and descriptions of the three books listed under Reading Corner. These are just a few selections from the Theme Booklist, chosen to help motivate students to want to read. Have the books available for students to look at. Prompt discussion about which book each student would like to read and why. Allow students to sign up for turns with the books. Use this experience to get your students excited about reading.

 **Activating prior knowledge; self-assessment.** Students complete chart before and after lesson. Teaching suggestions are provided in the Skills Journal annotation.

3 • EXTEND

SOCIAL STUDIES Describing one's family. Invite students to write a paragraph or draw a picture to tell about their families. Have them share their work with the class.

SOCIAL STUDIES Making a chart. Have students make charts to show the members of their families. Students might enjoy compiling information from

YOUR FAMILY, MY FAMILY

THEME 2

Reading Corner
Try these terrific books!

The Emperor and the Kite
by Jane Yolen
A Chinese girl helps her father escape from a tower.

Journey To the Bright Kingdom
by Elizabeth Winthrop
A Japanese folktale about family love.

The Two-Thousand-Pound Goldfish
by Betty Byars
What do you do if your mother is wanted by the FBI?

23

★ **BOOKBYTES**
Have students use the BookBytes software as motivation for reading and writing about what they've read.

★ **LANGUAGE NOTE**
Help students as necessary with terms for family members, for example:
father's father = grandfather
grandmother's mother = great grandmother
mother's brother = uncle
aunt's or uncle's son or daughter = cousin

individual charts into a class chart to see just how large the class "family" is. (CALLA: Grouping)

ART Making a family tree. Provide an example of a family tree for students to use as a model in constructing a tree of their own family.

Discovering the library. Lead students on a tour of your school or local library. With students, gather the books recommended for this theme in the Theme Booklist. Students will enjoy participating in this search and, in so doing, will practice basic library and research skills. In the classroom, plan to read aloud to students each day. You may wish to record the books on tape and let students read the books as they listen to the tapes. Encourage students to read independently whenever possible.

ONGOING ASSESSMENT

PERFORMANCE Oral and written language.
Evaluate students' oral, written, and pictorial descriptions of their families.

LESSON 2
IN MY MOTHER'S HOUSE

📷 STUDENT BOOK/SKILLS JOURNAL
PAGES 24–27

★ KEY EXPERIENCES

- Reading/responding to free verse
- Describing/comparing homes
- Discussing New Mexico
- Understanding figurative language

★ KEY LANGUAGE

- simple present tense
- prepositions of place
- rooms of the house
- *fire, fireplace, make ready for feasting*
- *plaza*

★ MATERIALS

- pictures of different types of housing and rooms
- map of the U.S.
- photos of the Southwest

IN MY MOTHER'S HOUSE
EXCERPTED FROM THE BOOK
BY ANN NOLAN CLARK
This story is about a Tewa Indian girl from New Mexico.
• • •

In my Mother's house
All day
I play and work;
All night
I sleep.

The walls come close around me
In a good way
I can see them;
I can feel them;
I live with them.

24   Theme 2

1 ◆ INTRODUCE

★ **Excerpted literature:** "In My Mother's House" has been excerpted from *In My Mother's House* by Ann Nolan Clark. Copyright © 1941 by Ann Nolan Clark, renewed © 1969 by Ann Nolan Clark. Used by permission of Viking Penguin, a division of Penguin Books USA, Inc.

Rationale: Some of the text from the book has been deleted, but the material tells the entire story. Copy was cut for space reasons.

Building background: Describing a home. Show pictures of different types of housing and rooms within a house or apartment. Ask students to describe the homes and identify the rooms. Invite students to suggest activities that might be done in and around the home.

MULTI-LEVEL TEACHING STRATEGIES

You can include all students by asking questions appropriate to each student's language level.

Speech Emergence: *Show me the kitchen. Where do you sleep in the house?*

What can you do in the kitchen? Where do you play? What do you like to do in the living room?

Developing Fluency: *What's your favorite room? What do you enjoy doing in that room? Are there other houses (apartments) near yours? Who lives there? What do you enjoy doing with your neighbors?*

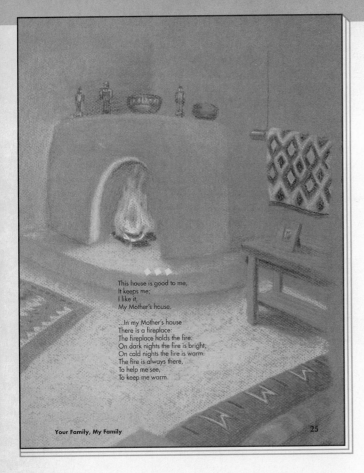

This house is good to me,
It keeps me;
I like it,
My Mother's house.

...In my Mother's house
There is a fireplace:
The fireplace holds the fire.
On dark nights the fire is bright;
On cold nights the fire is warm.
The fire is always there,
To help me see,
To keep me warm.

Your Family, My Family   25

Making a "house" word web. With students, brainstorm a list of rooms and activities associated with those rooms in a house or apartment. Create a word web on the board or on a large sheet of paper.

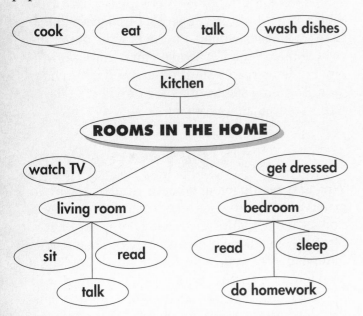

SOCIAL STUDIES Discussing New Mexico. Tell students that they are going to read a story about a Tewa Indian girl who lives in New Mexico. Ask students to find New Mexico on a map of the U.S. Find out what students know about the climate and vegetation in that part of the country. If possible, use photos of the Southwest to prompt discussion. As part of the discussion, ask students what they think houses might look like in that type of climate.

2 ◆ EXPLORE

Activating prior knowledge. Open to page 24. Ask a volunteer to read the title and the first sentence. Have students look at the pictures on pages 24–27. To prompt discussion, ask multi-level questions such as *Who do you think lives here? What objects do you see inside the house? Does this home look like your home? What is different from your home? Would you like to live here? Why or why not?*

GUIDED READING Reading free verse. Read or play the tape for the poem as students follow along in their books. Ask students whether they think "In My Mother's House" is more like a story or more like a poem. Point out that, although free verse does not rhyme, its punctuation is that of a poem. Read the poem again, stopping to ask multi-level questions. You may wish to pose the following display/comprehension questions to prompt discussion of each page and monitor students' understanding.

Display/Comprehension Questions

Pages 24–25
   What does the girl do all day in the house? (play and work)
   When does she sleep? (all night)
   Does she like the walls? (yes)
   How do the walls make her feel? (good)
   Who else lives in the house? (her mother - inference)
   Where is the fire? (in the fireplace)
   How does the fire help the girl? (helps her see and keeps her warm)

When does the girl like the fire? (on cold and dark nights)

Pages 26–27

What do people do in the plaza? (work, play, sing, dance, make ready for feasting)
Does everybody use the plaza? (yes)
What are behind the houses? (the mountains)
Are the houses alone or are they together? (together)
Is this town like a big family? (yes)
What does the girl call the other houses in the town? (sister houses)

Pronunciation. Make sure students understand that *close* in line 1 of the second stanza is pronounced with an *s* sound, not with a *z* sound. Elicit that this word means *near*. Use your hand or a pointer to mark the cadence as students reread the poem chorally.

Understanding figurative language. Ask students what they think the poet is comparing the house to. Call on volunteers to read the following lines from page 27: *With their backs to the mountains, Stand facing the plaza,* and *Its sister houses.* Elicit that the poet describes the houses using human terms. Ask students for other examples of human characteristics that could be used to describe a house.

Independent reading. Have students reread the poem silently. Then have volunteers read the poem aloud.

Understanding pronoun reference. Ask students to locate examples of the pronouns *it, its, them,* and *their.* Call on volunteers to read the context sentences aloud and have students identify the noun referent for each.

Your Turn. With the class, read the instructions under "Your Turn." Have students work with partners as they talk about their homes and activities they enjoy doing at home. Be sensitive to personal privacy. Do not insist on participation if some students seem reluctant to share information about their home life. Depending on the level of the class, you may want to follow up by having students

describe their partner's home for the class.

Page 24: Cloze exercise. Students complete cloze of Student Book text. **Page 25: Reading comprehension; using a chart.** Students complete chart with words from the story. **Page 26: Distinguishing true-false statements; writing.** Students write about their own homes. **Page 27: Reading for a purpose; writing.** Students read a short essay, then write their own. Teaching suggestions are provided in the Skills Journal annotations.

3 ◆ EXTEND

Writing a description of a house. Students work in groups of three to take turns telling about their homes and activities they enjoy doing at home. Students help each other as needed. Then students independently write about their houses and associated family activities. Some students may be willing to write free verse; others will feel more comfortable writing in paragraph form. Encourage stu-

In the plaza the people work;
In the plaza the people play
And sing and dance
And make ready for feasting.
It is the place
For all the people.

The plaza keeps the people together,
And the houses
With their backs to the mountains;
Stand facing the plaza
And shut it in.

My Mother's house,
It does not stand alone;
Its sister houses
Are all around it.

YOUR TURN Tell a partner about your house. What do you
like about it? What do you like to do in your
house?

Your Family, My Family 27

dents find the word on page 25. Ask a volunteer to explain the meaning and point out the two words in the compound. Ask if students can think of other compound words related to homes such as: *bedroom, bathroom, upstairs, downstairs, backyard.* (CALLA: Selective attention)

 **PROCESS WRITING PORTFOLIO** See the ideas and writing topics related to this theme.

ONGOING ASSESSMENT

PERFORMANCE Oral language. Have students reread the part of the story that they like the best. Ask students to explain what they like about their own homes.

PORTFOLIO Writing. Save Skills Journal pages 26 and 27 as examples of independent writing.

dents to think about ways they can use figurative language in their descriptions. Remind students to check paragraph (or poetry) form, punctuation, and capitalization. Then have students regroup and share what they have written. Students help each other correct, clarify, and, if necessary, expand their descriptions. Students can make corrections on their drafts. When finished, have students copy their descriptions, making corrections and revisions. Students can also illustrate their descriptions.

SOCIAL STUDIES Making comparisons. Students can work in pairs to compare their homes to the Tewa Indian girl's home. Encourage students to use a Venn diagram to show the similarities and differences. (CALLA: Comparing)

SOCIAL STUDIES Research and report. Students can work alone or with partners to find out more about the Pueblo Indians or other Native Americans—the Sioux, Cherokee, Arapaho, Seminole, etc.

Identifying compound words. Write the following compound word on the board: *fireplace.* Have stu-

 COMPUTER CONNECTION
Have students use a multimedia CD-ROM encyclopedia to find pictures and information about the Pueblo Indians and New Mexico.

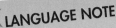 **LANGUAGE NOTE**
Some students may not be familiar with the word *plaza.* Introduce other parallel terms such as *town square, market place, public square, park.*

 PREDICTABLE PROBLEM
Students may be confused with *its* and *it's* when they write about the story.

LESSON 3
LANGUAGE POWER

STUDENT BOOK/SKILLS JOURNAL PAGES 28–29

⭐ **KEY EXPERIENCES**

■ Describing location

■ Playing a location guessing game

■ Following oral/written directions

■ Distinguishing between true/false statements

⭐ **KEY LANGUAGE**

■ prepositions of place

⭐ **MATERIALS**

■ index cards

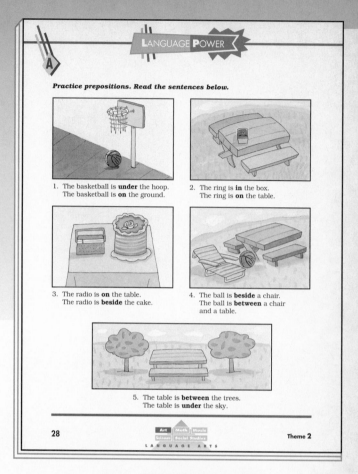

Practice prepositions. Read the sentences below.

1. The basketball is **under** the hoop. The basketball is **on** the ground.
2. The ring is **in** the box. The ring is **on** the table.
3. The radio is **on** the table. The radio is **beside** the cake.
4. The ball is **beside** a chair. The ball is **between** a chair and a table.
5. The table is **between** the trees. The table is **under** the sky.

28

LANGUAGE ARTS

Theme 2

1 ♦ INTRODUCE

Building background: Describing location. Use objects in the classroom to involve students in questions and answers using the prepositions of place *in, on, under, beside, between.* Write the prepositions on the board. Place a book on a desk and say, *The book is on the desk.* Then ask, *What is on the shelf?* (point to the word on the board) Continue in this manner, using other objects and prepositions of place.

MULTI-LEVEL TEACHING STRATEGIES

You can include all students by asking questions appropriate to each student's language level.

Speech Emergence: *What is in/on/under/beside/between the ...?*

Developing Fluency: *Where is the ...?*

Playing a location guessing game. Have students work in small groups to play a game. The starter thinks of an object in the room and then describes its location, using one of the prepositions of placement. For example, *I'm thinking of something that is between the chalkboard and the clock.* The turn rotates to the next person after a correct guess.

2 ♦ EXPLORE

Activating prior knowledge. Open to page 28. To prompt discussion, ask multi-level questions such as *What things do you see in the first picture? Where is the basketball?*

Grammar in context. Read aloud the sentences on page 28 as students follow silently. Ask students to look at the picture on page 29. Ask questions about the location of objects in the picture, such as *Is the basketball in or on the ground?* Continue in the same manner with the remaining pictures on the page. Have students work in pairs to ask and answer questions about the pictures.

True/False statements. Have students work in teams. Mix up index cards with *in, on, under, beside* and *between* on them, and place them face down in a pile. Students take turns drawing a card. Each time a student draws a card, he or she must use the preposition in a sentence to tell the location of an object in the room. The sentence can be true or deliberately false. A student on the other team

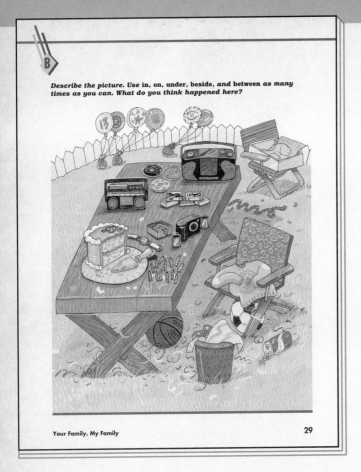

Describe the picture. Use in, on, under, beside, and between as many times as you can. What do you think happened here?

Your Family, My Family   29

must tell whether the statement is true or false. If the player identifies and corrects a false statement, award an extra point. If students are ready, add new prepositions such as *on top of*, *inside*, *next to*, *at the bottom*, etc.

**SKILLS JOURNAL
PAGES 28-29**

Page 28: Prepositions of location; comparing/contrasting. Students answer questions about an illustration. **Page 29: Reading for a purpose; describing quantity.** Students read a dialogue and answer questions. Teaching suggestions are provided in the Skills Journal annotations.

3 ◆ EXTEND

Following oral directions. Play a TPR game with the students by having them follow directions for placement. Give directions such as, *Put a book on your head. Put your thumb between two fingers.* After students have caught on, split them into small groups and have them continue the game, taking turns giving the directions.

ART Following written directions. Prepare and distribute a sheet of directions for students to follow, such as *Draw a tree on your paper. Put a bird in the tree. Draw a house beside the tree. Show a person sleeping under the tree. Draw a dog between the person and the house.* Have students exchange papers to check that they correctly followed directions for placement of the objects in their pictures. (CALLA: Imagery)

Describing location. Select an item in the classroom and ask students to use as many of the prepositions of place as they can to describe its location. Vary the activity by turning it into a round-robin game played in small groups. The first student picks an object and uses one preposition of place to describe its location. Each subsequent student must give a description different from those preceding. If a student cannot come up with a new description, he or she retires from the game. The last student remaining in the game starts over with a new object.

ONGOING ASSESSMENT

PERFORMANCE Oral and written language. Observe students' ability to follow oral and written directions to evaluate their understanding of prepositions of place.

LESSON 4
EXPLORE...SCIENCE

STUDENT BOOK/SKILLS JOURNAL
PAGES 30–31

 KEY EXPERIENCES

- Reading for information
- Discussing nutrition
- Interpreting a graph
- Planning meals
- Following a recipe
- Keeping a food diary
- Practicing math skills

 KEY LANGUAGE

- *calcium, dairy products, food pyramid, grains, recommended daily servings, vegetables, vitamin*

MATERIALS

- pictures of the different food groups

- ingredients for salsa: tomatoes, onion, green pepper, cucumber, vinegar, oil, oregano, parsley, tortilla chips

- large mixing bowl, paring knives, chopping block

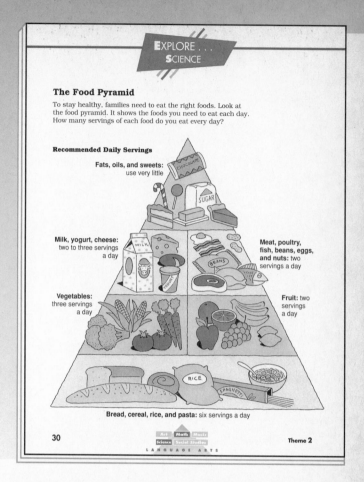

EXPLORE . . . SCIENCE

The Food Pyramid

To stay healthy, families need to eat the right foods. Look at the food pyramid. It shows the foods you need to eat each day. How many servings of each food do you eat every day?

Recommended Daily Servings

Fats, oils, and sweets: use very little

Milk, yogurt, cheese: two to three servings a day

Meat, poultry, fish, beans, eggs, and nuts: two servings a day

Vegetables: three servings a day

Fruit: two servings a day

Bread, cereal, rice, and pasta: six servings a day

30

Theme 2

1 • INTRODUCE

Building background: Discussing nutrition. Discuss the importance of a good diet. Begin by encouraging students to talk about food. Ask, *What are your favorite foods?* Display pictures of the various food groups and have students identify the foods. Ask questions that encourage students to make inferences about the importance of a balanced diet.

MULTI-LEVEL TEACHING STRATEGIES

You can include all students by asking questions appropriate to each student's language level.

Speech Emergence: *What are some good foods? What foods do you think would make a good meal?*

Developing Fluency: *Why do you think some foods are better for you than others? Why is it important to eat healthy meals?*

Exploring key vocabulary. Have students create a food word chart, listing as many foods as they can under the headings: dairy, meats, vegetables, fruits, grains, sweets. (CALLA: Grouping)

2 • EXPLORE

Activating prior knowledge. Open to page 30. Invite students to comment on the page. To prompt discussion, ask multi-level questions such as *Have you seen this shape before? Do you know what this shape is called? Why do you think the foods are shown in a pyramid, or triangle?*

Interpreting graphic information. Discuss the food pyramid. Ask multi-level questions such as *Name the foods shown in the pyramid. How many servings of bread, cereal, rice or pasta should we eat each day? Which foods are shown at the top of the pyramid? Why should we eat very few sweets? What do you eat every day?*

SCIENCE Planning a meal. Have students work in small groups to plan a meal. Remind them to

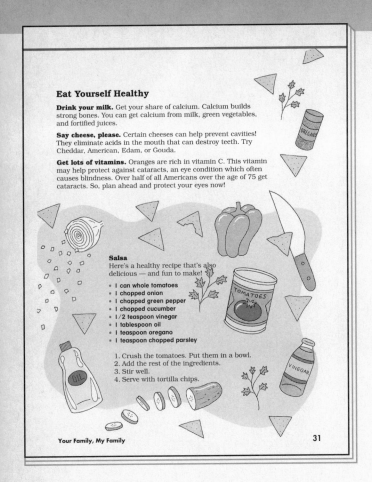

Eat Yourself Healthy

Drink your milk. Get your share of calcium. Calcium builds strong bones. You can get calcium from milk, green vegetables, and fortified juices.

Say cheese, please. Certain cheeses can help prevent cavities! They eliminate acids in the mouth that can destroy teeth. Try Cheddar, American, Edam, or Gouda.

Get lots of vitamins. Oranges are rich in vitamin C. This vitamin may help protect against cataracts, an eye condition which often causes blindness. Over half of all Americans over the age of 75 get cataracts. So, plan ahead and protect your eyes now!

Salsa

Here's a healthy recipe that's also delicious — and fun to make!

- 1 can whole tomatoes
- 1 chopped onion
- 1 chopped green pepper
- 1 chopped cucumber
- 1/2 teaspoon vinegar
- 1 tablespoon oil
- 1 teaspoon oregano
- 1 teaspoon chopped parsley

1. Crush the tomatoes. Put them in a bowl.
2. Add the rest of the ingredients.
3. Stir well.
4. Serve with tortilla chips.

Your Family, My Family   31

include servings recommended in the food pyramid. Have the groups share their menus with the class, explaining why they chose certain foods.

GUIDED READING Reading for information. Read "Eat Yourself Healthy" on page 31 as students follow along. Use multi-level questions to check understanding: *Why should you drink milk? What other foods have calcium? What's a cavity? Why do some cheeses help prevent cavities? How does vitamin C help you stay healthy?*

Following recipe directions: Making salsa. Direct students' attention to the salsa recipe. Call on volunteers to read the ingredients and directions. Discuss why this recipe is healthy. Prepare the salsa recipe. Later, call on students to tell how they divided up the preparation and cleanup chores. If a kitchen is not available in your school, groups of volunteers can do the preparation at home and bring the salsa to class the next day to share. (CALLA: Cooperation)

SKILLS JOURNAL PAGES 30-31

Page 30: Food vocabulary; using a chart; describing quantity. Students complete a daily meal chart. **Page 31: Math skills; data collection; interviewing.** Students write friends' orders from a menu and tally costs. Teaching suggestions are provided in the Skills Journal annotations.

3 ◆ EXTEND

SCIENCE Keeping a food diary. Encourage students to keep a diary for one week of all the foods and servings they eat at each meal. Then have students chart their daily meals into the four basic food groups. Ask students to analyze their eating habits to see if they are eating the recommended daily servings of the food groups. Have them report their findings and whether they think they might change their eating habits. (CALLA: Grouping/Self-assessment)

MATH Comparing geometric shapes. Have volunteers draw different geometric shapes on the board. Then invite students to figure out what the food pyramid would look like if it were depicted using a different shape. Discuss whether the graphic representation would be as effective.

PROCESS WRITING PORTFOLIO

See the ideas and writing topics related to this theme.

- - - **ONGOING ASSESSMENT** - - -

PERFORMANCE Oral language. Have students describe a healthy meal in their own words.

TEACHER TO TEACHER

Work with a health teacher to promote a Healthy Eating Week (or Month). Have mainstream students from health and ESL classes team up to make posters that remind students to eat healthy. Posters can be in English and the native language(s) of the students in ESL classes.

LESSON 5
INSIDE... OUTSIDE...

📷 STUDENT BOOK/SKILLS JOURNAL
PAGES 32–33

⭐ **KEY EXPERIENCES**

- Discussing family activities
- Reading/responding to a photo essay
- Making an activities chart
- Describing a favorite family activity

⭐ **KEY LANGUAGE**

- present progressive
- chores
- leisure activities

⭐ **MATERIALS**

- pictures of families involved in household chores and leisure activities

1 ◆ INTRODUCE

Building background: Discussing family activities.
Show pictures of families doing different chores and leisure activities. Have students identify and describe the activities. Invite students to suggest places and times for the activities.

┌─ **MULTI-LEVEL TEACHING STRATEGIES** ─┐

You can include all students by asking questions appropriate to each student's language level.

Speech Emergence: *Who is washing the dishes? Are they in the house or outside? Where are they painting?*

Developing Fluency: *What can you do in the kitchen? Where do you study? When do you study? What do you like to do with your family?*

└─────────────────────────────────┘

2 ◆ EXPLORE

Activating prior knowledge. Open to pages 32 and 33. Have students look at the pictures. To prompt discussion, ask multi-level questions such as *Point to the TV. Who is watching the TV? What is he doing? What room are they in? What do you like to do inside? Where are they planting a garden?*

What else is the family doing outside? Which activities do you like to do? Why?

Previewing. Ask a volunteer to read the titles on pages 32 and 33. Have students look at the pictures and identify the "inside" activities and "outside" activities. One of the students can list the activities on the board in two columns; have classmates help out with spelling. (CALLA: Advance organization)

📷 **GUIDED READING Reading a photo essay.**
Read or play the tape for the selection as students follow along in their books. Read the selection again. Ask multi-level questions to check students' understanding.

Display/Comprehension Questions

Page 32

Can you find families reading inside the house? (yes)
Are families playing games or playing soccer inside the house? (playing games)
What can families listen to? (music, radio)
What else can families do inside the house?

OUTSIDE...
Families wash windows, sweep steps, and empty trash. Families plant gardens, paint fences, and have barbeques. Families walk, swim, and ride bikes. What else do families do outside?

AROUND THE NEIGHBORHOOD...
Families are busy everywhere. Look around... at the supermarket, the dry cleaners, and the library ... at the hospital and the drugstore ... at restaurants and movie theaters ... at the hairdresser, the flower shop, and the bakery. Families are busy everywhere.

YOUR TURN   Talk about the pictures with a partner. What do you see in each picture? Tell about your family, too.

Your Family, My Family   33

Page 33

What are they washing outside the house? (windows)

Are families having barbecues inside or outside the house? (outside)

Which things are fun?

Which things are chores/work?

Do you do these things with your family?

What does your family like to do outside the house?

Rereading. Arrange students in pairs or small groups and have them read the selection together. Circulate, helping students as needed.

Independent reading. Have students read the selection silently. You may want to ask volunteers to read parts of the selection aloud.

Your Turn. With the class, read the instructions under "Your Turn." Have students work with partners as they talk about what they see in each picture and talk about activities that they do with their families.

SKILLS JOURNAL
PAGES 32-33

Reading for a purpose; writing. Students read two short essays, answer questions, and write about their families. Teaching suggestions are provided in the Skills Journal annotation.

3 ♦ EXTEND

SOCIAL STUDIES Making an activities chart. Create a chart titled "Inside and Outside Activities." Have students list additional family activities. You may want to have students add details to the activities, such as Inside: washing dishes in the kitchen, reading in my room; Outside: riding my bike in the park, swimming at the beach. (CALLA: Grouping)

Grammar in context. Have students answer a variety of information questions that prompt the use of *-ing* forms and singular personal pronouns. Students may still be forgetting to use *is*, e.g., *He playing*, or dropping the *-ing*, e.g. *He is play*.

ART/SOCIAL STUDIES Describing a favorite family activity. Students can talk about a favorite activity. Encourage students to tell who does the activity, when and where they do it, and why they enjoy it. Students can create drawings or collages made from magazine photos of items associated with the activities. Later, invite students to make comparisons among family interests and activities.

- - - **ONGOING ASSESSMENT** - - -

PERFORMANCE Oral language. With books closed, have students talk about inside and outside activities they do with their families.

MULTICULTURAL AWARENESS
Ask students about inside and outside activities in their cultures. For example, cooking is an outside activity in some cultures. Explain, if necessary, that a barbecue is traditional summer activity for many American families. Discuss food common to the occasion.

LESSON 6
MY BIRD DAY

📖 **STUDENT BOOK/SKILLS JOURNAL PAGE 34**

⭐ **KEY EXPERIENCES**

■ Discussing birthdays and family celebrations

■ Reading/responding to a poem

■ Writing a poem

■ Practicing math skills

⭐ **KEY LANGUAGE**

■ *birthday, good luck*

⭐ **MATERIALS**

■ party decorations or pictures of parties in different cultures

My Bird Day
JANET S. WONG

When my grandfather says *birthday*
in his Chinese accent,
it sounds like "bird day,"
which is closer to truth—
for us, anyway.

At my birthday parties
we never have
paper streamers,
piñatas in trees,
balloons taped up
on the wall.
We decorate with platters
of peking duck,
soy sauce chicken and squab
in lettuce cups.
Food is all
that matters.

Other Chinese families
might do things
differently,
but my grandfather,
whose name is Duck,
thinks it's good
luck to make
a bird day
special.

1 ◆ INTRODUCE

Building background: Discussing birthdays and family celebrations. Ask students what kinds of parties they have in their homes. List student ideas on the board in chart form. Also ask about typical decorations and food for the parties. (CALLA: Classifying)

┌─ **MULTI-LEVEL TEACHING STRATEGIES** ─┐

You can include all students by asking questions appropriate to each student's language level.

Speech Emergence: *When is your birthday? Do you like parties? When does your family have parties? Who comes to family parties?*

Developing Fluency: *Why do you like parties? What special foods do people eat at parties?*

└──────────────────────────────────┘

2 ◆ EXPLORE

Activating prior knowledge. Open to page 34. Ask a volunteer to read the title of the poem. To prompt discussion, ask multi-level questions about the picture such as *Who do you see in the picture? What food do you see? What else do you see?* Encourage students to suggest reasons for the title. Tell students to listen to find out why this poem is called "bird day."

📖 **GUIDED READING Reading a poem.** Read or play the tape for the poem as students follow along in their books. Ask multi-level questions such as *Who says "bird day?" What word is he trying to say? Is "bird day" a good name for the celebration? Why? Do you think that a "squab" is a bird or a fish? How can we find the answer?*

Pronunciation. Contrast the pronunciation of *bird day* and *birthday* for the students. Practice this contrast with other pairs such as *din/thin, hard/hearth,* and *mad/math.*

Independent reading. Have students read the poem silently. Then ask volunteers to read the poem aloud.

Discussing a poem. Discuss what makes a poem different from a prose story. Reread the poem to students, emphasizing its line breaks and cadence. Ask students what they like about this poem. Have them explain their answers.

Math skills. Students use an order form to answer questions of quantity and price. Teaching suggestions are provided in the Skills Journal annotation.

3 ♦ EXTEND

ART/SOCIAL STUDIES Describing a family celebration. Ask students to describe a special family celebration. Students can write a description of the event and then draw pictures to illustrate it.

Writing. Have students write a poem about their favorite celebration. Invite volunteers to share their poems.

See the list of ideas and writing topics related to this theme.

★ MULTICULTURAL AWARENESS
This is a good time to compare different types of parties and celebrations around the world. In some cultures and some religions, birthdays are not considered important. Encourage students to share other family celebrations such as name days or religious holidays.

★ LANGUAGE NOTES
Students may not be familiar with some of the culture-specific vocabulary in the poem. Squab is a young pigeon. Peking duck is duck prepared in the northern Chinese style. Soy sauce is a commonly used seasoning in Oriental cooking

♦ TEACHER'S NOTES ♦

LESSON 7
THE DANCE

 **STUDENT BOOK/SKILLS JOURNAL**
PAGE 35

⭐ **KEY EXPERIENCES**

- Reading/responding to a poem
- Understanding figurative language
- Writing a poem
- Designing a kite
- Measuring

⭐ **KEY LANGUAGE**

- *dance, hummingbird, kite, wind, hitting, hover, soaring, swooping*

⭐ **MATERIALS**

- kite or pictures of kites
- picture of a hummingbird

1 ♦ INTRODUCE

Building background: Describing a kite. Display a kite or pictures of kites. Encourage students to talk about what kites look like and what they do.

┌─ **MULTI-LEVEL TEACHING STRATEGIES** ─┐

You can include all students by asking questions appropriate to each student's language level.

Speech Emergence: *Draw a kite. Can a kite fly high? Where can you fly a kite?*

Developing Fluency: *What does a kite look like in the sky? How do you fly a kite?*

└───────────────────────────────────────┘

2 ♦ EXPLORE

Activating prior knowledge. Open to page 35. Ask a volunteer to read the title aloud. Invite students to comment on the page. Ask, *How do you know this is a poem?*

🖼 **GUIDED READING Reading a poem.** Read or play the tape as students follow along. Students who are able to should read the poem independently. Point out the words *soaring* and *swooping* and how the arrangement of the words make a picture of the way a kite moves. Ask multi-level ques-

tions such as *Are they inside or outside? What are they doing? Who is dancing: the father and son or the kite?*

Understanding figurative language (simile). Reread the poem chorally. Point out the lines, "The kites stop in the sky, like hummingbirds in motion." Discuss the way hummingbirds move; explain that this type of comparison is called a simile. Provide additional examples and have students come up with others.

Your Turn. Have students write their names in different designs. Encourage students to experiment.

📖 **SKILLS JOURNAL PAGE 35** **Reading and following directions; measuring.** Students make kites. Teaching suggestions are provided in the Skills Journal annotation.

3 ♦ EXTEND

Writing a poem. Students write a poem about a special activity. Encourage students to use at least one simile or to write a shape poem. Students can also illustrate the poems with drawings or photographs. Display in class.

ART Designing a kite. Students can make and decorate kites. Ask students to include a word or phrase on their kites describing what the kite looks like or how it moves. For example: *like an eagle, soaring, swooping, flying, falling, catching the wind, hitting the ground.* (CALLA: Imagery)

⭐ **COMPUTER CONNECTION**

Students can use computer graphics software to enter their names and manipulate the shape so that the letters bend and twist on a page.

The Dance

JOSÉ KAMHI

Look! A father and son are
flying kites together.
Watch them catch the wind!

Look, there they go!
Up, up
in a dance,
s
 o
  a
   r
    i
     n
      g
       i
        n g
         i
          p
         o
        o
       w
s

down,
nearly hitting the ground.

Then up again,
the kites stop in the sky,
like hummingbirds in motion;
they don't move — then
Swoop down again.

YOUR TURN   Write your name in a soaring, swooping design.

Your Family, My Family

Art Math Music
Drama Social Studies
LANGUAGE ARTS

35

TEACHER'S NOTES

LESSON 8
ALL STAR NEWS

📷 **STUDENT BOOK/SKILLS JOURNAL**
PAGES 36–37

⭐ **KEY EXPERIENCES**

- Reading for information and pleasure

- Interpreting graphs and charts

- Taking a poll

- Process writing

⭐ **KEY LANGUAGE**

- recreational activities

- *country, family, myself, proud, school, subject, team*

1 ◆ INTRODUCE

Building background: Discussing things to be proud of. Write *pride* and *proud of* on the board and use both expressions with some examples, such as a good group effort on an assignment or in a sporting event. Have students share things that they are proud of. You may want to create a word web on the board to record student ideas.

MULTI-LEVEL TEACHING STRATEGIES

You can include all students by asking questions appropriate to each student's language level.

Speech Emergence: *What are you proud of? What do you like about your country? town? school? family? yourself?*

Developing Fluency: *How do you feel when you are proud? What do people say to you when they are proud of something you do?*

2 ◆ EXPLORE

Previewing reading selections. Have students find and read the article headings on pages 36 and 37. Ask students to guess what the articles will be about. You may want to have students use article titles to form questions about the content. For example, for "Saturday Morning": *What do fami-*

lies do on Saturday morning? Is Saturday morning different from other days?

Scanning for information. Do rapid scanning practice by asking questions such as *Which selection mentions the country, Russia? Which day is in a selection title? Find the chart about birthdays.* (CALLA: Selective attention)

📷 **GUIDED READING Reading for information.**
Play the tape or read the selections, pausing occasionally to ask multi-level questions. Students who are able to should read the pages independently. You may want to pose the following display/comprehension questions to prompt discussion of each page and to monitor students' understanding.

Display/Comprehension Questions

Page 36
Where is Alex from? (Russia)
Why is Terry proud of her school? (great basketball team and teachers)
Who likes to read? (Nadia)
Is Nadia's favorite subject math or French? (math)

Whose mother is a teacher? (Chris)

What do most kids watch on Saturday morning? (cartoons)

How many kids did they ask? (50)

What other things do kids do on Saturday morning?

Page 37

What were movie theaters called a long time ago? (nickelodeons)

How much did they cost? (a nickel/five cents)

True or false: More than 100 million calls are made on Mother's Day. (true)

How many peanut butter sandwiches does the average kid eat before age 18? (1,500)

SOCIAL STUDIES/MATH Taking a poll. Have students conduct a poll of Saturday activities, birthdays, hours of TV watching, or another idea from the *All Star News.* Students prepare a survey questionnaire. Then students work in groups to compile the results and prepare graphs or charts.

SKILLS JOURNAL PAGES 36-37 **Process writing; computer connection.** Students read a sample newspaper article and write a first draft of their own article on the same topic. Teaching suggestions are provided in the Skills Journal annotation.

3 ◆ EXTEND

ART Making a class pride display. Have students brainstorm and write about something they are proud of. Students can use the TeenSpeak selections as models. Encourage students to illustrate their writing with drawings or magazine pictures. Make a bulletin board display or collage titled: *What We Are Proud Of.*

MATH Calculating percentages. Use the graph to determine the number of responses for each of the activities. For example, 80% of 50 kids = 40 kids watched Saturday morning cartoons.

ONGOING ASSESSMENT

PERFORMANCE Reading. Check student responses for ability to scan for information.

PORTFOLIO Writing. Save Skills Journal pages 36–37 as an example of independent writing.

★ **MULTICULTURAL AWARENESS**
Keep in mind that in some cultures it is considered rude to talk about one's own accomplishments.

★ **COMPUTER CONNECTION**
Have students use spreadsheet or graphics software to create a chart of the data they collect. Have students use a multimedia CD-ROM encyclopedia to find more information about nickelodeons, Mother's Day, twins, and Zuni Indians.

LESSON 9
ALL STAR NEWS

STUDENT BOOK/ SKILLS JOURNAL PAGES 38–39

★ KEY EXPERIENCES

■ Reading for information and pleasure

■ Responding to a letter

■ Working in collaborative groups:

- photo essays
- polling and charting
- research

■ Practicing science process skills

★ KEY LANGUAGE

■ *club, pen pal, stuff*

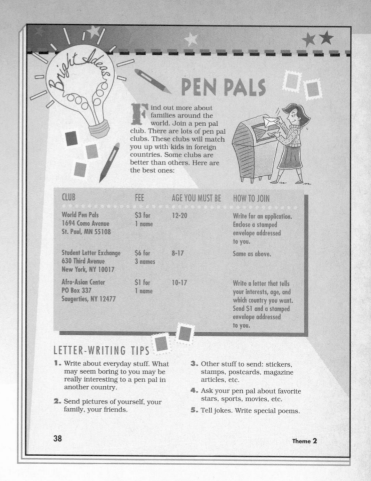

1 ◆ INTRODUCE

Building background: Discussing letter writing.
Encourage students to share ideas and experiences about letter writing. Find out if students know how to begin and end letters and how to address an envelope. As needed, provide a model and allow students to practice addressing real envelopes.

MULTI-LEVEL TEACHING STRATEGIES

You can include all students by asking questions appropriate to each student's language level.

Speech Emergence: *Have you ever received a letter? Do you write letters? What do you write on the envelope?*

Developing Fluency: *How do you begin a letter? How do you end a letter? What do you write about? Why do people write letters?*

Scanning for information. Have students scan page 38 of the Student Book to find the following key words: *pen pal, club,* and *stuff.* Ask students if they know any of these words. Encourage volunteers to give simple definitions and explanations.

2 ◆ EXPLORE

Activating prior knowledge. Open to pages 38–39. To prompt discussion, ask multi-level questions such as *What is a pen pal? What type of club is a pen pal club? What do you think this page is about?* Invite students to comment on the pages and to predict what the short selections will be about. (CALLA: Predicting)

GUIDED READING Reading for information. Read the selections as students follow along. Invite students who are able to do so to read independently. Reread, pausing to ask multi-level questions and do activities such as those that follow.

Reading a chart. Ask questions about the paragraph and chart: *How old do you have to be to join the World Pen Pals club? How much does it cost to join the Student Letter Exchange? Which club is least expensive to join?* Have students practice reading the addresses aloud. (CALLA: Comparing)

Bright Ideas. Ask questions about the letter-writing tips: *Why would you send pictures to a pen pal?*

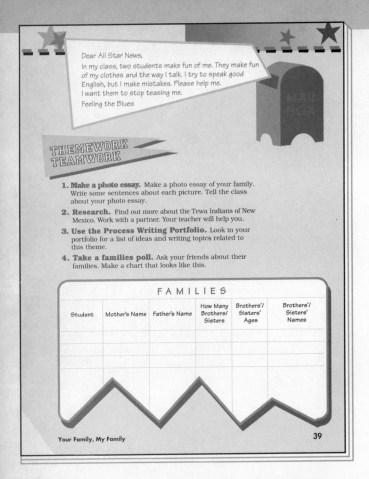

Dear All Star News,
In my class, two students make fun of me. They make fun of my clothes and the way I talk. I try to speak good English, but I make mistakes. Please help me. I want them to stop teasing me.
Feeling the Blues

THEMEWORK TEAMWORK

1. **Make a photo essay.** Make a photo essay of your family. Write some sentences about each picture. Tell the class about your photo essay.
2. **Research.** Find out more about the Tewa Indians of New Mexico. Work with a partner. Your teacher will help you.
3. **Use the Process Writing Portfolio.** Look in your portfolio for a list of ideas and writing topics related to this theme.
4. **Take a families poll.** Ask your friends about their families. Make a chart that looks like this.

FAMILIES

Student	Mother's Name	Father's Name	How Many Brothers/ Sisters	Brothers'/ Sisters' Ages	Brothers'/ Sisters' Names

Your Family, My Family   39

What would you tell a pen pal about yourself? What would you want to know about a pen pal? Encourage students to use the "Letter-Writing Tips" to plan a letter. Have them make notes about what they might write about for each of the five tips.

Mailbox. Ask questions to prompt discussion of the letter: *Why do people tease the letter writer? Do you think that's fair? How would you feel if people treated you that way? What are "the blues"? Have you ever felt that way? How would you help the letter writer?*

Writing a response. Have students split into small groups to discuss solutions for the letter writer. Have them write a response to "Feeling the Blues." Provide time for groups to share their letters of response with the class.

Themework/Teamwork. Read through the projects and encourage students to choose one or more to complete. Students can work independently or in cooperative groups. Allow time for students to share their completed projects with the class.

 **SKILLS JOURNAL PAGES 38-39** **Page 38: Expressing opinions; letter writing; process writing.** Students reread and answer the Mailbox letter on page 38 of the Student Book. **Page 39: Science skills.** Students read a cartoon experiment and draw conclusions. Teaching suggestions are provided in the Skills Journal annotation.

3 ✦ EXTEND

ART Designing a letterhead. Students may enjoy designing their own stationery. Show some examples with a letterhead and some with other types of designs.

Writing formal letters. As a group, write a letter to one of the pen pal clubs, requesting information. Brainstorm what to include and discuss how to organize the letter. You may want to write the letter as a group.

Writing to a friend or pen pal. Encourage students to use the notes they made on letter-writing tips to compose a letter. The letter can be to an imaginary or real pen pal or to a friend or relative.

 **PROCESS WRITING PORTFOLIO** See the list of ideas and writing topics related to this theme.

ONGOING ASSESSMENT

PORTFOLIO Writing. Add drafts and copies of final versions of letters to the students' portfolios. You may want to have students share their letters with others in the class or with you before sending. Also save Skills Journal page 39.

COMPUTER CONNECTION
Students will enjoy creating their own stationery on the computer, designing their own letterhead, and using clip art. If possible, use software that combines word processing and graphics.

53

LESSON 10 HOLISTIC ASSESSMENT

STUDENT BOOK/SKILLS JOURNAL PAGES 40–41

★ KEY EXPERIENCES

- Demonstrating comprehension
- Summarizing
- Thinking critically
- Self-assessment
- Writing about oneself

★ KEY LANGUAGE

- *fever, flu, skating, competition*

1 ◆ INTRODUCE

These two pages offer a variety of assessment opportunities. The left-hand page consists of listening and speaking activities that follow a taped presentation. In the speaking activity, students are asked to summarize what they have heard. The right-hand page consists of writing and critical thinking activities. These follow a reading passage that completes the listening component. You can use the activities to assess listening, speaking, reading, writing, and critical thinking skills. Have students work as a class or in small groups as you circulate and record observations on the **Anecdotal Record Form,** the **Reading Checklist,** and the **Writing Checklist** in the *All Star Assessment Package.*

Observing and recording student performance. Note the level of participation and the particular abilities of each student. How much do students understand? How well can they express themselves orally? What language structures do they use? What new words and concepts do they use? How actively do they participate? Use the **Anecdotal Record Form** in the *All Star Assessment Package* to record your observations and note areas for further development. Place in students' **portfolios.**

2 ◆ EXPLORE

Previewing. Open to pages 40 and 41 and let the students comment on the illustrations. Read the title "Mike's Problem" or call on a volunteer to do so. Give students time to read the listening questions.

Listening. Read or play the tape for the first part of "Mike's Problem." You will find the tapescript in the Appendix. Have students work independently to answer the listening questions. Read or play the tape again for students to check their work.

Speaking. Discuss what students have heard up to this point. Ask multi-level questions such as *How old is Mike? What was wrong with Mike yesterday? Did he have the flu or a headache?* If some students are struggling, play the tape again and summarize the story once yourself. Ask questions again. When you are satisfied with this stage, go on to the next.

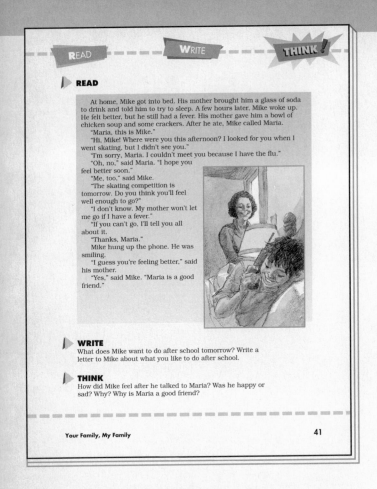

READ WRITE THINK!

▶ **READ**

At home, Mike got into bed. His mother brought him a glass of soda to drink and told him to try to sleep. A few hours later, Mike woke up. He felt better, but he still had a fever. His mother gave him a bowl of chicken soup and some crackers. After he ate, Mike called Maria.

"Maria, this is Mike."

"Hi, Mike! Where were you this afternoon? I looked for you when I went skating, but I didn't see you."

"I'm sorry, Maria. I couldn't meet you because I have the flu."

"Oh, no," said Maria. "I hope you feel better soon."

"Me, too." said Mike.

"The skating competition is tomorrow. Do you think you'll feel well enough to go?"

"I don't know. My mother won't let me go if I have a fever."

"If you can't go, I'll tell you all about it.

"Thanks, Maria."

Mike hung up the phone. He was smiling.

"I guess you're feeling better," said his mother.

"Yes," said Mike. "Maria is a good friend."

▶ **WRITE**
What does Mike want to do after school tomorrow? Write a letter to Mike about what you like to do after school.

▶ **THINK**
How did Mike feel after he talked to Maria? Was he happy or sad? Why? Why is Maria a good friend?

Your Family, My Family 41

teacher. Students may take a copy of this page home to share with families. You may want to save this page in students' **Assessment Portfolios**. Teaching suggestions are provided in the Skills Journal annotation.

3 ◆ EXTEND

SCIENCE Discussing colds and flu. Students work in small groups to come up with a list of ways to avoid catching a cold or the flu and a list of things to do if one does get sick. Later, groups share their ideas with the class.

ART/SCIENCE Making a colds and flu display. Students can work as a group to turn their lists into a bulletin board display for the classroom or for the whole school. Students decide who will be responsible for art, design, lettering.

📼 **Reading.** Read or play the tape for the story on page 41 as the students listen and follow along in their books. Pause occasionally to ask multi-level questions. Then have the students do partner reading, alternating paragraphs.

Writing. Encourage students to tell you what they have heard and read. Do not look for word-for-word retelling, even from your best students. Have students write their summaries in outline form. (CALLA: Summarizing)

Thinking. Ask students questions such as *What would you do if you felt sick at school? Who do you think Mike went to see at school when he felt sick?*

SKILLS JOURNAL PAGES 40-41 **Page 40: Assessment; reinforcing key vocabulary.** Students circle the word that doesn't belong in each of ten vocabulary groups, then write about their favorite foods. **Page 41: Self-assessment; Home-School Connection.** Students complete a chart of their accomplishments to be checked by the

LESSON 11
WHEN IS YOUR BIRTHDAY?

STUDENT BOOK/SKILLS JOURNAL
PAGE 42

★ **KEY EXPERIENCES**

- Reviewing the theme
- Singing a song
- Reading and following directions
- Singing birthday songs from other cultures

★ **KEY LANGUAGE**

- *dance, chance*

WHEN IS YOUR BIRTHDAY
WORDS AND MUSIC BY ANDY VALLARIO AND LARRY MILTON

Hey, hey. When is your birthday?
Can you tell me the day, the month, the year?
We'd like to know about your birthday.
We'll have a party
Do happy things
Blow out the candles as we dance and sing.

Please, please. Talk about your birthday.
Does it come in the winter, spring, summer, or fall?
We'd like to know about your birthday.'

Is it in January?
February?
March or April, May, June or July?
Is it in August?
September?
October? November?
Or maybe in December?

Hey, hey. When is your birthday?
Can you tell me the day when you were born?

42   Theme **2**

1 ◆ INTRODUCE

Activating prior knowledge: Reviewing the theme.
Review the theme by asking volunteers to retell or describe different stories in the theme. Encourage students to tell which story or activity was their favorite.

┌─ **MULTI-LEVEL TEACHING STRATEGIES** ─┐

You can include all students by asking questions appropriate to each student's language level.

Speech Emergence: *Did you like the stories in this theme? Which story or activity did you like best? Least? Why?*

Developing Fluency: *Why do you think this theme was called "Your Family, My Family"?*

2 ◆ EXPLORE

Building background. Open to page 42. To prompt discussion, ask multi-level questions such as *What is the title of this song? Do you know any other birthday songs?*

Singing the song. Read through the song several times with students. Then play the tape of the song several times, inviting students to sing along as soon as they are ready.

SKILLS JOURNAL PAGE 42 **Reading and following directions; Home-School Connection.** Students make birthday cards. Teaching suggestions are provided in the Skills Journal annotation.

3 ◆ EXTEND

SOCIAL STUDIES/MUSIC Singing birthday songs.
Encourage students to write down the lyrics for birthday songs in their native language. Then students can teach the songs to their classmates.

Home-School Connection: Sharing with families.
Invite students to take their Student Books home to share with family members. Students can read stories to younger siblings, a parent, or a friend. Ask them to keep a record of who they read to and the person's reaction.

┌─ **ONGOING ASSESSMENT** ─┐

PERFORMANCE Oral language. As students give their opinions about the theme content, evaluate their comprehension and oral expression.

Wrap Up

ASSESSMENT

You have been collecting assessment data through the ongoing and holistic assessment options (Oral Language Checklist, Reading Checklist, Anecdotal Record Form) in this theme. Following are some additional assessment strategies that will help you evaluate your students' progress as well as adapt your instruction to meet their needs.

Student Self-Assessment. Self-assessment surveys are a means for students to have input into their own learning process. Students can use them to reflect on the work they have done and the learning strategies they have used during this theme. Be sure to check students' self-assessment pages for each theme in the Skills Journal.

Informed Instruction. Evaluate the checklists, anecdotal records, and Process Writing Portfolio collections from this theme as a means of informing your instruction.

- In which areas are students showing confidence and enthusiasm?
- In which areas are they hesitant or confused?
- Should you provide more classroom opportunities for oral language or writing?
- Would certain students (or the whole class) benefit from a focused mini-lesson on a certain area or skill?
- Remember to recycle skills as you teach the next theme and provide students with many opportunities to gain competence.

READING

Don't forget to check on and encourage students' independent reading. Students who weren't ready for independent reading in English at the beginning of this theme may be ready now. Students who continue to read in their first language should be encouraged to do first language book reviews and be an attentive audience for other students' reviews in English.

BOOKBYTES

Have students been able to use the *All Star BookBytes* CD-ROM software? The BookBytes' book list includes the titles on the Theme Booklists for all levels of *All Star English.* BookBytes helps students choose a book to read based on their responses to a short questionnaire, then prompts students to think about and respond to what they've read through writing, drawing, and drama. Students can print out their work and share it with others. They can also choose to see other students' work on-screen in a gallery presentation.

THEME CELEBRATION

If your class is participating as an All Star Team, the end of theme is a good time to review students' accomplishments with the Theme Booklist and Theme Projects. Consider posting a chart in the classroom where students may check off their accomplishments and, if you are using a point system, total their points for the theme. Students should strive to do their best and outdo their *own* scores, not compete with each other. Encourage students to present their All Star projects to the class to allow more oral practice and to sharpen students' presentation skills. You might invite other classes or families to attend the presentations.

PREVIEW

GETTING ALONG TOGETHER • •

CONCEPTS
- questioning gender roles
- team sports
- teamplay
- how kids spend their time and money
- making decisions

LITERATURE

- A Win for Sung Hee
  (*fiction*)
- I Love Baseball
  (*poem*)
- Let's Play Soccer
  (*photo essay*)
- All Star News
  (*short nonfiction articles*)
- No, No, No
  (*song*)

READING/WRITING SKILLS

- summarizing a story
- reading for information and pleasure
- classifying information
- making comparisons
- critical thinking
- reading comprehension
- process writing
- reading/responding to a photo essay
- reading/responding to a poem
- writing a poem
- understanding print conventions
- understanding poetic language
- reading a bar graph
- reading a schedule
- reading/following directions
- writing a letter

CONTENT

- **Math:** Math: taking a poll, charting results, solving problems
- **Social Studies:** researching a topic, describing actions, making a calendar of events
- **Art/Music:** writing and illustrating a poem, exploring string and percussion instruments, designing a uniform/logo, making a diagram, making a scale drawing
- **Science:** demonstrating vibration, creating a prototype, drawing conclusions from an experiment

---

KEY LANGUAGE/KEY EXPERIENCES

- days of the week
- simple present tense
- taking a poll
- self-assessment
- using a chart
- telling time
- expressing opinions
- understanding humor
- practicing math skills
- following/giving oral instructions
- working in collaborative groups
- practicing science process skills
- researching
- vocabulary development
- learning language through song

THEME BOOKLIST/ THEME PROJECTS

As this new theme begins, photocopy the Theme Booklist/Theme Projects pages (following spread) for students. Encourage students to read as many books as they like from the Booklist, and to complete any of the assignments on the Project list as homework for this theme.

AWARDING POINTS FOR ALL STAR TEAMS

This is a good opportunity to motivate students through an All Star Team approach. Consider assigning point values to each project, including reading books from the booklist. Explain to students that they will accumulate points for each book they read or project they complete during the theme. Students will try to top their own scores as they work through each theme, competing against themselves, not each other. Remind students that they will have the opportunity to present their *All Star* projects to the class at the end of the theme.

BOOKBYTES

If you have a computer with a CD-ROM drive available, introduce students to the *All Star BookBytes* software which is correlated to the Theme Booklists throughout *All Star English*. *BookBytes* categorizes the books by genre and helps students choose a book to read based on their answers to a short questionnaire. It then prompts students to think about and respond to what they've read through writing, drawing, and drama activities. Students can print out their work and share it with others or view work on-screen in a gallery presentation.

THEME BOOKLIST

HERE ARE SOME BOOKS YOU MIGHT LIKE TO READ.
LOOK FOR THEM IN YOUR LIBRARY.

Book of Rhythms, by Langston Hughes. Oxford, 1995. How poetry and jazz beat through our lives.

Forward Pass, by Thomas Dygard. William Morrow, 1989. A football coach finds a cure for his mediocre team—a wide-receiver named Jill!

Gymnasts, The, by Elizabeth Levy. Scholastic, Inc., 1989-1992. A series of books about girls on a gymnastics team.

Just for Kicks, by Paul Baczewski. J.B. Lippincott, 1990. A spoof of sports books.

Sports, by Tim Hammond. Alfred A. Knopf, 1988. Everything you want to know about the most popular sports—even archery!

The Toilet Paper Tigers, by Gordon Corman. Scholastic, Inc., 1993. A baseball team tries to get it together.

The Trading Game, Alfred Slote. J.B. Lippincott, 1990. A baseball card collection is a boy's only interest.

The Way Things Work, by David Macaulay. Houghton Mifflin, 1988. A visual guide to the world of machines.

What's the Opposite of a Best Friend?, by A. Bates. Scholastic, Inc., 1993. Two girls have problems growing up.

Who Ran My Underwear Up the Flagpole?, by Jerry Spinelli. Scholastic, Inc., 1992. Four misfits suddenly score big during the football season.

Wilma Rudolph, by Tom Biracree. Chelsea House, 1988. The life of the great Olympic athlete.

BOOKS IN LANGUAGES OTHER THAN ENGLISH

Una semana en Lugano (A Week in Lugano), by Francisco Hinojosa. Barcelona, España: ediciones sm.

El puente de piedra (The Bridge of Stone), by Alfredo Gómez Cerdá. Barcelona, España: ediciones sm.

Noma Ui Plagyon, by Orini ch' olhak yon 'guso (Korean). Los Angeles, CA: Jeong-Eum-Sa Imports, Inc. (The Korea Book Center).

Chinese Proverbs, by R. McCunn and YS Tang (Chinese). Arcada, CA: Shen's Books and Supplies.

★ THEME PROJECTS

YOU MAY WANT TO WORK ON THESE PROJECTS ALONE OR WITH A PARTNER OR SMALL GROUP.

☆ Make a set of vocabulary cards that show vocabulary words learned in the theme on one side and illustrations of the words on the other.

☆ Write dialogues that use vocabulary or grammatical structures learned in the theme.

☆ Write original sentences or stories using key vocabulary words.

☆ Create a word search or crossword puzzle that uses vocabulary from the theme.

☆ Translate a song, poem, or prose selection from your native language into English.

☆ Create paintings, drawings, or dioramas of stories or readings within the theme.

☆ Produce scripts or dramatizations of information presented in the theme.

☆ Create a collage, mobile, or other three-dimensional art project that illustrates key concepts from the theme.

☆ Take a survey and present graphs and charts that explore questions related to the theme.

☆ Write journal entries for five to ten days about key concepts or ideas in the theme.

☆ Paste news clippings onto blank paper and write a short statement explaining how the article relates to the theme.

☆ Write a letter to the editor, the school government, City Hall, or the President of the United States about issues and ideas in the theme.

☆ Create maps that show the location of places mentioned in the theme.

☆ Create a time line that shows what happened in a story from the theme.

☆ Make a story chart that clearly labels the characters, plot, setting, climax, and ending of a story from the theme.

☆ Present a dramatic reading of one of the stories in the theme.

☆ Write a letter that gives advice or constructive criticism to a character in a story from the theme.

LESSON 1
THEME OPENER

STUDENT BOOK/SKILLS JOURNAL PAGE 43

★ KEY EXPERIENCES

- Talking about sports
- Talking about cooperation
- Previewing theme content and titles
- Exploring key vocabulary
- Playing a team game
- Self-assessment
- Discovering the library

★ KEY LANGUAGE

- *sports, team*
- names of team sports

1 ◆ INTRODUCE

Theme 3, Getting Along Together, introduces sports and the concept of team effort. Students will read and talk about baseball and soccer. They will practice the present tense and learn sports terms.

Building background: Talking about team cooperation. To introduce the theme "Getting Along Together," ask questions to prompt discussion of working together as a team: *Do you belong to any teams? Which ones? What activities need people working together in teams?*

MULTI-LEVEL TEACHING STRATEGIES

You can include all students by asking questions appropriate to each student's language level.

Speech Emergence: *Do you know how to play (baseball)? Can you play (baseball) by yourself? What is your favorite sport? How many people are on a (baseball) team?*

Developing Fluency: *How do people on a (baseball) team work together to play the game?*

2 ◆ EXPLORE

Activating prior knowledge. Open to page 43. To prompt discussion of the theme content, ask multi-level questions such as *What is the title of this theme? What does the picture show? What do you think this theme will be about?* (CALLA: Predicting)

Reading Corner. Have students read the titles, authors, and descriptions of the three books listed under Reading Corner. These are just a few selections from the Theme Booklist, chosen to help motivate students to want to read. Have the books available for students to look at. Prompt discussion about which book each student would like to read and why. Allow students to sign up for turns with the books. Use this experience to get your students excited about reading.

Previewing theme content and titles. Guide students as they look through the unit, inviting them to comment on the titles, photos, and art. Have students predict how each of the titles is connected with the theme of "Getting Along Together."

Exploring key vocabulary. During a discussion of the theme titles, introduce vocabulary for the names of team sports by asking students to list their favorite sports or games. Write student responses on the board.

Activating prior knowledge; self-assessment. Students complete chart before and after lesson. Teaching suggestions are provided in the Skills Journal annotation.

3 ◆ EXTEND

Playing a team game. In order to experience working together, have students play a team game of their choosing. If it's not possible to take the class outside to a playground for this activity, invite them to play an indoor game such as Twenty Questions or Charades. Afterwards, encourage students to describe how they worked together as a team.

GETTING ALONG TOGETHER

THEME 3

Reading Corner
Try these terrific books!

What's the Opposite of a Best Friend?
by A. Bates
Two girls have problems growing up.

The Toilet Paper Tigers
by Gordon Korman
A baseball team tries to get it together.

Who Ran My Underwear Up the Flagpole?
by Jerry Spinelli
Four misfits suddenly score big during the football season.

43

★ **BOOKBYTES**
Have students use the BookBytes software as motivation for reading and writing about what they've read.

◆ TEACHER'S NOTES ◆

Discovering the library. Lead students on a tour of your school or local library. With students, gather the books recommended for this theme in the Theme Booklist. Students will enjoy participating in this search and, in so doing, will practice basic library and research skills. In the classroom, plan to read aloud to students each day. You may wish to record the books on tape and let students read the books as they listen to the tapes. Encourage students to read independently whenever possible.

╌ ╌ **ONGOING ASSESSMENT** ╌ ╌

PERFORMANCE Oral language. Evaluate students' oral language abilities as they discuss working together as a team.

LESSON 2
A WIN FOR SUNG HEE

📷 STUDENT BOOK/SKILLS JOURNAL
PAGES 44–46

⭐ **KEY EXPERIENCES**

- Discussing baseball
- Understanding print conventions
- Summarizing a story
- Making comparisons

⭐ **MATERIALS**

- baseball equipment or pictures of equipment: bat, ball, glove
- pictures of baseball field and players

⭐ **KEY LANGUAGE**

- *do my best...*
- *baseball, champion, coach, double, first base, home run, Ping-Pong, pitch, runner, batter, try-out*
- *hit, swing, throw, field the ball*
- *simple present with -s and -es*

1 ◆ INTRODUCE

Building background: Discussing baseball. Show baseball equipment or pictures of baseball items. Ask students to describe or demonstrate how the items are used in baseball. If students are not familiar with the game, model TPR commands related to a baseball game and have students do the actions.

┌─ **MULTI-LEVEL TEACHING STRATEGIES** ─┐

You can include all students by asking questions appropriate to each student's language level.

Speech Emergence: *What do you do after you hit the ball with the bat? Where do people play baseball? Is baseball a summer or winter sport?*

Developing Fluency: *What is the glove used for? When do you use a bat? How do you use the bat?*

└────────────────────────────────────┘

Making a baseball word web. With students, brainstorm a list of words about baseball. Create a word web using categories such as: things you use to play, where you play, how you play. Fill in the words that students suggest under the proper categories. Add additional categories as needed.

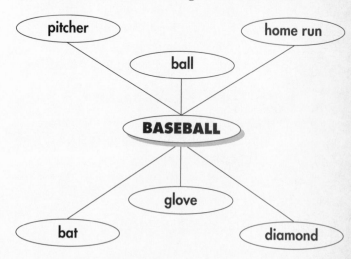

2 ◆ EXPLORE

Activating prior knowledge. Open to page 44. Ask a volunteer to read aloud the title, "A Win for Sung Hee." Have students look at the pictures on pages 44–46. To prompt discussion, ask multi-level questions such as *Which person is Sung Hee? What does she look like? Do you think she likes baseball? How do you know?*

GUIDED READING Reading nonfiction. Read or play the tape for the story as students follow along in their books. Read the story again, stopping to ask multi-level questions. Students who are able to should read the story independently. You may want to pose the following display/comprehension questions to prompt discussion of each page and monitor students' understanding.

Display/Comprehension Questions

Page 44
Is Sung Hee a girl or a boy? (girl)
Where does she go to school? (Sunny Brooke Junior High)

What grade is she in? (seventh grade)
Does Sung Hee like to play first or second base? (first base)
Who is Sung Hee's brother? (Doo Jin)
What sport is he good at? (Ping-Pong)
Can girls play on the school baseball team? (no)
Who doesn't want girls on the team? (the coach)

Page 45
Is Sung Hee going to try out for the team? (yes)
Why? (She wants to play on the team.)
Who can hit the ball better than the boys? (Sung Hee)
Where does Sung Hee hit the ball? (over the fence)
Where does Sung Hee throw the ball? (to home plate)
What does Doo Jin's friend say about Sung Hee? (She is better than the boys.)

Page 46
Did Sung Hee get on the team? (yes)
How will her parents feel? (proud)
How do you think Sung Hee feels?
Why do you think the coach put Sung Hee on the team?
Do you think the coach has changed his mind?

Understanding print conventions/quotes. Help students locate the quotation marks on page 44 with questions such as *How do you know when someone in a story is giving another person's exact words? What are the marks called? Find some quotation marks in this story.* Show examples of quotation marks in other stories as well.

Understanding print conventions/capital letters. Arrange students in pairs and have them reread the story together. Point out on page 45 the sentence "Your sister really IS better..." Explain that "IS" is there in capital letters for emphasis, to state a strong opinion. When reading, make sure students put stress on the word. Go around the room assisting as needed.

Independent reading. Have students read the story silently. Then have volunteers read the story aloud.

THEME 3: GETTING ALONG TOGETHER

Your Turn. With the class, read the instructions under "Your Turn." Have students work with partners as they talk about girls and boys playing sports. Depending on the level of the class, you may want to follow up by having students summarize their partner's opinions.

Page 44: Reading comprehension. Students complete multiple choice sentences. **Page 45: Sequencing.** Students put sentences from the story in correct order. **Page 46: Summarizing.** Students complete a summary chart for the story. Teaching suggestions are provided in the Skills Journal annotation.

3 ◆ EXTEND

Watching a baseball game. If possible, students can watch a local baseball team practice or play a game. Alternatively, you may want to bring in a video about baseball or videotape some news segments of professional baseball games and play them in class.

Making comparisons. Students can work in pairs to compare baseball to another sport they may enjoy. Encourage students to use a Venn diagram to show the similarities and differences. (CALLA: Comparing)

Grammar in context. Write the following compound words on the board: *baseball, tryouts*. Have students find the words on pages 44 and 45. Ask a volunteer to explain the meanings and point out the two words in the compounds. Ask if students can think of other compound words related to sports such as *football, volleyball, basketball, shortstop*. Go back to Themes 1 and 2 to find more compound words. (CALLA: Selective attention)

Personalizing. Encourage students to find out if there are any girls in your school who play football or baseball. If not, have there ever been? Have any students ever tried out but not made the team? Students can interview various coaches and report back to the class on their findings. Discuss students' feelings about girls playing on *boys'* teams.

 Can girls play sports as well as boys? Talk about it with a partner.

46   Theme 3

SOCIAL STUDIES Researching women in sports. Encourage interested students to investigate the topic of women in sports. Brainstorm with students a list of possible areas of investigation and resources. Possible topics might include a comparison of men's and women's events in the Olympics, women in tennis, women's sports in other countries, salaries of professional women athletes compared to men. Students can present their findings orally or in writing.

PROCESS WRITING PORTFOLIO See the list of ideas and writing topics related to this theme.

ONGOING ASSESSMENT

PERFORMANCE Oral language. With books closed, have students retell the story in their own words. Check the sequence of events.

◆ TEACHER'S NOTES ◆

 LANGUAGE NOTES

Some words can be used as both a verb and a noun. Students may be familiar with a sports *field*, but not with the action to *field* a ball. Sung Hee hit a *pitch* (a ball that was pitched) and the player will *pitch* (throw in a specific direction) the ball.

 MULTICULTURAL AWARENESS

Although many Americans think that baseball is played just in the United States, the sport is very popular in other countries around the world, including Japan and Cuba. In fact, the American team does not usually win the baseball event in the Olympics!

LESSON 3
I LOVE BASEBALL

📼 STUDENT BOOK/SKILLS JOURNAL PAGE 47

⭐ **KEY EXPERIENCES**

- Reading/responding to a poem
- Understanding poetic language
- Writing and illustrating a poem

⭐ **KEY LANGUAGE**

- *fans, players, umpire, vendors*
- *cheer, hot dogs, national anthem, peanuts, flag*

⭐ **MATERIALS**

- pictures of a baseball stadium

1 ◆ INTRODUCE

Building background: Discussing baseball. Show pictures of a baseball field or stadium. Encourage students to point out where different people are during a game: spectators, players, umpires, and coaches. Students can suggest what people do during the game.

MULTI-LEVEL TEACHING STRATEGIES

You can include all students by asking questions appropriate to each student's language level.

Speech Emergence: *Who is in the field? Are they playing or watching the game?*

Developing Fluency: *Why do people watch baseball games? What sounds can you hear at a baseball game?*

---

2 ◆ EXPLORE

Activating prior knowledge. Open to page 47. Ask a volunteer to read the title of the poem. To prompt discussion, ask multi-level questions about the picture such as *What are the players doing? Where do the fans sit?*

📼 **GUIDED READING** **Reading a poem.** Read or play the tape for the poem as students follow along in their books. Read the poem again. Ask multi-level questions such as *What can you smell at a baseball game? What can the fans buy to eat? Are there many things to hear at the game? Who shouts "Play ball?" When do the fans cheer?*

Independent reading. Have students read the poem silently. Then ask volunteers to read the poem aloud.

Understanding poetic language. Explain that a poem paints a picture with words. Elicit that this poem uses the sights, smells, and sounds of a baseball stadium to paint a picture. Make a chart on the board of the five senses. Ask students to look back in the poem for examples of how the five senses are used at a baseball game.

 **SKILLS JOURNAL PAGE 47** **Creative writing.** Students write and illustrate a poem about their favorite sport. Teaching suggestions are provided in the Skills Journal annotation.

3 ◆ EXTEND

MUSIC **"Take Me out to the Ball Game" and "The Star Spangled Banner."** Play recordings of the national anthem and songs associated with baseball games. You may want to teach the words to the songs.

ART **Writing and illustrating a poem.** Encourage students to write a poem about a favorite sporting event or activity. Students can use the five senses to describe the scene. Invite students to illustrate their poems. Display in class.

ONGOING ASSESSMENT

PERFORMANCE **Oral language.** With books closed, have students talk about the sights and sounds of a baseball game.

PORTFOLIO **Writing.** Save Skills Journal page 47 as an example of students' guided writing.

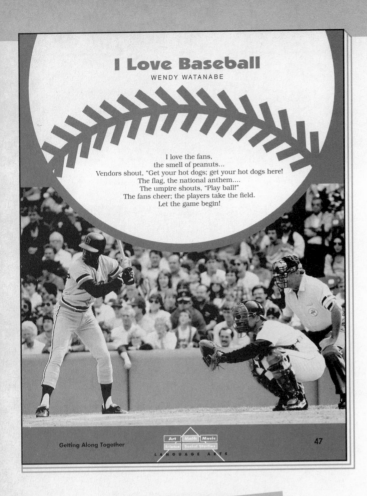

I Love Baseball
WENDY WATANABE

I love the fans,
the smell of peanuts...
Vendors shout, "Get your hot dogs; get your hot dogs here!
The flag, the national anthem....
The umpire shouts, "Play ball!"
The fans cheer; the players take the field.
Let the game begin!

Getting Along Together

47

LANGUAGE ARTS

✦ TEACHER'S NOTES ✦

★ MULTICULTURAL AWARENESS

Students may not understand why so many Americans enjoy watching or playing baseball. Encourage students to compare fans and spectators of a popular sport in their native countries (such as soccer) to understand the feelings and excitement that many Americans experience at a baseball game.

LESSON 4
LANGUAGE POWER

STUDENT BOOK/SKILLS JOURNAL
PAGES 48–49

★ KEY EXPERIENCES

- Talking about weekly activities
- Making Weekly Planners
- Reading a schedule
- Using a chart
- Taking a poll

★ KEY LANGUAGE

- *What does he/she do on ....*
- days of the week
- simple present with -s and -es

★ MATERIALS

- newspapers, magazines

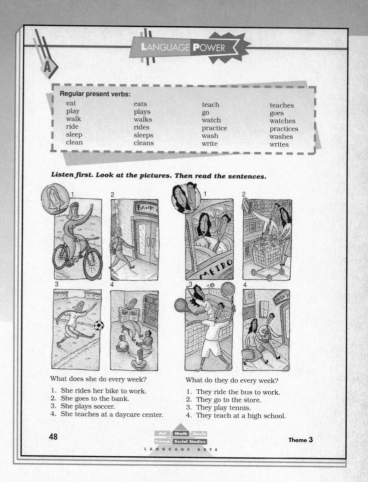

1 ♦ INTRODUCE

Building background: Talking about weekly activities.
Model for students your usual weekly activities:
This is what I do every week. I teach school. I go to the store. I clean house.... Then invite volunteers to tell what they do every week.

⌐ MULTI-LEVEL TEACHING STRATEGIES ¬

You can include all students by asking questions appropriate to each student's language level.

Speech Emergence: *Do you go to school every week? Do you ride your bike every week?*

Developing Fluency: *What do you do every week? Write a list of your weekly activities.*

Making Weekly Planners. Students make charts showing what they plan to do for the week.

Monday	Tuesday	Wednesday	Thursday	Friday	Saturday	Sunday
Go to school	Go to school	Go to school	Go to school	Go to school	Clean my room	Go to church
Band practice	Dentist appointment	Watch TV	Play soccer	Go to dance	Go to the store	Visit Grandma
					Go to the movies	

2 ♦ EXPLORE

Activating prior knowledge. Open to pages 48–49. To prompt discussion, ask multi-level questions such as *What is the woman doing in the pictures? Does she ride a bike? What do the pictures tell us about her? What are the man and woman doing? Do they play tennis?*

Exploring key language. Ask students to follow along as volunteers read the sentences. Ask multi-level questions to check students' comprehension: *What game does the woman play? Where do the two people teach?* Encourage students to respond with complete sentences.

Grammar in context. Contrast the use of *she plays* with *they play*, *she goes* with *they go*, etc. If students need more practice, have them make statements with *I*, *he*, *you*, and *we* as well.

Using the Word Bank. Direct students' attention to the Word Bank. Ask for volunteers to read the words in the chart. Elicit that the words in the

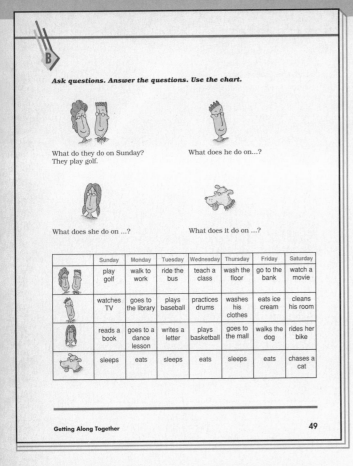

Ask questions. Answer the questions. Use the chart.

What do they do on Sunday?
They play golf.

What does he do on...?

What does she do on ...?

What does it do on ...?

	Sunday	Monday	Tuesday	Wednesday	Thursday	Friday	Saturday
	play golf	walk to work	ride the bus	teach a class	wash the floor	go to the bank	watch a movie
	watches TV	goes to the library	plays baseball	practices drums	washes his clothes	eats ice cream	cleans his room
	reads a book	goes to a dance lesson	writes a letter	plays basketball	goes to the mall	walks the dog	rides her bike
	sleeps	eats	sleeps	eats	sleeps	eats	chases a cat

Getting Along Together   49

chart are action words, or verbs: *Do all these words describe actions? What do we call this kind of word? Which form of the word* play *do we use with the words* he, she, *and* they?

Reading a schedule. Elicit that the chart on page 49 is a schedule that shows what family members do each day of the week. Read aloud the first example as the students follow along. Then ask, *What do the parents do on Monday? What does the son do on Friday?* Encourage students to respond with complete sentences. Continue asking questions until it is clear that students have caught on to the activity. Then have students work with partners to ask and answer questions about the chart.

Page 48: Data collection; comparing/contrasting; using a chart.
Students complete an activity chart about themselves and compare answers with a partner. **Page 49: Telling time; daily schedules.** Students answer questions about a sample schedule. Teaching suggestions are provided in the Skills Journal annotations.

3 ✦ EXTEND

SOCIAL STUDIES Describing actions. Ask students to look through magazines to find action pictures. In pairs, students ask and answer questions about the pictures: *What does (he/she) do? What do they do?* Extend the activity by having students write their questions as captions below the pictures. They can then exchange pictures with another pair and continue the activity by answering the questions.

MATH Home-School Connection: Taking a poll. Encourage students to poll family members and friends independently to find out what they do every Saturday. Students can then work collaboratively in small groups or as a class to compile the poll results and chart them to find out the most/least common activities, the most unusual, the greatest number of activities per person, and so on. (CALLA: Classifying)

- - - **ONGOING ASSESSMENT** - - -

PERFORMANCE Oral language. Ask students to tell you what they do each week. Listen for correct usage of the present tense.

⭐ **TEACHER TO TEACHER**
Students may enjoy using inexpensive pocket planners. Bring in some examples for the class to look at and show how you would fill one out yourself.

⭐ **PREDICTABLE PROBLEMS**
Students may have a difficult time with third person -s on singular verbs. Remind students that the question word *does* usually requires a final -s on the verb that answers the question, while the question word *do* is usually a signal for not using -s.
Some students will continue to use the *am, is, are* of the present continuous with the present tense. Remind students to use only the verbs *am, is, are* with -ing words.

71

LESSON 5
EXPLORE...SCIENCE

STUDENT BOOK/SKILLS JOURNAL
PAGES 50–51

 KEY EXPERIENCES

- Reading/following directions
- Forming a hypothesis
- Investigating vibration in musical instruments
- Practicing math skills

KEY LANGUAGE

- *bat, cork, salt, string, sweet spot, vibrate, wood*

MATERIALS

- 2 chairs with arms; string; wooden board approximately 3/4" thick, 2" wide, 24" long; salt; pencil; cork; baseball bat and ball; cardboard

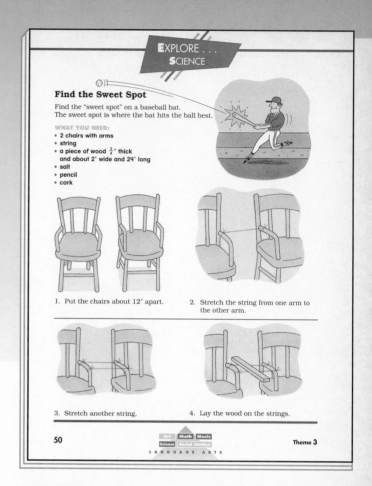

1 ◆ INTRODUCE

Activating prior knowledge: Talking about baseball. Remind students that earlier in this theme they read a story titled "A Win for Sung Hee." Invite volunteers to retell the story. As needed, reread the story. Then review what students know about baseball and the equipment used.

MULTI-LEVEL TEACHING STRATEGIES

You can include all students by asking questions appropriate to each student's language level.

Speech Emergence: *Did Sung Hee play baseball or soccer? Do you like baseball?*

Developing Fluency: *What things do you need to play baseball? What do you call the different players on a baseball team?*

---

2 ◆ EXPLORE

Activating prior knowledge. Open to pages 50–51. To prompt discussion, ask multi-level questions such as *What is the title of this lesson? What do you think this activity is about? Have you ever heard of a "sweet spot"? Can you guess what it is? What things will we need for the activity?*

Exploring key vocabulary. Ask volunteers to read the title, paragraph, and list of materials. Ask questions to check that students understand the key vocabulary: *What is the "sweet spot" on a baseball bat? Why do you think it's called a "sweet spot"? What is a cork?*

GUIDED READING Reading directions for an experiment. Have students follow along as you read the directions for the experiment. Ask multi-level questions to check understanding: *What do we do first? What do we do with the string? Why do we tap the wood?*

SCIENCE Demonstrating vibration. Ask volunteers to describe vibration. Encourage them to demonstrate several types of vibration using objects in the classroom. For example, they might run their fingers down the teeth of a comb to cause the teeth to vibrate, or students might pluck a tightly stretched string or rubber band.

Following directions/Forming a hypothesis. Divide students into as many groups as you have sets of

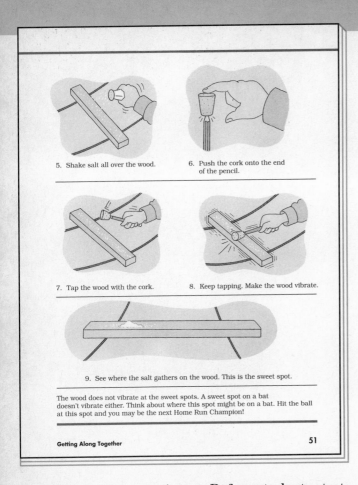

5. Shake salt all over the wood.

6. Push the cork onto the end of the pencil.

7. Tap the wood with the cork.

8. Keep tapping. Make the wood vibrate.

9. See where the salt gathers on the wood. This is the sweet spot.

The wood does not vibrate at the sweet spots. A sweet spot on a bat doesn't vibrate either. Think about where this spot might be on a bat. Hit the ball at this spot and you may be the next Home Run Champion!

Getting Along Together   51

---

materials for the experiment. Before students start the activity, ask each group to guess where the sweet spot will be. Ask students to explain why they made their predictions. Have students draw circles on the wooden board to show their predictions. Discuss and explain that a scientific prediction is called a *hypothesis*. Write the word on the board. Encourage students to work cooperatively in performing the activity. When they have completed the experiment, have them check their predictions. Ask multi-level questions: *Where was the sweet spot on the board? Did you predict correctly?* (CALLA: Predicting)

SKILLS JOURNAL
PAGES 50-51

Page 50: Reading for a purpose; math skills. Students read and solve a math word problem. **Page 51: Practicing conversations.** Students practice a sample dialogue about school activities. Teaching suggestions are provided in the Skills Journal annotations.

3 ◆ EXTEND

PHYSICAL EDUCATION Batting practice. Take students to a playground or playing field. Provide a baseball bat and ball and have students take turns trying to hit the "sweet spot" on the bat. Encourage students to rotate turns as pitcher, fielders, and batters.

SCIENCE Finding more sweet spots. Have students discuss what effect the size and shape of an object might have on its sweet spot. Supply sheets of cardboard. Ask students to cut the sheets into various shapes. Encourage students to repeat the experiment with the different pieces of cardboard. Ask them to predict the location and size of the sweet spot before the experiment. Have students write summaries of their predictions and observations.

MUSIC/SCIENCE Making sweet vibrations. Have students research how vibration causes sound and how sound is turned into different musical tones with stringed instruments such as the piano, violin, harp, guitar; with percussion instruments such as drums, xylophones, and castanets; and with woodwind and brass horns. (CALLA: Resourcing)

PROCESS WRITING PORTFOLIO

See the list of ideas and writing topics related to this theme.

ONGOING ASSESSMENT

PERFORMANCE Oral and written language. Evaluate students' abilities to follow directions and their oral and written predictions and observations of their experiments.

★ **TEACHER TO TEACHER**

Invite students from a music class to demonstrate how various musical instruments use vibration to produce their different sounds.

LESSON 6
LET'S PLAY SOCCER

📼 STUDENT BOOK/SKILLS JOURNAL
PAGES 52–55

⭐ **KEY EXPERIENCES**

- Reading/responding to a photo essay
- Discussing soccer
- Summarizing information on a chart
- Following/giving oral instructions
- Classifying information
- Reading a bar graph

⭐ **KEY LANGUAGE**

- *goal, goalkeeper, net, kick, heading, dribble, pass, tackle, mark, foul, fake*

⭐ **MATERIALS**

- soccer ball or pictures of soccer players in action
- different types of sports equipment

1 ♦ INTRODUCE

Building background: Discussing soccer. Show pictures of soccer players and games. Invite students to share their experience and knowledge of soccer. You may want to ask students to explain and demonstrate different soccer skills. On the board, create a chart about soccer to organize student ideas. (CALLA: Organizing)

Soccer				
number of players	positions	where played	scoring	how much time
11	goalie	soccer field		half

MULTI-LEVEL TEACHING STRATEGIES

You can include all students by asking questions appropriate to each student's language level.

Speech Emergence: *Have you ever played soccer? What position do you like to play? How many people are on a soccer team?*

Developing Fluency: *What do you know about soccer? Who can touch the ball with their hands? How can you move the ball in soccer?*

2 ♦ EXPLORE

Activating prior knowledge. Open to pages 52–55. Ask a volunteer to read the title aloud, "Let's Play Soccer." Then have students look through the story, commenting on the pictures. To prompt discussion, ask multi-level questions about the pictures such as *Is this baseball or soccer? Where is the goal? Find someone who is kicking the ball.*

Here's how to kick a soccer ball. Put one foot next to the ball. Swing the other leg toward the ball. Point your toes and hit the ball with the side of your foot. Let your kicking leg continue swinging in the direction you want the ball to go.

Getting Along Together   53

Where is he/she trying to put the ball? Is anyone heading the ball?

GUIDED READING Reading a description. Read or play the tape for the photo essay as students follow along in their books. Reread the selection, pausing at the end of each paragraph to discuss. Students who are able to should read independently. You may want to pose the following display/comprehension questions to prompt discussion of each page and monitor students' understanding.

Display/Comprehension Questions

Page 52

How many teams play? (two)
How many players are on a team? (eleven)
What does the team try to do? (get the ball across the field to the opposite goal)
Where do you kick the ball to score? (into the net)

Page 53

How do you kick a soccer ball? (If indoors, have

student demonstrate the movement without lifting the ball off the ground.)
Do you kick the ball with your toes or the side of your foot? (side of your foot)
If you want the ball to go to the right, do you swing your leg to the left or right? (right)

Page 54

Who can touch the ball with their hands when the ball's in play? (goalkeepers)
What parts of the body can the other players use? (feet, legs, bodies, head)
Describe what the goalie in the picture is doing. What happens if someone on the field touches the ball? (A foul is called—background knowledge.)
When the ball is in the air, is it easier to use your head or your feet to hit the ball? (head—background knowledge)

Page 55

What is dribbling? (kicking the ball along the ground while running)
Do you tackle or dribble to take the ball away from an opponent? (tackle)

Rereading. Arrange students in pairs or small groups to reread the essay together.

Discussing the selection. Discuss with students the popularity of soccer in their countries. Ask them if they think soccer is as popular in the U.S. Have students discuss some reasons why they think soccer is or is not a popular sport in this country. Do they think this is changing? Why might soccer be a good sport for kids in the U.S. to play? What are the advantages and disadvantages of coed teams?

Summarizing information. Go back to the chart at the beginning of the lesson. See if students can fill in any additional information about soccer that they learned from the selection.

Acquiring new vocabulary. Encourage students to add to the soccer terms listed under "Soccer Talk" and to write their own definitions. Suggest that students include words such as *penalty* and alternates such as *goalie* for *goalkeeper.*

Your Turn. With the class, read the instructions under "Your Turn." Have students work with partners as they talk about their favorite sports.

SKILLS JOURNAL PAGES 52-55 **Page 52: Vocabulary development.** Students match names of animals with pictures of school mascots. **Page 53: Reading a bar graph; writing.** Students discuss a bar graph and write a paragraph explaining the information in the graph. **Page 54: Reading for a purpose; writing.** Students read about sports safety rules and write about safety rules they follow. **Page 55: Solving a puzzle; reinforcing key vocabulary.** Students solve a word search puzzle. Teaching suggestions are provided in the Skills Journal annotations.

3 ◆ EXTEND

Following/giving oral instructions. Bring in different sports equipment and give simple TPR directions on how to use each piece. Invite volunteers to follow the directions as you give them. Invite pairs of students to teach the group how to use some sports equipment or how to do some action related to a favorite sport. Encourage students to think carefully how to break the instructions down into small steps. Students may want to write out the steps first and check the sequence before giving the instructions to the class. (CALLA: Sequencing)

Grammar in context. Point out the use of *score* as both a noun and a verb. Present other words in the essay that also can be both nouns and verbs: *kick, run, time, point, swing, hit, head, tackle, dribble, pass, mark, fake.* Encourage student pairs to use these words in oral and written sentences.

Organizing a soccer event. Find out if students are interested in scrimmaging with students from other classes in your school or in a neighboring school. Your students will enjoy thinking of a name for their team. If soccer is not yet popular in your area, you might like to help students get some teams organized. Students can begin by brainstorming what the steps would be in getting a local league started.

Goalkeepers are the only players who can touch the ball with their hands when it's in play. Other players use their feet, legs, bodies, or heads to hit the ball.

Heading is a great way to pass the ball when it comes at you through the air. Hit the ball with your forehead, but be careful!

54   Theme 3

ART Designing a uniform/logo. Soccer fans may enjoy designing a uniform and team logo. Display student work in the classroom. Your local league may be interested in looking at your students' logo ideas for possible adoption as patches that can be exchanged at soccer tournaments.

ART Making a diagram/Acquiring new vocabulary. Students can draw a soccer player on a field and label all of the parts of the uniform and equipment including such things as the *shirt, shorts, shin guards, cleats, net, ball.* Students with a sense of humor may enjoy drawing and labeling some common soccer bumps and bruises.

Preparing a sports handbook. Have students work cooperatively in groups. Each group chooses a different sport to research. Suggest some ideas for sports that not everyone knows a lot about, such as lacrosse or field hockey. Groups can prepare diagrams of the playing fields and mark player positions, define or draw pictures of equipment, and describe basic skills used in the sports. Groups

Soccer Talk

Dribble
Kick the ball along the ground while running.

Tackle
Use your feet to take the ball away from an opponent.

Pass
Kick the ball to your team members. Remember—no hands!

Mark
Guard the ball and make it hard for an opponent to get it.

Foul
When a player breaks a rule.

Fake
Pretend to kick or pass the ball. Then do something different.

 Tell a partner about your favorite sport. Why do you like this sport? Talk about your partner's favorite sport.

Getting Along Together 55

★ MULTICULTURAL AWARENESS
Soccer, which is called "football" in many countries, is the most popular sport in the world.

★ COMPUTER CONNECTION
Students can use the computer to do research on sports as they are preparing their sports handbooks.

can share their information with the class. You may want to compile the information from the different sports to create a sports dictionary or handbook. (CALLA: Cooperating/resourcing)

Classifying information. Have students brainstorm a list of sports. Students can create a chart and categorize the sports by seasons, similarities in the way they are played, numbers of players, etc.

PROCESS WRITING PORTFOLIO See the list of ideas and writing topics related to this theme.

ONGOING ASSESSMENT

PERFORMANCE Reading. Check student responses for ability to read for information. **Oral Language.** With books closed, have students talk about basic soccer skills or describe another sport they like better.

LESSON 7
ALL STAR NEWS

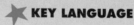 STUDENT BOOK/SKILLS JOURNAL
PAGES 56–57

★ KEY EXPERIENCES

- Reading for information and pleasure
- Discussing spending money
- Understanding humor
- Expressing opinions
- Taking a poll/charting results
- Process writing

★ KEY LANGUAGE

- *spending money, allowance*

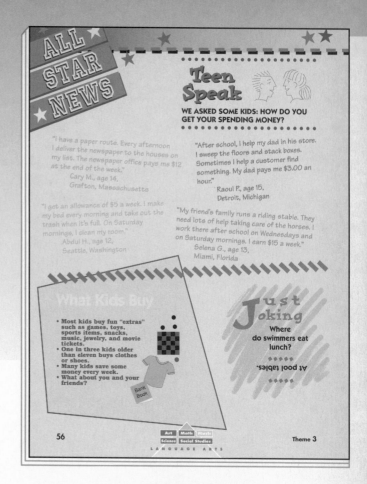

1 ◆ INTRODUCE

Building background: Discussing spending money.
Have students share ideas for how to spend money. You may want to bring in store flyers and have students identify items they would like to buy. Be sensitive to the fact that some students may not get allowances or have any spending money. Invite students to share ideas on how to get or earn money. You may want to create a flow chart on the board to record student ideas of where they can get money and what to do with the money.

```
┌─ MULTI-LEVEL TEACHING STRATEGIES ─┐

  You can include all students by asking ques-
  tions appropriate to each student's language
  level.

  Speech Emergence: Do you like to go shopping?
  What do you like to buy? Where do you go to
  shop?

  Developing Fluency: How do you get money?
  Would you rather spend or save money? Why?
  What is an "allowance?"
└────────────────────────────────────┘
```

2 ◆ EXPLORE

Activating prior knowledge. Open to pages 56 and 57. By now, students should be familiar with the format of the *News*. To prompt discussion, ask multi-level questions.

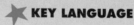 **GUIDED READING Reading for information.**
Play the tape or read the selections, pausing occasionally to ask multi-level questions. Students who are able to should read the pages independently. You may want to pose the following display/comprehension questions to prompt discussion of each page and monitor students' understanding.

Display/Comprehension Questions

Page 56
How does Raoul get his spending money? (helps his Dad)
Does Gary have a morning paper route? (no, afternoon)
True or false: Abdul gets an allowance of $10. (false—$5)
Who has the most spending money? (Selena)

News From All Over

SPORTS TEAMS AND THEIR NAMES

AMAZING FACTS!

Hundreds of professional and amateur sports teams use Native American Indian names. Many Native Americans don't like it. Native Americans protested at the 1995 World Series between the Atlanta Braves and the Cleveland Indians. The protesters objected to the team names, the team mascots, and the team symbols—tomahawks, bows and arrows, and feather headdresses. They say that use of these things dishonors their culture. Other Americans disagree. They don't see anything wrong with using Native American Indian names or symbols.

In the town of Mukwonago, Wisconsin, the high school's football team is "The Mukwonago Indians." The town held a hearing about the team's name. Students voted 410 to 32 to keep the name.

What's your opinion? Should sports teams use Native American names? Why or why not?

- Track athletes are most likely to break records late in the day when their body temperatures are highest.
- Olympic athletes work hard to win gold medals. But, guess what? The gold medals are made mostly of silver. Only about 0.2 ounces of pure gold coats the outside of the medal.

Getting Along Together   57

Page 57
What teams use Native American Indian names? (professional and amateur sports teams)
Who has objected to these names? (Native Americans)
When do track athletes usually break records? (late in the day)
Who wins gold medals? (Olympic athletes)
What metals are used in making the medals? (gold and silver)

Understanding humor. Read the joke on page 56 as students follow along in their books. Be prepared to explain the answer. Invite students to share other jokes that they know.

MATH Taking a poll/charting results. Have students prepare and conduct a poll of how much money kids have to spend weekly, what kids buy, or another idea from the *All Star News* pages. Students can prepare questions or a survey questionnaire to give to others in the school. Then students can work in groups to compile the results and prepare a pie chart.

Expressing an opinion. With the class, read the questions at the end of "Sports Teams and Their Names." Have students work in pairs or small groups to discuss their opinions about Native American names used by sports teams. You may want to introduce some functional language for giving opinions such as *I think that..., I believe that..., I agree with (someone) that..., I disagree.*

SKILLS JOURNAL PAGES 56-57 **Process writing; computer connection.** Students read a sample newspaper article and write their own article on the same topic. Teaching suggestions are provided in the Skills Journal annotations.

3 ◆ EXTEND

SOCIAL STUDIES Researching sports and athletic events. Students can work in small groups to find out more information about the Olympics and track events. *When did the Olympics start? What events are included in track and field?* Students can prepare oral or written reports to present to the class. (CALLA: Resourcing)

ONGOING ASSESSMENT

PERFORMANCE Reading. Check student responses for ability to scan for information.

PORTFOLIO Writing. Save Skills Journal pages 56–57 as an example of independent writing.

COMPUTER CONNECTION
Have students use a multi-media CD-ROM encyclopedia to find more information about football, the Olympics, Native Americans, and track and field events.

LESSON 8
ALL STAR NEWS

STUDENT BOOK/SKILLS JOURNAL
PAGES 58–59

★ KEY EXPERIENCES

- Reading for information and pleasure
- Reading/responding to a poem
- Writing a letter
- Working in collaborative groups:
  - photo essays
  - taking polls
  - charting/graphing results
  - comparing/contrasting information
- Practicing science process skills

★ KEY LANGUAGE

- *inventor, model, smile*

★ MATERIALS

- straws, ice cream sticks, rubber bands
- glue, Tinkertoys or Legos

1 ◆ INTRODUCE

Building background: Talking about inventions.

Prompt a discussion of inventions by asking: *What would it be like without telephones, cars, airplanes, electricity, computers? Do you know who invented these things? If you could invent something, what would it be?*

MULTI-LEVEL TEACHING STRATEGIES

You can include all students by asking questions appropriate to each student's language level.

Speech Emergence: *Do you use electricity? How does electricity help you? Have you ever thought about making a special tool to help you do something? What is it?*

Developing Fluency: *What would it be like without electric lights? Without cars? Do you know who invented these things?*

Charting inventions. As students discuss inventions, make a chart on the board.

Invention	Inventor	How it helps us
Telephone	Alexander Grahm Bell	Communication
Bifocals	Benjamin Franklin	Vision

2 ◆ EXPLORE

Activating prior knowledge. Open to pages 58–59. To prompt discussion, ask multi-level questions such as *What do inventors do? What do you put in a mailbox?*

Bright Ideas. Have students follow along as you read the selection. Explore the vocabulary: *What is a prototype? Why is it useful to make a prototype? What is a scale drawing?*

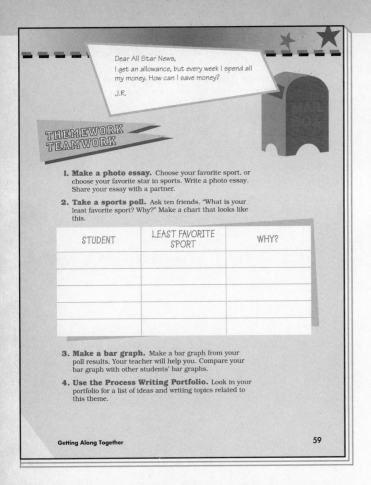

THEMEWORK
TEAMWORK

Dear All Star News,
I get an allowance, but every week I spend all
my money. How can I save money?

J.R.

1. **Make a photo essay.** Choose your favorite sport, or
choose your favorite star in sports. Write a photo essay.
Share your essay with a partner.

2. **Take a sports poll.** Ask ten friends, "What is your
least favorite sport? Why?" Make a chart that looks like
this.

STUDENT	LEAST FAVORITE SPORT	WHY?

3. **Make a bar graph.** Make a bar graph from your
poll results. Your teacher will help you. Compare your
bar graph with other students' bar graphs.

4. **Use the Process Writing Portfolio.** Look in your
portfolio for a list of ideas and writing topics related to
this theme.

Getting Along Together   59

Using context. If students have trouble with the
vocabulary, read through the selection again.
Demonstrate how context clues will help them figure out the meaning of new or unfamiliar words.
Make sure students understand that a term like
"surf chair" is an invented term, used in this case to
describe an invention.

Brainstorming. Have students brainstorm ideas for
new inventions. Write their suggestions on the
board. Save this list for use with an Extend project.

Poetry corner. Ask a volunteer to read the short
poem aloud. Discuss the "chain reaction" the poet
cites. Does this also happen with frowns? What
other emotions or body language can work this
way?

Mailbox. Direct students' attention to the mailbox
letter on page 59. Invite a volunteer to read it
aloud. Ask: *What's J.R.'s problem? Do you have the
same problem?* Split students into small groups
and have them discuss how J.R. could save money,
then share their solutions with the class.

Students write letters to J.R. on page 59 of the
Skills Journal.

Themework/Teamwork. Ask volunteers to read
through the list of projects. Students may choose
one or more projects to complete independently or
as a collaborative effort. Have them share their
completed projects with the class.

 **Page 58: Expressing opinions; letter
writing.** Students answer the letter
in Mailbox on Student Book page
58. **Page 59: Science skills; using a chart.** Students
read a cartoon science experiment, then try it
themselves. Teaching suggestions are provided in
the Skills Journal annotations.

3 ♦ EXTEND

SCIENCE/ART Creating a prototype. Invite students
to create a prototype for an invention. Suggest that
they create the prototype with Tinkertoys, Legos,
straws, ice cream sticks, or any other suitable
materials they find. Have students share and
explain their models to the class. (CALLA:
Organizational Planning/Imagery)

MATH/ART Making a scale drawing. Encourage students to make a scale drawing. They can make the
drawing of the prototype from the preceding activity or of any other object. When they share their
work with the class, have students explain the
mathematics involved in working to scale. (CALLA:
Imagery)

**PROCESS
WRITING
PORTFOLIO** See the list of ideas and writing
topics related to this theme.

- - - ONGOING ASSESSMENT - - -

PERFORMANCE Oral language. Evaluate students' oral language abilities as they share and
explain their projects to the class.

PORTFOLIO Writing. Save Skills Journal page 58
as an example of independent writing.

LESSON 9
HOLISTIC ASSESSMENT

 STUDENT BOOK/SKILLS JOURNAL
PAGES 60–61

★ **KEY EXPERIENCES**

- Demonstrating comprehension
- Summarizing
- Thinking critically
- Self-assessment
- Writing about oneself
- Researching a topic

★ **KEY LANGUAGE**

- *medals, race, speed skating, retired*

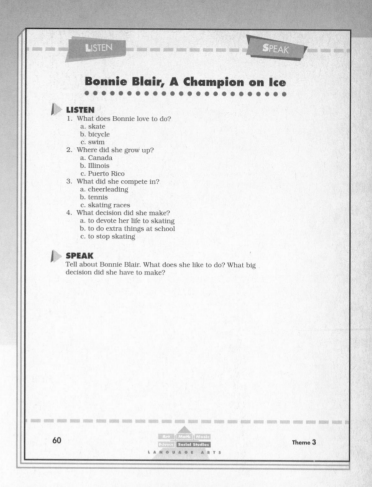

1 ◆ INTRODUCE

These two pages offer a variety of assessment opportunities. The left-hand page consists of listening and speaking activities that follow a taped presentation. In the speaking activity, students are asked to summarize what they have heard. The right-hand page consists of writing and critical thinking activities. These follow a reading passage that completes the listening component. You can use the activities to assess listening, speaking, reading, writing, and critical thinking skills. Have students work as a class or in small groups as you circulate and record observations on the **Anecdotal Record Form,** the **Reading Checklist,** and the **Writing Checklist** in the *All Star Assessment Package.*

Observing and recording student performance. Note the level of participation and the particular abilities of each student. How much do students understand? How well can they express themselves orally? What language structures do they use? What new words and concepts do they use? How actively do they participate? Use the **Anecdotal Record Form** in the *All Star Assessment Package* to record your observations and note areas for further development. Place in students' **portfolios.**

2 ◆ EXPLORE

Previewing. Open to pages 60 and 61 and let the students comment on the illustrations. Read the title "Bonnie Blair, A Champion on Ice" or call on a volunteer to do so. Give students time to read the listening questions.

 **Listening.** Read or play the tape for the first part of "Bonnie Blair, A Champion on Ice." You will find the tapescript in the Appendix. Have students work independently to answer the listening questions. Read or play the tape again for students to check their work.

Speaking. Discuss what students have heard up to this point. Ask multi-level questions such as *Was Bonnie active in school? What did she do? Did she grow up in Illinois or Indiana?* If some students are struggling, play the tape again and summarize the story once yourself. Ask questions again. When you are satisfied with this stage, go on to the next.

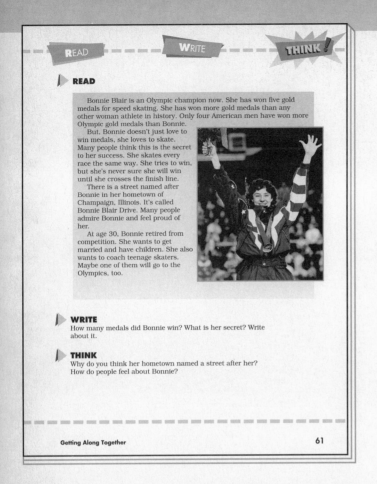

READ   WRITE   THINK!

READ

Bonnie Blair is an Olympic champion now. She has won five gold medals for speed skating. She has won more gold medals than any other woman athlete in history. Only four American men have won more Olympic gold medals than Bonnie.

But, Bonnie doesn't just love to win medals, she loves to skate. Many people think this is the secret to her success. She skates every race the same way. She tries to win, but she's never sure she will win until she crosses the finish line.

There is a street named after Bonnie in her hometown of Champaign, Illinois. It's called Bonnie Blair Drive. Many people admire Bonnie and feel proud of her.

At age 30, Bonnie retired from competition. She wants to get married and have children. She also wants to coach teenage skaters. Maybe one of them will go to the Olympics, too.

WRITE

How many medals did Bonnie win? What is her secret? Write about it.

THINK

Why do you think her hometown named a street after her? How do people feel about Bonnie?

Getting Along Together   61

Reading. Read the story on page 61 or play the tape as the students listen and follow along in their books. Pause occasionally to ask multi-level questions. Then have the students do partner reading, alternating paragraphs.

Summarizing. Encourage students to tell you what they have heard and read. Do not look for word-for-word retelling, even from your best students. (CALLA: Summarizing)

Writing. Encourage students to write a short paragraph about Bonnie Blair's secret to success.

Thinking. Discuss the text questions as well as *How many hours a day do you think Bonnie practiced? What do you think winters are like in Illinois?*

 **SKILLS JOURNAL PAGES 60-61** **Page 60: Assessment; reinforcing key vocabulary.** Students circle words that don't belong in vocabulary groups. **Page 61: Self-assessment; Home-School connection.** Students check off things they can do and

---

words they know. Teaching suggestions are provided in the Skills Journal annotations.

3 ◆ EXTEND

Pronunciation: Voiceless *th*. Work with students on the pronunciation of the two-syllable word *athlete*. Practice other words with the voiceless *th* such as *three* and *think*, also found in the story. Also help students with the pronunciation of *Illinois* and *Champaign*. Make sure students understand that these words do have unusual spellings, even for English. The Illinois were Native Americans, and the French who in settled the region are responsible for the spelling of both words.

SOCIAL STUDIES Researching a topic. Students can work in small groups to research a topic related to this lesson. Possible topics include speed skating, figure skating, the state of Illinois, the Illinois tribe, the French settlers, or another topic of the students' choosing.

★ **TEACHER TO TEACHER**

Students may be unfamiliar with concepts relating to school life in the U.S. This is an excellent opportunity to discuss extra-curricular activities such as cheerleading and student council, both activities that Bonnie Blair participated in.

THEME 3: GETTING ALONG TOGETHER

LESSON 10
NO, NO, NO

📼 **STUDENT BOOK/SKILLS JOURNAL PAGE 62**

⭐ **KEY EXPERIENCES**

■ Reviewing the theme

■ Talking about making decisions

■ Singing a song

■ Playing charades

■ Writing new verses

⭐ **KEY LANGUAGE**

■ *make up your mind*

■ *yes, no , maybe*

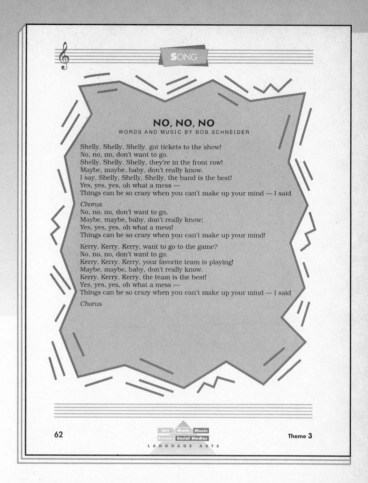

1 ◆ INTRODUCE

Building background: Talking about making decisions. To prompt a discussion about making decisions, model asking students if they want to go to a baseball game. Write and model the responses: "Yes, I want to go." "Maybe. I don't know." "No, I don't want to go." on the board. Ask students to choose a response to the question. Ask why they chose their answers.

┌─ **MULTI-LEVEL TEACHING STRATEGIES** ─┐

You can include all students by asking questions appropriate to each student's language level.

Speech Emergence: *What does* yes *mean? What does* no *mean? What does* maybe *mean?*

Developing Fluency: *What happens when you can't decide yes or no? How do you make a decision?*

└──────────────────────────────────┘

2 ◆ EXPLORE

Activating prior knowledge. Open to page 62. To prompt discussion, ask multi-level questions such as *What do you see on this page? How do you know this is a song?* (CALLA: Making predictions)

📼 **MUSIC Singing the song.** Have a volunteer read through the song lyrics. Then play the tape several times, inviting students to sing along when they are ready.

 **SKILLS JOURNAL PAGE 62** **Providing information about self; writing.** Students write answers to short essay questions. Teaching suggestions are provided in the Skills Journal annotation.

3 ◆ EXTEND

Writing new verses. It's easy to add new verses to this song. Show students how to replace the name (Shelley), the event (tickets for the show), the detail (in the front row), and the summation (the band is the best) in the verse. Give students more help, if necessary, and lots of time for creative thinking. Allow all students who want to perform the original song and/or their own verses to do so. Students will enjoy teaching their song to other groups.

WRAP UP

ASSESSMENT

You have been collecting assessment data through the ongoing and holistic assessment options (Oral Language Checklist, Reading Checklist, Anecdotal Record Form) in this theme. Following are some additional assessment strategies that will help you evaluate your students' progress as well as adapt your instruction to meet their needs.

Student Self-Assessment. Self-assessment surveys are a means for students to have input into their own learning process. Students can use them to reflect on the work they have done and the learning strategies they have used during this theme. Be sure to check students' self-assessment pages for each theme in the Skills Journal.

Informed Instruction. Evaluate the checklists, anecdotal records, and Process Writing Portfolio collections from this theme as a means of informing your instruction.
- In which areas are students showing confidence and enthusiasm?
- In which areas are they hesitant or confused?
- Should you provide more classroom opportunities for oral language or writing?
- Would certain students (or the whole class) benefit from a focused mini-lesson on a certain area or skill?
- Remember to recycle skills as you teach the next theme and provide students with many opportunities to gain competence.

READING

Don't forget to check on and encourage students' independent reading. Students who weren't ready for independent reading in English at the beginning of this theme may be ready now. Students who continue to read in their first language should be encouraged to do first language book reviews and be an attentive audience for other students' reviews in English.

BOOKBYTES

Have students been able to use the *All Star BookBytes* CD-ROM software? The BookBytes' book list includes the titles on the Theme Booklists for all levels of *All Star English*. BookBytes helps students choose a book to read based on their responses to a short questionnaire, then prompts students to think about and respond to what they've read through writing, drawing, and drama. Students can print out their work and share it with others. They can also choose to see other students' work on-screen in a gallery presentation.

THEME CELEBRATION

If your class is participating as an All Star Team, the end of theme is a good time to review students' accomplishments with the Theme Booklist and Theme Projects. Consider posting a chart in the classroom where students may check off their accomplishments and, if you are using a point system, total their points for the theme. Students should strive to do their best and outdo their *own* scores, not compete with each other. Encourage students to present their All Star projects to the class to allow more oral practice and to sharpen students' presentation skills. You might invite other classes or families to attend the presentations.

PREVIEW
HOPES AND DREAMS······

CONCEPTS
- ancestral roots
- the pursuit of dreams
- the Chippewa culture
- civil rights

LITERATURE

- Africa Dream
  (narrative poem)
- The Magic of Dance
  (photo essay)
- I Have a Dream
  (speech excerpt)
- All Star News
  (short nonfiction articles)
- When You Dream a Dream
  (song)

READING/WRITING SKILLS

- summarizing a story
- reading for information and pleasure
- classifying information
- making comparisons
- critical thinking
- reading comprehension
- process writing
- reading/responding to a poem
- reading/responding to a photo essay
- understanding poetic language
- writing and illustrating a poem/story
- reading/following directions
- reading/responding to an excerpt from a speech
- understanding figurative language
- writing a letter
- writing original song verses

CONTENT

- **Social Studies:** attending a dance performance, researching dancers, describing cultural dances, learning about the African American culture, learning about professions, researching a topic, making a timeline, listening to a speech

- **Art/Music:** illustrating a story, making and displaying dream catchers, listening to dance music, taking photographs, singing a song
- **Science:** researching dreams and dreaming, learning about cameras/photographers, drawing conclusions from an experiment about time zones

KEY LANGUAGE/KEY EXPERIENCES

- past tense
- self-assessment
- asking and answering questions
- understanding a sequence
- completing a story board
- using a chart
- taking a poll
- working in collaborative groups
- expressing opinions
- practicing science process skills
- vocabulary development
- learning language through song

THEME BOOKLIST/ THEME PROJECTS

As this new theme begins, photocopy the Theme Booklist/Theme Projects pages (following spread) for students. Encourage students to read as many books as they like from the Booklist, and to complete any of the assignments on the Project list as homework for this theme.

AWARDING POINTS FOR ALL STAR TEAMS

This is a good opportunity to motivate students through an All Star Team approach. Consider assigning point values to each project, including reading books from the booklist. Explain to students that they will accumulate points for each book they read or project they complete during the theme. Students will try to top their own scores as they work through each theme, competing against themselves, not each other. Remind students that they will have the opportunity to present their *All Star* projects to the class at the end of the theme.

BOOKBYTES

If you have a computer with a CD-ROM drive available, introduce students to the *All Star BookBytes* software which is correlated to the Theme Booklists throughout *All Star English*. *BookBytes* categorizes the books by genre and helps students choose a book to read based on their answers to a short questionnaire. It then prompts students to think about and respond to what they've read through writing, drawing, and drama activities. Students can print out their work and share it with others or view work on-screen in a gallery presentation.

THEME BOOKLIST

HERE ARE SOME BOOKS YOU MIGHT LIKE TO READ.
LOOK FOR THEM IN YOUR LIBRARY.

B-Ball: The Team That Never Lost a Game, by Ron Jones. Bantam Books, 1990. The great true story of the San Francisco Special Olympics basketball team.

Come a Stranger, by Cynthia Voigt. Simon & Schuster, 1995. The story of a girl's dream to be a dancer.

Dancing Is, by George Ancove. Dalton, 1981. More than 50 international dances you can move to.

The Dream Keeper, by Langston Hughes. Knopf, 1945. A collection of poems by the noted black poet.

Glass Slippers Give you Blisters, by Mary Jane Auch. Holiday House, 1989. A girl's life seems to be falling apart when she doesn't get a part in "Cinderella."

Go Free or Die, by Jeri Ferros. Lerner Publications, 1989. Harriet Tubman's story.

Martin L. King: The Peaceful Warrior, by Edward Clayton. Prentice-Hall, 1968.

Of Swans, Sugarplums and Satin Slippers, by Violette Verdy. Scholastic, Inc., 1991. Great art and beautiful ballet stories.

Pass It On: African-American Poetry for Children, comp. by Wade Hudson, illustrated by Floyd Cooper. Scholastic, 1993.

Seven Candles for Kwanzaa, by Andrea Davis Pinkney. Dial Books, 1993. An African American family celebrates Kwanzaa.

Uncle Jed's Barbershop, by Margaree King Mitchell. Simon and Schuster, 1993. A story of hope from the segregated South in the 1920s.

BOOKS IN LANGUAGES OTHER THAN ENGLISH

La niña que escribió un sueño (The Girl Who Wrote a Dream), by José Luis Olaizola. Madrid, España: Susaeta Ediciones, S. A.

Las mujeres: Mexican American/Chicana Women (bilingual), developed by National Women's History Project, Windsor, CA.

China's Bravest Girl, by Charlie Chin (English/Chinese). Arcadia, CA: Shen's Books and Supplies.

Hyonyo Simch' ong (Blindman's Daughter), by Edward B. Adams, ed. (Korean). Los Angeles, CA: Jeong-Eum-Sa Imports, Inc. (The Korea Book Center).

★ THEME PROJECTS

YOU MAY WANT TO WORK ON THESE PROJECTS
ALONE OR WITH A PARTNER OR SMALL GROUP.

☆ Make a set of vocabulary cards that show vocabulary words learned in the theme on one side and illustrations of the words on the other.

☆ Write dialogues that use vocabulary or grammatical structures learned in the theme.

☆ Write original sentences or stories using key vocabulary words.

☆ Create a word search or crossword puzzle that uses vocabulary from the theme.

☆ Translate a song, poem, or prose selection from your native language into English.

☆ Create paintings, drawings, or dioramas of stories or readings within the theme.

☆ Produce scripts or dramatizations of information presented in the theme.

☆ Create a collage, mobile, or other three-dimensional art project that illustrates key concepts from the theme.

☆ Take a survey and present graphs and charts that explore questions related to the theme.

☆ Write journal entries for five to ten days about key concepts or ideas in the theme.

☆ Paste news clippings onto blank paper and write a short statement explaining how the article relates to the theme.

☆ Write a letter to the editor, the school government, City Hall, or the President of the United States about issues and ideas in the theme.

☆ Create maps that show the location of places mentioned in the theme.

☆ Create a time line that shows what happened in a story from the theme.

☆ Make a story chart that clearly labels the characters, plot, setting, climax, and ending of a story from the theme.

☆ Present a dramatic reading of one of the stories in the theme.

☆ Write a letter that gives advice or constructive criticism to a character in a story from the theme.

LESSON 1
THEME OPENER

STUDENT BOOK/SKILLS JOURNAL
PAGE 63

⭐ **KEY EXPERIENCES**

- Talking about hopes and dreams
- Making a word web
- Previewing theme content and titles
- Taking a poll
- Self-assessment
- Discovering the library

⭐ **KEY LANGUAGE**

- *Africa, dance, dreams, hopes, magic, Olympics*

Categorizing information. Have students use the list you wrote on the chalkboard to create a word web that categorizes the information. (CALLA: Grouping)

1 ◆ INTRODUCE

Theme 4, Hopes and Dreams, taps students' imaginations. Students will read and talk about sleeptime dreams and dreams for the future. They will practice the past tense and learn about an important dream in U.S. history.

Building background: Talking about hopes and dreams. Ask students to tell about their hopes and dreams for the future. Get the discussion started by modeling: *When I was young, I wanted to be .... but now I want to be ....* As students describe their hopes, list them on the board.

┌─ **MULTI-LEVEL TEACHING STRATEGIES** ─┐

You can include all students by asking questions appropriate to each student's language level.

Speech Emergence: *What do you want to do when you finish school?*

Developing Fluency: *What can you do to make your dreams reality?*

└──────────────────────────────────────┘

Exploring key vocabulary. Help students understand the two meanings of *dream* used in this theme. Elicit that the word can be used to mean a hope, goal, or aim. It can also mean the images or thoughts we have when we are sleeping.

2 ◆ EXPLORE

Activating prior knowledge. Open to page 63. To prompt discussion, ask multi-level questions such as *What does the picture show? What do you think this theme is about?*

Reading Corner. Have students read the titles, authors, and descriptions of the three books listed under Reading Corner. These are just a few selections from the Theme Booklist, chosen to help motivate students to want to read. Have the books available for students to look at. Prompt discussion about which book each student would like to read and why. Allow students to sign up for turns with the books. Use this experience to get your students excited about reading.

Previewing theme content and titles. Guide students as they look through the unit, inviting them to comment on the titles, photos, and art. Ask students to tell which titles sound like selections they will be interested in, and why.

THEME 4

HOPES AND DREAMS

Reading Corner
Try these terrific books!

Of Swans, Sugarplums and Satin Slippers
by Violette Verdy
Great art and beautiful ballet stories.

Uncle Jed's Barbershop
by Margaree King Mitchell
A story of hope from the segregated South in the 1990's.

B-Ball: The Team That Never Lost a Game
by Ron Jones
A great, true story of the San Francisco Special Olympics basketball team.

63

Making predictions. Have students work with partners to make predictions about what they think each selection will be about. Encourage them to write down each headline and their predictions. They will check their prediction list at the end of the unit. (CALLA: Making predictions)

SKILLS JOURNAL PAGE 43

Activating prior knowledge; self-assessment. Students complete chart before and after lesson. Teaching suggestions are provided in the Skills Journal annotation.

3 ◆ EXTEND

Planning for the future. Encourage students to think about their hopes and dreams for the future. What must they do to fulfill their dreams? Have students write a paragraph or make an outline about their aspirations and plans for fulfilling them. Allow volunteers to share their plans.

Home-School Connection: Taking a poll. Have students poll friends and family members to find out

what their hopes and dreams are. Students might ask questions to determine what people's dreams were when they were young, what they are now, if any dreams were fulfilled, and what they are doing to fulfill current dreams. Students can make a chart to report on results of the poll. (CALLA: Grouping)

Discovering the library. Lead students on a tour of your school or local library. With students, gather the books recommended for this theme in the Theme Booklist. Students will enjoy participating in this search and, in so doing, will practice basic library and research skills. In the classroom, plan to read aloud to students each day. You may wish to record the books on tape and let students read the books as they listen to the tapes. Encourage students to read independently whenever possible.

ONGOING ASSESSMENT

PERFORMANCE Writing. Use the Writing Checklist to assess students' performance in compiling their list of predictions for theme content.

BOOKBYTES
Have students use the BookByte software as motivation for reading and writing about what they've read.

TEACHER TO TEACHER
Remind students of the two meanings of the word *dream* (the literal concrete meaning of dreams during sleep and the more abstract meaning of fantasy or of goals, aims, and plans for the future) as you work through the selections of this theme.

LESSON 2
AFRICA DREAM

STUDENT BOOK/SKILLS JOURNAL
PAGES 64-67

⭐ **KEY EXPERIENCES**

■ Reading/responding to a narrative poem

■ Discussing Africa

■ Understanding poetic language

■ Distinguishing fantasy from reality

■ Writing and illustrating a poem/story

⭐ **KEY LANGUAGE**

■ *Africa, crowds, donkey, drums, long-ago, marketplace, song, village*

■ past tense

⭐ **MATERIALS**

■ pictures of urban and rural life in Africa, map of the world

1 ◆ INTRODUCE

Building background: Describing Africa. Show a map of the world. Ask students to find Africa on the map. Encourage students to share what they know about Africa. You may want to show pictures of urban and rural life in Africa to start the discussion. Students can describe the buildings, people, clothing, customs, and way of life.

┌─ **MULTI-LEVEL TEACHING STRATEGIES** ─┐

You can include all students by asking questions appropriate to each student's language level.

Speech Emergence: *Where is Africa? Are there many countries in Africa? Is it usually hot or cold in Africa?*

Developing Fluency: *How is life in Africa different from here? How is it the same? Would you like to visit Africa? What would you like to see?*

└─────────────────────────────────────┘

Making an African word web. With students, brainstorm a list of words associated with Africa and life in Africa. Create a word web on the board using categories such as: people, clothing, cities, village, customs. Fill in the words that students suggest under the appropriate categories. Add other categories as needed.

2 ◆ EXPLORE

Activating prior knowledge. Open to pages 64–65. Ask a volunteer to read the title, "Africa Dream." Ask if this is going to be about a real trip or an imagined trip. Have students look at the pictures on pages 64 to 67. To prompt discussion, ask multi-level questions such as *Who is dancing? Do you think they are friends? How do you know? How do you know that this is about a dream?*

GUIDED READING **Reading a story.** Read or play the tape for the story as students follow along in their books. Read the story again stopping to ask questions. You may want to pose the following display/comprehension questions to prompt discussion of each page and monitor students' understanding.

And rode through the crowds
On a donkey's back

Hopes and Dreams   65

Display/Comprehension Questions

Pages 64–65

Where did the girl go? (Africa)

Was it real or in a dream? (in a dream)

How did she cross the ocean? (she jumped)

Where did she go to shop? (in the marketplace)

What did she buy? (pearls and perfume)

What kind of words were in the old books? (strange words)

Did she understand the words? (yes)

How did she feel next to the stone buildings? (small)

Were there many people? (yes)

How do you know? (there were crowds)

How did she travel? (on a donkey's back)

Pages 66–67

Where did she go now in her dream? (to a village)

What kind of a dance did she do? (a hello dance)

Who played the drums? (her uncles)

Who did she sing a hello song with? (with new-old friends)

Where did she walk with her cousins? (all over Africa)

What was she wearing? (a long dress)

Can you really step across countries? (no)

When did the girl turn into a baby? (when she was tired)

Who held her? (her long-ago grandma)

Who did the grandma look like? (her mother)

Why did the grandma rock her? (to make her go to sleep)

How did the girl feel?

Independent reading. Have students read the story silently. Then have volunteers read the poem aloud.

Understanding poetic language. Explain that writers often choose or combine words to paint a picture. Point out the example *long-ago Africa* on page 64. Explain that usually writers say, *Long ago I went to Africa.* In this story the writer wants to give a new meaning to the words. The writer uses *long-ago Africa* to describe ancient Africa. Ask students to find other examples of hyphenated words that the writer has used to create different images, such as *lonesome-still* and *new-old* on page 66.

Your Turn. With the class, read the instructions under "Your Turn." Have students work with partners as they talk about a place they might dream about. Depending on the level of the class, you may want to follow up by having students describe their partner's dream for the class.

Pages 64–65: Guided writing; cloze exercise. Students complete cloze of poem. **Page 66: Summarizing; process writing.** Students fill in summary chart about poem. **Page 67: Recalling details; creative writing.** Students answer questions about the poem, then write about their families and dreams. Teaching suggestions are provided in the Skills Journal annotations.

3 ◆ EXTEND

Writing about a dream. Students work in groups of three to take turns telling about their dream places.

Students help each other as needed. Then each student independently writes a paragraph about the place. Remind students to check paragraph form, punctuation, and capitalization. Then have students regroup and share stories. Students help each other correct, clarify, and if necessary expand the descriptions of their trips. Students can make corrections on their drafts. When finished, have students recopy their stories, making corrections and revisions. Students can also illustrate their stories. (CALLA: Cooperating)

Distinguishing fantasy from reality. Students can work in pairs to compare the girl's vision of Africa to what a real trip would be like. Students can go back through the story on pages 64–67 and point out which things are possible and which things could never happen. Encourage students to list the real and unreal events on a chart. For each fantasy event from the story, have students suggest what the real experience might be.

Understanding poetic language. Introduce alliteration. On page 64, point out the lines *I crossed the ocean in a slow, smooth jump.* Ask students to listen as you read the line and decide what letter sound is important in the sentence. Explain that writer often use the sounds of letters and words to add to the music and meaning of their poems. Encourage students to look back through the story for other examples of alliteration such as *I shopped in the marketplace for pearls and perfume* and *danced a hello dance to the drums.*

ART Illustrating the story. Reread or play the tape for the story as students listen with their eyes closed. Suggest that they allow their imaginations to roam freely. Invite students to illustrate the story based on the images that form in their own minds as they read it.

PROCESS WRITING PORTFOLIO See the list of ideas and writing topics related to this theme.

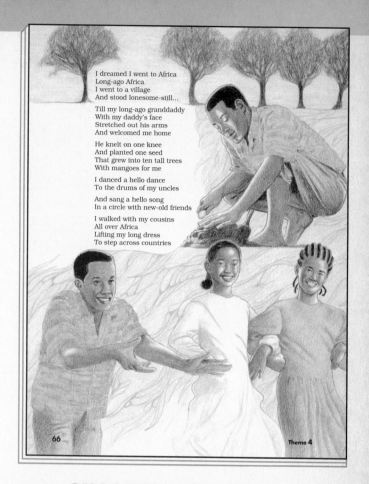

I dreamed I went to Africa
Long-ago Africa
I went to a village
And stood lonesome-still...

Till my long-ago granddaddy
With my daddy's face
Stretched out his arms
And welcomed me home

He knelt on one knee
And planted one seed
That grew into ten tall trees
With mangoes for me

I danced a hello dance
To the drums of my uncles

And sang a hello song
In a circle with new-old friends

I walked with my cousins
All over Africa
Lifting my long dress
To step across countries

66   Theme 4

ONGOING ASSESSMENT

PERFORMANCE Oral language. Have students reread the part of the story that they like the best. Ask students to tell about a dream that they had.

PORTFOLIO Writing. Save students' descriptions of dreams as an example of independent writing. You may want to include both the rough draft and the final copy to assess the student's writing process.

And when I got tired
I turned into a baby
And my long-ago grandma
With Mama's face
Held me in her arms
And rocked me
Rocked me
To sleep

 YOUR TURN Do you dream about a place of long-ago? Where is that place? Talk to a partner about it. Then share your dream with another pair of classmates.

Hopes and Dreams   67

♦ TEACHER'S NOTES ♦

★ MULTICULTURAL AWARENESS
"Africa Dream" is a lovely poem about racial and ethnic roots. Discuss the importance for many people to recognize and celebrate their origins and culture. Invite students to share their views of their own countries and culture.

★ TEACHER TO TEACHER
You may want to help students learn more about figurative language such as hyperbole and alliteration.

LESSON 3
LANGUAGE POWER

STUDENT BOOK/SKILLS JOURNAL
PAGES 68–69

⭐ **KEY EXPERIENCES**

- Talking/reading about sleep dreams
- Asking and answering questions
- Performing a skit
- Researching dreams
- Choosing verb forms

⭐ **KEY LANGUAGE**

- past tense

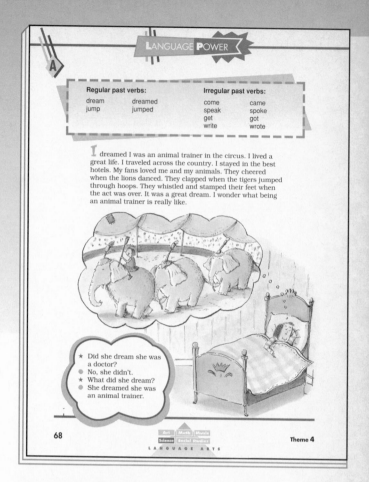

1 ◆ INTRODUCE

Building background: Talking about sleep dreams.
Encourage students to tell about a dream they had in their sleep. Compare students' dreams. How did they feel in their dreams? Did their dreams seem real or silly?

> **MULTI-LEVEL TEACHING STRATEGIES**
>
> You can include all students by asking questions appropriate to each student's language level.
>
> **Speech Emergence:** *Do you remember your dreams? What is the funniest/scariest/most interesting dream you have had?*
>
> **Developing Fluency:** *Why do you think people dream when they are asleep?*

2 ◆ EXPLORE

Activating prior knowledge. Open to page 68. To prompt discussion, ask multi-level questions such as *What does the picture show? What is the girl doing? What is she dreaming about? What do you think this lesson will be about?*

GUIDED READING Reading the paragraph. Have students follow along as you read or a volunteer reads

the paragraph. Ask, *Is the girl telling about something in the present or something in the past? How can we tell she is talking about something in the past?* Elicit that the action words, or verbs, all end in *ed*, and that this shows past action. Have volunteers read each sentence and point out the simple past tense verbs.

Pronunciation: -ed endings. Work with students on the pronunciation of the past tense endings. By lengthening and overemphasizing slightly the preceding vowel sound, students can achieve a better distinction of endings.

Asking and answering questions. Have students read the questions and answers about the dream. Let them work with partners to ask and answer questions about the girl's dream. Remind students to use the questions and answers on page 68 as a model.

Telling about dreams. Have students work in small groups. Students can take turns telling about dreams they have had. Tell students that they can describe real dreams they have had or they can

ALL STAR ENGLISH LEVEL 2

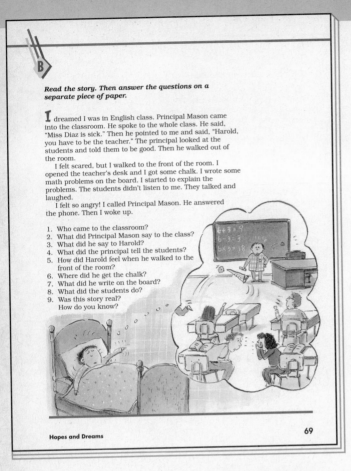

B

*Read the story. Then answer the questions on a
separate piece of paper.*

I dreamed I was in English class. Principal Mason came
into the classroom. He spoke to the whole class. He said,
"Miss Diaz is sick." Then he pointed to me and said, "Harold,
you have to be the teacher." The principal looked at the
students and told them to be good. Then he walked out of
the room.

I felt scared, but I walked to the front of the room. I
opened the teacher's desk and I got some chalk. I wrote some
math problems on the board. I started to explain the
problems. The students didn't listen to me. They talked and
laughed.

I felt so angry! I called Principal Mason. He answered
the phone. Then I woke up.

1. Who came to the classroom?
2. What did Principal Mason say to the class?
3. What did he say to Harold?
4. What did the principal tell the students?
5. How did Harold feel when he walked to the
   front of the room?
6. Where did he get the chalk?
7. What did he write on the board?
8. What did the students do?
9. Was this story real?
   How do you know?

Hopes and Dreams   69

---

make up dreams—in fact the wilder, the better.
After each dream is described, others in the group
ask and answer questions about it. Remind students to use simple past tense verbs in their questions and answers.

Reading the story. Have students turn to page 69.
Read aloud the story as students follow along.
Read the questions at the bottom of the page. Call
on volunteers to answer the questions. Be sure students answer in full sentences for verb practice.

Writing answers. Have students work independently and write answers to the questions on a separate
sheet of paper. Students can work with partners to
check their answers.

**Page 68: Choosing verb forms; cate-
gorizing.** Students complete cloze
of student book text with correct
verb forms. **Page 69: Creative writing.** Students
write about a dream. Teaching suggestions are provided in the Skills Journal annotations.

---

3 ◆ EXTEND

DRAMA Performing dreams. Have students work in
small groups to prepare a skit in which they act out
a dream. The dream can be an actual dream that
one of the students has had or a dream that is
made up by the group. Students might enjoy video-
taping their performance.

SCIENCE Learning about dreams. Have students use
the library and other resources to learn more about
dreams: *What causes them? How can you tell
when a person is dreaming? Do people ever
dream while awake?* Ask students to share their
findings with classmates.

Staging a contest. Have students work in small
groups to compete in a "Can You Top This?" contest. Each person, in turn, tells the weirdest dream
they ever had, trying to top the previous dream.
(Students should be encouraged to use their imaginations and not necessarily stick to the truth in this
activity.) Members of the group vote for the crazi-
est, funniest, or weirdest dream. Then the groups
present the dream they selected to the class to
compete for the grand winner.

ONGOING ASSESSMENT

PERFORMANCE Oral language. Evaluate students' abilities to respond to questions and participate during class discussions.

PORTFOLIO Writing. Save Skills Journal page 69
as an example of independent writing.

LESSON 4
EXPLORE...SOCIAL STUDIES

STUDENT BOOK/SKILLS JOURNAL
PAGES 70–71

★ **KEY EXPERIENCES**

- Reading/following directions
- Learning about the Chippewa
- Understanding a sequence
- Making a dream catcher
- Completing a story board

★ **KEY LANGUAGE**

- *dream catcher, web, feathers, crisscross*

★ **MATERIALS**

- white paper plates, 12-inch sections of yarn, beads, feathers, masking tape, pencil, scissors

EXPLORE...
SOCIAL STUDIES

Chippewa Dream Catcher

The Chippewa make dream catchers from wooden hoops with webs and feathers. Bad dreams get caught in the web. Good dreams float through the web and down the feathers into the sleeper's mind.

WHAT YOU NEED:
- a white paper plate
- 12 inches of yarn
- beads
- feathers
- masking tape, pencil, scissors

1. Draw a large ring inside the rim of the paper plate.
2. Cut out the center of the plate.
3. Punch about 16 holes around the ring.
4. Wrap masking tape around one end of the yarn. Poke the taped end through a hole and pull through, leaving about 3 inches at the end.

70

Art Math Music
Science Social Studies
LANGUAGE ARTS

Theme 4

1 ◆ INTRODUCE

Building background: Discussing dreaming. Continue your discussion of students' dreams from the previous lesson. Encourage them to share their ideas and personal experiences. Have students create a word web of dream ideas.

┌─ **MULTI-LEVEL TEACHING STRATEGIES** ─┐

You can include all students by asking questions appropriate to each student's language level.

Speech Emergence: *Do you like to dream? Do you dream in black and white or in color? What language do you dream in?*

Developing Fluency: *Have you had a funny dream? What was it about?*

└──────────────────────────────────────┘

SOCIAL STUDIES Learning about the Chippewa.
Explain that students are going to make Chippewa dream catchers. The Chippewa are a Native-American tribe that lived in Minnesota in the area around the Great Lakes. Have students locate this area on a map. Ask students to think about how they could catch a dream. Then ask students to draw what they think a dream catcher might look like.

2 ◆ EXPLORE

Activating prior knowledge. Open to pages 70 and 71. To prompt discussion, ask multi-level questions such as *What do the illustrations show? How do you think this object could catch dreams?*

GUIDED READING Reading directions. Read the introduction on page 70 aloud. Then have students reread the introduction independently. Check understanding with multi-level questions, such as *What do you use to make dream catchers? What gets caught in the web?* Have students skim the page. Ask, *What are we going to do? How many steps are there? What materials will we need?*

Exploring key vocabulary. On the board, write the words for the materials needed. Hold up each item, model the word, and have students repeat.

Following directions/Understanding a sequence. Read aloud and demonstrate the directions. Make sure students understand what *crisscrossing* means. Have students read through the directions independently. Then ask students to tell you what

5. Begin creating the web by crisscrossing the yarn through the rest of the holes in the ring. Leave the center open.

6. Take the taped end of the yarn back to the first hole and tie it to the loose, 3-inch end.

7. Cut a piece of yarn about 8 inches long. Loop it through a hole opposite the first hole. Pass several beautiful beads up the yarn. Add a feather or two, and knot the end of the yarn.

8. Share your dream catcher with your friends. Then hang it over your bed. Sweet dreams!

Hopes and Dreams   71

Language experience writing. Encourage students to keep their own "dream logs." Tell them to keep a pencil and some paper next to their beds. As soon as they wake up, they write down what happened in their dreams. If they want, after a week, they can bring their "dream logs" to class to share, or they can choose just one dream to share.

ART Displaying the dream catchers. Help the students make a display of their dream catchers in a hall of the school for all to admire. Compile more information about the Chippewa to include in the display.

PROCESS WRITING PORTFOLIO See the list of ideas and writing topics related to this theme.

╺╺╺ **ONGOING ASSESSMENT** ╺╺╺

PERFORMANCE Oral language. Ask individual students to explain how to make a dream catcher. Observe different students' levels. Check for sequence words such as *first, next, then.*

PORTFOLIO Writing. Save Skills Journal page 71 as an example of independent writing.

to do in what sequence, using words such as *first, next, then.*

Cooperative learning. In pairs, students help each other make the dream catchers, rereading the directions as needed. (CALLA: Cooperation)

SKILLS JOURNAL PAGES 70-71 **Completing a storyboard; writing.** Students draw last two frames of a storyboard, then write what happened in the story. Teaching suggestions are provided in the Skills Journal annotation.

3 ◆ EXTEND

SCIENCE Dreaming. Help students use resource materials to look up REM (rapid eye movement) sleep and find out what happens to our bodies when we dream. Challenge more proficient students to find out what happens if we don't dream. Compile the information on a chart. Pair students of varying abilities and have them write a paragraph about what they learned. (CALLA: Resourcing)

★ **PREDICTABLE PROBLEM**
Keep in mind that students who have experienced personal trauma may not want to share troubling dreams.

★ **MULTICULTURAL AWARENESS**
In the Chippewa culture, dream catchers are often given to newlyweds or parents of newborn babies.

LESSON 5
THE MAGIC OF DANCE

**STUDENT BOOK/SKILLS JOURNAL
PAGES 72–74**

⭐ **KEY EXPERIENCES**

- Reading/responding to a photo essay
- Discussing dance
- Using a chart

⭐ **KEY LANGUAGE**

- *ballet, cooperation, magic, perform, performance, scholarship, sweat*

⭐ **MATERIALS**

- pictures of dancers and dance performances including ballet

Jacques d'Amboise was a very famous dancer. He was the main dancer for the New York City Ballet for many years. Later, he became a teacher and started the NDI—National Dance Institute. He wanted to teach kids the magic of dance.

72

Theme 4

1 ◆ INTRODUCE

Building background: Discussing dance. Show pictures of dance performances and dancers. Invite students to describe the people and dances. Students can comment on costumes, sets, and actions. Encourage students to think about how the dancers prepare for the performances.

MULTI-LEVEL TEACHING STRATEGIES

You can include all students by asking questions appropriate to each student's language level.

Speech Emergence: *Do you like to dance? What kind of dance do you like? What kind of music do you dance to?*

Developing Fluency: *Why do some dancers wear special costumes at performances? Name some different kinds of dance.*

Making a dance word web. With students, brainstorm a list of words for dance. Encourage students to include names of dances in their own languages. Create a word web using question words as categories: who, when, where, why, how.

2 ◆ EXPLORE

Activating prior knowledge. Open to pages 72 and 73. Ask a volunteer to read the title, "The Magic of Dance." Have students look at the pictures on pages 72–74. To prompt discussion, ask multi-level questions such as *Are they singing? What are they doing? Is this a performance or practice? Where is the dance teacher? Who can be a dancer? Would you like to be a dancer? Why or why not?*

Previewing a story. Ask students if they think this story is real or a dream/fantasy. Have students explain their answers.

GUIDED READING Reading an essay. Read or play the tape for the selection as students follow along in their books. Read the selection again. You may want to pose the following display/comprehension questions to prompt discussion of each page and monitor students' understanding.

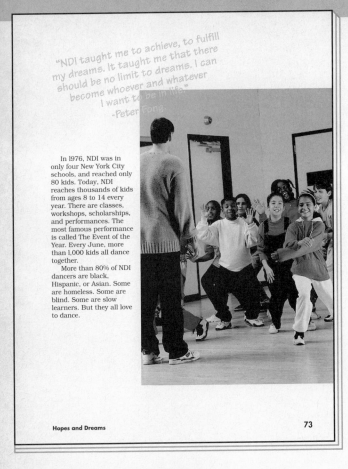

"NDI taught me to achieve, to fulfill my dreams. It taught me that there should be no limit to dreams. I can become whoever and whatever I want to be in life."
-Peter Fong

In 1976, NDI was in only four New York City schools, and reached only 80 kids. Today, NDI reaches thousands of kids from ages 8 to 14 every year. There are classes, workshops, scholarships, and performances. The most famous performance is called The Event of the Year. Every June, more than 1,000 kids all dance together.

More than 80% of NDI dancers are black, Hispanic, or Asian. Some are homeless. Some are blind. Some are slow learners. But they all love to dance.

Hopes and Dreams   73

Display/Comprehension Questions

Page 72

Who is Jacques d'Amboise? (a famous dancer)
Where was he a dancer? (at the New York City Ballet)
Why did he become a teacher? (he wanted to teach kids the magic of dance)
What is the name of the institute that he started? (the National Dance Institute)
What do you think is magic about dance?

Page 73

How many kids did he teach in 1976? (80)
How many kids does NDI teach now? (thousands)
How old are the kids? (8–14 years old)
What is the most famous performance of NDI? (The Event of the Year)
When is it? (every June)
Do many kids dance in it? (yes, more than 1,000)
Are the NDI dancers all Hispanic? (no)
What other groups of people are in NDI? (black, Asian, homeless, blind)

The kids are all different, but what do they all love? (to dance)

Page 74

Is it important to work together at NDI? (yes)
What else do the kids learn about at NDI? (practice, hard work, believing in yourself, pride)
Do you think these kids will stop dreaming?
Do you think they will continue to work hard in the future?

Rereading. Arrange students in pairs or small groups and have them read the selection together. Go around the room helping students as needed.

Independent reading. Have students read the selection silently. Then ask volunteers to read parts of it aloud.

SKILLS JOURNAL PAGES 72-74 **Page 72: Reading comprehension; using a diagram.** Students complete a Venn diagram about the text then mark statements true or false. **Page 73: Vocabulary development; creating a dance.** Students work with partners to describe a new dance. **Page 74: Using a chart; providing information about self.** Students complete a chart about themselves then write about their goals. Teaching suggestions are provided in the Skills Journal annotations.

3 ◆ EXTEND

MUSIC Listening to dance music. Bring in examples of music associated with various styles of dance and different cultural groups. Encourage students to discuss how the different musics makes them feel.

SOCIAL STUDIES Attending a dance performance. If possible, arrange for the class to attend a dance performance. Later, have students compare the different styles of dance and performances.

SOCIAL STUDIES Researching famous dancers. If students are interested, invite them to find information about other famous dancers such as Maria Tallchief or Barishnikov. Do not limit to classical dance, however.

SOCIAL STUDIES Describing cultural dances.
Encourage students to share information about
dance in their native cultures. Students can bring
in pictures or samples of music used in dances.

**PROCESS
WRITING
PORTFOLIO**

See the list of ideas and writing
topics related to this theme.

ONGOING ASSESSMENT

PERFORMANCE Oral language. With books
closed, have students talk about why the kids
work hard and practice so much. Ask what the
kids learn from NDI.

PREDICTABLE PROBLEM

Make sure students understand that the *t*
at the end of *ballet* is silent.

MULTICULTURAL AWARENESS

Revisit Theme 1, Lesson 6 for activities
about the music and dance of Puerto
Rico. Extend to other popular dances:
the samba, meringue, contra dancing,
the two-step, etc. This is an opportunity
for lots of fun and active participation.

TEACHER TO TEACHER

Work with the music teacher to introduce students to different styles of music
and types of dance.

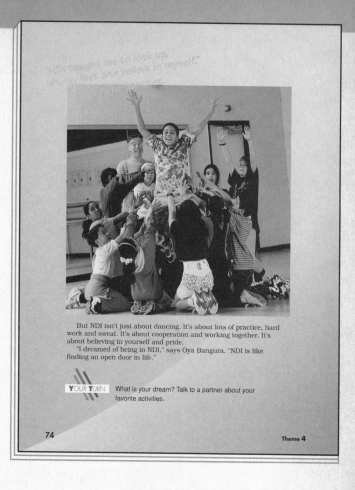

"NDI taught me to look up, lift my feet, and believe in myself."

But NDI isn't just about dancing. It's about lots of practice, hard
work and sweat. It's about cooperation and working together. It's
about believing in yourself and pride.
"I dreamed of being in NDI," says Oya Bangura. "NDI is like
finding an open door in life."

YOUR TURN What is your dream? Talk to a partner about your
favorite activities.

74

Theme **4**

◆ TEACHER'S NOTES ◆

LESSON 6
I HAVE A DREAM

 STUDENT BOOK/SKILLS JOURNAL
PAGE 75

⭐ KEY EXPERIENCES

- Reading/responding to an excerpt from a speech
- Understanding figurative language

⭐ KEY LANGUAGE

- brotherhood, character, color, equal, former, judged, nation, slave, slave-owner

1 ◆ INTRODUCE

Note: *This reading selection is an excerpt from Martin Luther King, Jr.'s speech in Washington, D.C., 1963.*

Building background: Martin Luther King, Jr.
Students' knowledge about the people and events of the civil rights movement may be limited. Explain that Martin Luther King, Jr. was a famous African American leader. Encourage students to share information they know about African Americans and their history. Give a brief background.

┌─ **MULTI-LEVEL TEACHING STRATEGIES** ─┐

You can include all students by asking questions appropriate to each student's language level.

Speech Emergence: *Have you ever heard of Martin Luther King, Jr.? What did he do?*

Developing Fluency: *Why is Martin Luther King, Jr. famous? What did he believe in?*

└──────────────────────────────────┘

2 ◆ EXPLORE

Activating prior knowledge. Open to page 75. Ask a volunteer to read the title of the poem, "I Have a Dream." To prompt discussion, ask multi-level questions about the title and pictures such as *Is this dream important to many people or just to*

this man? Why do you think he's telling everyone his dream? What do you think his dream is about? Is this about a sleep dream or a dream for the future?

 GUIDED READING Reading a speech. Read or play the tape as students follow along in their books. Read the speech again. Ask questions to check students' understanding. *Is the dream about one person or the whole country? Does he think all men are created equal? Who does he dream about? Who are the sons of former slaves? Who are the sons of former slave owners? What do these people do in his dream? How many children does this man have? What does he dream for them? Which is more important: the color of people's skin or their character?*

Rereading. Reread the poem chorally. Point out that his dream first is about the entire country, then it is about the state of Georgia, and, finally, it is about his family.

Independent reading. Have students read the speech silently. Then ask volunteers to read the speech aloud.

Your Turn. With the class, read the instructions under "Your Turn." Have students work with partners as they talk about Martin Luther King, Jr.'s dream. Depending on the level of the class, you may want to follow up by having students share their opinions with the entire class. *Can this dream come true? Who can make this dream come true?*

 **Cloze exercise.** Students complete a cloze poem. Teaching suggestions are provided in the Skills Journal annotation.

3 ◆ EXTEND

Writing about hopes and dreams. Ask students to describe their dreams for the school, their town, the United States, or another place. Students can write a description of their hopes and dreams. Encourage students to make drawings or use magazine pictures

I Have a Dream

MARTIN LUTHER KING, JR.

I have a dream
That one day this nation will rise up
And live out the true meaning of its creed;
"We hold these truths to be self-evident,
That all men are created equal."

I have a dream
That one day on the red hills of Georgia
The sons of former slaves
And the sons of former slave-owners
Will be able to sit down together
At the table of brotherhood.

I have a dream
That my four little children
Will one day live in a nation
Where they will not be judged
By the color of their skin
But by the content of their character.

(excerpted from a speech in Washington, D.C., 1963)

YOUR TURN What does the writer hope will happen in the future? This speech was written over 30 years ago. Has the writer's dream come true? Why or why not? Talk about it with your class and the teacher.

Hopes and Dreams   75
LANGUAGE ARTS

dents that the phrase *sit down together at the table of brotherhood* is a reference to segregated restaurants where blacks (*the sons of slaves*) could not eat with whites (*the sons of former slave owners*).

ONGOING ASSESSMENT

PERFORMANCE Oral language. With books closed, have students summarize the dream of Martin Luther King, Jr. and tell what their hopes and dreams are.

PORTFOLIO Writing. Save Skills Journal page 75 as an example of guided writing.

TEACHER TO TEACHER
Work with a social studies teacher, perhaps as a guest speaker, to provide background for the excerpt of Dr. King's speech.

to create a collage of their dreams. Create a bulletin board display of hopes and dreams.

SOCIAL STUDIES Learning about African Americans. Encourage students to find out more about Martin Luther King, Jr., his speech, or African American history. Students can prepare a short oral or written report to share their findings with the class. (CALLA: Resourcing)

Understanding figurative language. King's speech looks, reads, and sounds like a poem. Explain that King's speeches were written to inspire people. They lose much of their power when worded differently. Help students understand what King means by the nation's *creed*. (He is referring to the Declaration of Independence; the two lines following are direct quotes from it.) Present other words or phrases that could be difficult for students. Ask students why King might have chosen the words *the red hills of Georgia*. (Georgia is King's home state; the soil in Georgia is mostly red clay; Georgia was one of the states whose economy was most dependent on slaves and plantation life.) Explain to stu-

LESSON 7
ALL STAR NEWS

 **STUDENT BOOK/SKILLS JOURNAL
PAGES 76–77**

⭐ **KEY EXPERIENCES**

- Reading for information and pleasure

- Discussing jobs and professional goals

- Reading/responding to a poem

- Taking a poll

- Process writing

⭐ **KEY LANGUAGE**

- *gymnast, routine, flawless, vault, dismount, uneven bars, obstacle, ribbons, robots*

- professions

- gymnastic events

⭐ **MATERIALS**

- pictures of different professions

1 ◆ INTRODUCE

Building background: Discussing jobs and professional goals. Show pictures of different professions. Have students identify the jobs and talk about where and what these people do. Encourage students to comment on the jobs that they like.

> **MULTI-LEVEL TEACHING STRATEGIES**
>
> You can include all students by asking questions appropriate to each student's language level.
>
> **Speech Emergence:** *Where do lawyers work? What does an astronaut do? Would you like to be a movie star? Why or why not?*
>
> **Developing Fluency:** *What job would you like best? Why? Which jobs are dangerous? Which jobs are interesting?*

2 ◆ EXPLORE

Activating prior knowledge. Have students find and read the article headings on pages 76 and 77. Ask students to guess what the articles will be about. You may want to have students use article titles to form questions about the content. (CALLA: Predicting)

Scanning for information. Do rapid scanning practice by asking questions, such as *How many lines are in the poem? What kind of Olympics are mentioned in the article "What's So Special?" How many professions are listed in "Dream Job?" What's the fifth job on the list?* (CALLA: Selective attention)

■ **GUIDED READING Reading for information.** Play the tape or read the selections, pausing occasionally to ask multi-level questions. Students who are able to should read the pages independently. You may want to pose the following display/comprehension questions to prompt discussion of each page and monitor students' understanding.

Display/Comprehension Questions

Page 76
What would Ben do? (help the homeless)
Who wants to be an Olympic champion? (Karen)
Who lives in the Dominican Republic? (Joseph's grandparents)
Which jobs do you think are interesting? Why?

News From All Over

What's So Special?

Kelly Ann Kettles is a gymnast. She performs her floor exercises like a ballet dancer. Her routine on the uneven bars is flawless. She treats the vault like a bump in the rug.

"Piece of cake," said Kelly after a great dismount. "It's amazing what training can do!"

Why is Kelly so special? She has only been training for five years. And like 7.5 million other Americans, she was born mentally retarded.

Like the "regular" Olympics, the Special Olympics awards ribbons and medals. But at the Special Olympics, winning isn't important. Trying is important. Sharing the experience is important. Friendships are important. The Special Olympics help each athlete believe that no obstacle is too high to jump and no race is too far to run.

AMAZING FACTS!

- Robots are not new inventions. The Chinese people dreamed them up 750 years ago.
- The world's largest table was set up in Spain in 1986. It was nearly a mile long and had seats for 6,400 people!
- The human brain contains an estimated 100 billion cells. It is the most complex object in the universe.

Hopes and Dreams   77

Page 77

Is Kelly a dancer or a gymnast? (gymnast)
How does she look when she does the floor exercise? (like a ballet dancer)
How long has Kelly been training? (5 years)
What is special about Kelly? (She was born mentally retarded.)
What kinds of awards are given at the Special Olympics? (ribbons and medals)
Do you think the Special Olympic athletes try only easy things? Why?

Reading a poem. Read or play the tape for the poem as students follow along in their books. Ask multi-level questions to check students' understanding.

Where is the house? (in South Carolina)
Is it a big house or a small house? (big house)
How many beds are in the room? (one)
Is someone sleeping in the bed? (no)
Do you think the poet misses the house in South Carolina? Why?

MATH Taking a poll. Have students prepare and conduct a poll of professions that kids would like to enter. Students can prepare questions or a survey questionnaire to give to others in the school. Then students can work in groups to compile the results and prepare graphs or charts. If there is a school newspaper, encourage students to write an article to share the results of their polls.

SKILLS JOURNAL PAGES 76-77 **Process writing.** Students read a sample newspaper article then write an article of their own on the same topic. Teaching suggestions are provided in the Skills Journal annotations.

3 ◆ EXTEND

ART Discussing dreams/making a display. Students can work in groups to share their dreams and hopes for the future. Later, students can write about their dreams. Encourage students to choose a format they like: a poem, a paragraph, a picture essay. Display the work for others in the class to read and enjoy.

SOCIAL STUDIES Learning about professions. Have students select professions that they like. Students may want to research the types of training, education, and skills that are needed in these professions. If possible, have students interview someone of that profession. Encourage students to report their findings to the class. If possible, prepare a large chart to compare the information about different professions.

ONGOING ASSESSMENT

PERFORMANCE Reading. Check student responses for ability to scan for information.

PORTFOLIO Writing. Save Skills Journal pages 76–77 as an example of independent writing.

COMPUTER CONNECTION
Have students use a multimedia CD-ROM encyclopedia to find more information about Special Olympics or gymnastics.

LESSON 8
ALL STAR NEWS

STUDENT BOOK/SKILLS JOURNAL
PAGES 78-79

 KEY EXPERIENCES

- Reading for information and pleasure

- Working in collaborative groups:
  - family histories
  - photo essays
  - polls
  - collages

- Writing a letter

- Expressing opinions

- Taking photos

- Practicing science process skills

 **KEY LANGUAGE**

- *photographer, photography, camera, film, photo*

Bright Ideas

KID PHOTOS

Maybe you're dreaming of becoming a famous photographer. *Shooting Back* is a photography program for city kids. It helps kids express themselves through photography. Adult volunteers teach kids how to use a camera and develop their own film. The photographers keep journals and write about their photos, too. Below are photos taken by kids in Washington, D.C. and Minneapolis, Minnesota.

Tips for Taking Good Photos
1. RELAX. The camera is a friendly tool.
2. THINK BEFORE YOU SHOOT. What do you want to show in the photo?
3. LOOK FOR NEW AND DIFFERENT ANGLES TO SHOOT FROM. Take a photo from your knees or from up high.
4. ASK PERMISSION TO TAKE SOMEONE'S PICTURE FIRST.
5. AS YOU AIM, TAKE A DEEP BREATH. Exhale as you snap the photo. One last thing: Don't forget to take the lens cap off!

UNICEF

Since 1950, kids in the U.S. have raised more than 100 million dollars for UNICEF.

UNICEF is the United Nations' agency that gives help to children around the world. If your class wants to help, write to:

UNICEF
PO Box 182248
Chattanooga, TN 37422-7248

78   Theme 4

1 ◆ INTRODUCE

Building background: Discussing photography. Have students share what they know about photography and cameras. Ask students whether they have ever used a camera. What do they have to do to take good photos? Write student ideas on the board.

┌ MULTI-LEVEL TEACHING STRATEGIES ┐

You can include all students by asking questions appropriate to each student's language level.

Speech Emergence: *Have you ever taken a picture with a camera? What did you take a picture of? How did your picture turn out?*

Developing Fluency: *What makes a good photograph? What makes a bad photograph? What would you like to photograph?*

2 ◆ EXPLORE

Activating prior knowledge. Open to page 78. To prompt discussion, ask multi-level questions such as *What is the top selection about? Do you think these are good photos? Why? Which photo do you like best? Which is most interesting? Who do you think took these photos?* (CALLA: Making predictions)

Bright ideas. Ask students to follow along as you or volunteers read the paragraph and photography tips. Prompt discussion of the tips with questions: *Why should you plan your photo before you shoot? What tips help you take more interesting photos? Why should you ask permission to take a person's picture?*

Mailbag. Direct students' attention to page 79. Have a volunteer read the letter. Ask students to brainstorm ideas for solving Sleepy Sue's problem. Write down their ideas and help students categorize the problem as sleeplessness, or insomnia. Suggest that students research insomnia. Have stu-

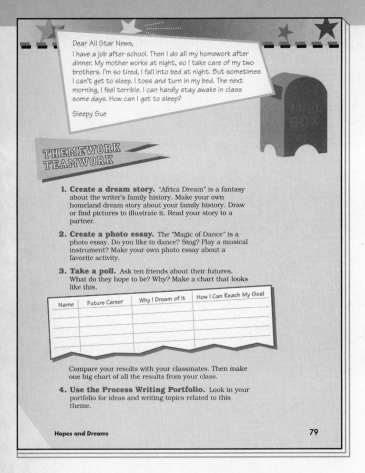

Dear All Star News,
I have a job after school. Then I do all my homework after dinner. My mother works at night, so I take care of my two brothers. I'm so tired, I fall into bed at night. But sometimes I can't get to sleep. I toss and turn in my bed. The next morning, I feel terrible. I can hardly stay awake in class some days. How can I get to sleep?

Sleepy Sue

THEMEWORK TEAMWORK

1. **Create a dream story.** "Africa Dream" is a fantasy about the writer's family history. Make your own homeland dream story about your family history. Draw or find pictures to illustrate it. Read your story to a partner.

2. **Create a photo essay.** The "Magic of Dance" is a photo essay. Do you like to dance? Sing? Play a musical instrument? Make your own photo essay about a favorite activity.

3. **Take a poll.** Ask ten friends about their futures. What do they hope to be? Why? Make a chart that looks like this.

Name	Future Career	Why I Dream of It	How I Can Reach My Goal

Compare your results with your classmates. Then make one big chart of all the results from your class.

4. **Use the Process Writing Portfolio.** Look in your portfolio for ideas and writing topics related to this theme.

Hopes and Dreams   79

---

dents work in small groups to compose a letter responding to Sleepy Sue. (See Skills Journal page 79.)

Themework/Teamwork. Have volunteers read the list of projects. Encourage students to pick one or more of the projects that interest them. Students can work independently or collaboratively to complete their projects. Ask students to share their completed projects with the class by explaining and displaying them.

SKILLS JOURNAL PAGES 78-79 **Page 78: Expressing opinions; letter writing; process writing.** Students answer the letter in Mailbox on student book page 78. **Page 79: Science skills.** Students read a cartoon science experiment then draw conclusions. Teaching suggestions are provided in the Skills Journal annotations.

3 ◆ EXTEND

SCIENCE Learning about cameras/famous photographers. Have students work in small groups to research how still cameras work and who some of the major inventors were. Other groups may want to read about famous photographers and find examples of their work. (CALLA: Resourcing)

SOCIAL STUDIES Making a timeline. Ask students to research the development of cameras, both still and motion. Have them present their information in the form of a timeline. (CALLA: Grouping)

ART Taking photographs. Allow students to use instant cameras or disposable cameras to take photos. (Students who own cameras should be invited to use them.) Students can prepare a display of their photos and information about them.

 **PROCESS WRITING PORTFOLIO** See the list of ideas and writing topics related to this theme.

ONGOING ASSESSMENT

PERFORMANCE Writing. Save copies of letters and reports in student's portfolios.

PORTFOLIO Writing. Save Skills Journal page 79.

★ **PREDICTABLE PROBLEM**
If you have only one or two instant cameras available, put up a sign-up sheet for their use and limit the number of exposures each student can take. Suggest that students plan all their photography projects by first sketching them out in "story board" form.

★ **COMPUTER CONNECTION**
Have students' photos put on photo CDs at your local photo shop. Students can view their photos on a computer with a CD-ROM drive and, with the right software, can manipulate their photos to create a multimedia presentation.

LESSON 9
HOLISTIC ASSESSMENT

📷 STUDENT BOOK/SKILLS JOURNAL
PAGES 80–81

⭐ KEY EXPERIENCES

- Demonstrating comprehension
- Summarizing
- Thinking critically
- Self-assessment
- Writing about oneself

⭐ KEY LANGUAGE

- arrested, demonstrations, minister, non-violence, protests

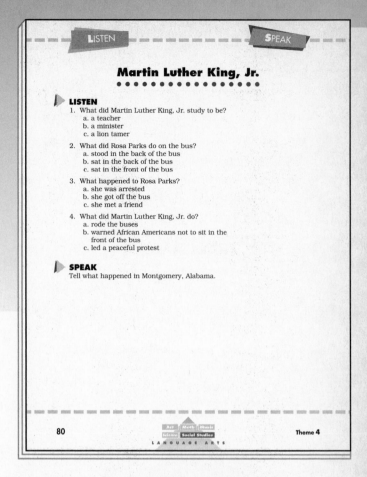

1 ◆ INTRODUCE

These two pages offer a variety of assessment opportunities. The left-hand page consists of listening and speaking activities that follow a taped presentation. In the speaking activity, students are asked to summarize what they have heard. The right-hand page consists of writing and critical thinking activities. These follow a reading passage that completes the listening component. You can use the activities to assess listening, speaking, reading, writing, and critical thinking skills. Have students work as a class or in small groups as you circulate and record observations on the **Anecdotal Record Form,** the **Reading Checklist,** and the **Writing Checklist** in the *All Star Assessment Package.*

Observing and recording student performance. Note the level of participation and the particular abilities of each student. How much do students understand? How well can they express themselves orally. What language structures do they use? What new words and concepts do they use? How actively do they participate? Use the **Anecdotal Record Form** in the *All Star Assessment Package* to record your observations and note areas for further development. Place in students' **portfolios.**

2 ◆ EXPLORE

Previewing. Open to pages 80 and 81 and let the students comment on the illustration. Read the title "Martin Luther King, Jr." or call on a volunteer to do so. Give students time to read the listening questions.

📷 **Listening.** Read or play the tape for the first part of "Martin Luther King, Jr." You will find the tapescript in the Appendix. Have students work independently to answer the listening questions. Read or play the tape again for students to check their work.

Speaking. Discuss what students have heard up to this point. Ask multi-level questions such as *When was King born? Was his father a school teacher or a minister? What does a minister do? What about his mother?* If some students are struggling, play the tape again and summarize the story once yourself. Ask questions again. When you are satisfied with this stage, go on to the next.

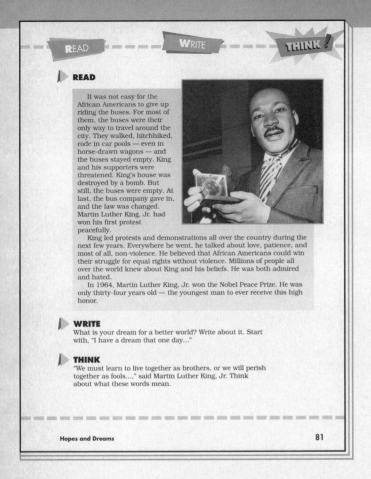

READ · WRITE · THINK!

READ

It was not easy for the African Americans to give up riding the buses. For most of them, the buses were their only way to travel around the city. They walked, hitchhiked, rode in car pools — even in horse-drawn wagons — and the buses stayed empty. King and his supporters were threatened. King's house was destroyed by a bomb. But still, the buses were empty. At last, the bus company gave in, and the law was changed. Martin Luther King, Jr. had won his first protest peacefully.

King led protests and demonstrations all over the country during the next few years. Everywhere he went, he talked about love, patience, and most of all, non-violence. He believed that African Americans could win their struggle for equal rights without violence. Millions of people all over the world knew about King and his beliefs. He was both admired and hated.

In 1964, Martin Luther King, Jr. won the Nobel Peace Prize. He was only thirty-four years old — the youngest man to ever receive this high honor.

WRITE

What is your dream for a better world? Write about it. Start with, "I have a dream that one day…"

THINK

"We must learn to live together as brothers, or we will perish together as fools…," said Martin Luther King, Jr. Think about what these words mean.

3 · EXTEND

SOCIAL STUDIES Listening to a speech. If possible, show the video of Martin Luther King, Jr.'s "I Have a Dream" speech. The language and repeated phrases will make this speech accessible to many of the students, and the message is one that many of the students will be able to appreciate as well.

Home-School Connection: Talking about leaders. Invite students to discuss the impact that a man like King has on all people. Then encourage students to talk about leaders in their own communities. Discuss what makes a good leader. Invite students to write their own definitions of a leader.

Reading. Read the story on page 81 or play the tape as the students listen and follow along in their books. Pause occasionally to ask multi-level questions. Then have the students do partner reading, alternating paragraphs.

Writing. Encourage students to tell you what they have heard and read. Do not look for word-for-word retelling, even from your best students. Have students write their answers to the question on page 81. (CALLA: Summarizing)

Thinking. Ask students questions such as *Do you think King changed history of the U.S.? Why or why not? What would life for African Americans be like if King had not lived?*

SKILLS JOURNAL PAGES 80-81 Page 80: Assessment; reinforcing key vocabulary. Students circle words that don't belong in vocabulary groups. **Page 81: Self-assessment; Home-School connection.** Students check off things they can do and words they know. Teaching suggestions are provided in the Skills Journal annotations.

LESSON 10
WHEN YOU DREAM
A DREAM

**STUDENT BOOK/SKILLS JOURNAL
PAGE 82**

★ **KEY EXPERIENCES**

- Reviewing the theme
- Listening to and singing a song
- Writing original verses

★ **KEY LANGUAGE**

- *queen, king, throne, singer*

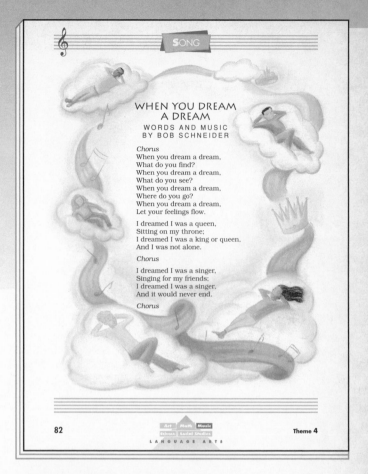

1 ◆ INTRODUCE

Building background: Discussing the theme. Engage students in a discussion and review of the things they learned in this theme.

┌─ **MULTI-LEVEL TEACHING STRATEGIES** ─┐

You can include all students by asking questions appropriate to each student's language level.

Speech Emergence: *What are two meanings of the word* dream*? What selection in this theme did you like best? Why?*

Developing Fluency: *What did you learn from this theme?*

└────────────────────────────┘

2 ◆ EXPLORE

MUSIC Listening to and singing the song. Read through the song several times with the students. Then play the tape of the song several times, inviting students to sing along as soon as they are ready.

Writing new verses. Encourage students to write new verses to the song. Use Skills Journal page 82 or separate paper that can be included in a class book called "Our Dreams."

 SKILLS JOURNAL PAGE 82

Creating an original song verse. Teaching suggestions are provided in the Skills Journal annotation.

3 ◆ EXTEND

Home-School Connection. Encourage students to take their books home to share with family and friends. They can read the stories in this theme to a younger sibling, a parent, or a friend. Have students keep a record of who they read to, which selections they read, and what the listeners thought about the selections.

Checking predictions. Have students take out the list of predictions they prepared for the first lesson of this theme. Ask them to check their predictions against the actual content of the unit. Were their predictions correct? (CALLA: Predicting)

Wrap Up

ASSESSMENT

You have been collecting assessment data through the ongoing and holistic assessment options (Oral Language Checklist, Reading Checklist, Anecdotal Record Form) in this theme. Following are some additional assessment strategies that will help you evaluate your students' progress as well as adapt your instruction to meet their needs.

Student Self-Assessment. Self-assessment surveys are a means for students to have input into their own learning process. Students can use them to reflect on the work they have done and the learning strategies they have used during this theme. Be sure to check students' self-assessment pages for each theme in the Skills Journal.

Informed Instruction. Evaluate the checklists, anecdotal records, and Process Writing Portfolio collections from this theme as a means of informing your instruction.
- In which areas are students showing confidence and enthusiasm?
- In which areas are they hesitant or confused?
- Should you provide more classroom opportunities for oral language or writing?
- Would certain students (or the whole class) benefit from a focused mini-lesson on a certain area or skill?
- Remember to recycle skills as you teach the next theme and provide students with many opportunities to gain competence.

READING

Don't forget to check on and encourage students' independent reading. Students who weren't ready for independent reading in English at the beginning of this theme may be ready now. Students who continue to read in their first language should be encouraged to do first language book reviews and be an attentive audience for other students' reviews in English.

BOOKBYTES

Have students been able to use the *All Star BookBytes* CD-ROM software? The BookBytes' book list includes the titles on the Theme Booklists for all levels of *All Star English*. BookBytes helps students choose a book to read based on their responses to a short questionnaire, then prompts students to think about and respond to what they've read through writing, drawing, and drama. Students can print out their work and share it with others. They can also choose to see other students' work on-screen in a gallery presentation.

THEME CELEBRATION

If your class is participating as an All Star Team, the end of theme is a good time to review students' accomplishments with the Theme Booklist and Theme Projects. Consider posting a chart in the classroom where students may check off their accomplishments and, if you are using a point system, total their points for the theme. Students should strive to do their best and outdo their *own* scores, not compete with each other. Encourage students to present their All Star projects to the class to allow more oral practice and to sharpen students' presentation skills. You might invite other classes or families to attend the presentations.

PREVIEW
STUDENT BOOK/SKILLS JOURNAL, PAGES 83–102
NEW FACES, NEW PLACES

CONCEPTS
- starting over
- feelings and emotions
- perseverance, courage, hope
- appreciating nature

LITERATURE

- The Family from Vietnam *(narrative story excerpt)*
- Flight Song *(poem)*
- All Star News *(short nonfiction articles)*
- Feelings and Emotions *(song)*

READING/WRITING SKILLS

- summarizing a story
- reading for information and pleasure
- classifying information
- making comparisons
- critical thinking
- reading comprehension
- process writing
- reading/responding to a narrative story
- writing a personal narrative
- writing about a past event
- reading/using a map
- reading/responding to a poem
- writing a poem
- understanding creative language
- reading and following directions
- responding to a letter
- writing about oneself
- writing new song verses

CONTENT

- **Math:** compiling information, calculating percentages, making graphs and charts
- **Social Studies:** learning about U.S. history, reading magazines and newspapers, learning about an Asian country, learning about current events, learning about immigration
- **Art/Music:** making a collage/display, writing directions for a craft, displaying craft objects, composing a rap song, singing a song
- **Science:** learning about animals of Asia, drawing conclusions from an experiment

---

KEY LANGUAGE/KEY EXPERIENCES

- modals
- past tense
- pronouns
- antecedents
- self-assessment
- feelings and emotions
- making a story map
- using a chart
- researching
- taking a poll
- understanding/making charts and graphs
- working in collaborative groups
- practicing science process skills
- practicing conversations
- note-taking
- learning language through song

THEME BOOKLIST/ THEME PROJECTS

As this new theme begins, photocopy the Theme Booklist/Theme Projects pages (following spread) for students. Encourage students to read as many books as they like from the Booklist, and to complete any of the assignments on the Project list as homework for this theme.

AWARDING POINTS FOR ALL STAR TEAMS

This is a good opportunity to motivate students through an All Star Team approach. Consider assigning point values to each project, including reading books from the booklist. Explain to students that they will accumulate points for each book they read or project they complete during the theme. Students will try to top their own scores as they work through each theme, competing against themselves, not each other. Remind students that they will have the opportunity to present their *All Star* projects to the class at the end of the theme.

BookBytes

If you have a computer with a CD-ROM drive available, introduce students to the *All Star BookBytes* software which is correlated to the Theme Booklists throughout *All Star English. BookBytes* categorizes the books by genre and helps students choose a book to read based on their answers to a short questionnaire. It then prompts students to think about and respond to what they've read through writing, drawing, and drama activities. Students can print out their work and share it with others or view work on-screen in a gallery presentation.

THEME BOOKLIST

HERE ARE SOME BOOKS YOU MIGHT LIKE TO READ.
LOOK FOR THEM IN YOUR LIBRARY.

And One For All, by Theresa Nelson. Orchard Books, 1989. A brother is killed fighting in Vietnam and his sister tries to cope.

A Boat to Nowhere, by Maureen Crane Wartski. Westminster Press, 1980. (Sequel—*A Long Way from Home*) A grandfather and his grandchildren are forced to leave their peaceful village in Vietnam.

The Brocaded Slipper and Other Vietnamese Folktales, by Lynette Dyer Vuong. J.B. Lippencott, 1982.

Cooking the Vietnamese Way, by Chi Nguyen and Judy Monroe. Lerner Publications, 1985. Easy-menu ethnic cookbook.

Fallen Angels, by Walter Dean Myers. Scholastic, 1988. A young man's tour of Vietnam.

In the Year of the Boar and Jackie Robinson, Bette B. Lord, Harper & Row, 1984. The delightful story of Shirley Temple Wong's first year in America.

Journey to Topaz, by Yoshiko Achida. Atheneum. A Japanese-American family is forced into a concentration camp.

The Land I Lost, Huynh Quang Nhuong. Harper and Row, 1986. The author's own story about growing up in and leaving Vietnam.

Lupita Manana, by Patricia Bealty. William Morrow, 1981. An orphaned brother and sister leave Mexico for the U.S.

Once Upon a Time in Junior High, by Lisa A. Norment. Scholastic, Inc., 1994. Two boys want to be "cool" in their new school.

A Tree is Nice, by Janice May Udry. Harper & Row, 1956.

BOOKS IN LANGUAGES OTHER THAN ENGLISH

Mai (Mai), by Hilda Perera. Barcelona, España: ediciones sm.

Doi song moi tren dat moi (A New Life in a New Land), by Nguyen Thi Duc Hien (Vietnamese). Fall River, MA: National Dissemination Center.

Island: Poetry and History of Chinese Immigrants on Angel Island 1910-1940, by Him Mark Lai, ed. (English/Chinese). Arcadia, CA: Shen's Books and Supplies.

Aekyung's Dream, by Min Paek (English/Korean). San Francisco, CA: Children's Book Press.

THEME PROJECTS

YOU MAY WANT TO WORK ON THESE PROJECTS
ALONE OR WITH A PARTNER OR SMALL GROUP.

☆ Make a set of vocabulary cards that show vocabulary words learned in the theme on one side and illustrations of the words on the other.

☆ Write dialogues that use vocabulary or grammatical structures learned in the theme.

☆ Write original sentences or stories using key vocabulary words.

☆ Create a word search or crossword puzzle that uses vocabulary from the theme.

☆ Translate a song, poem, or prose selection from your native language into English.

☆ Create paintings, drawings, or dioramas of stories or readings within the theme.

☆ Produce scripts or dramatizations of information presented in the theme.

☆ Create a collage, mobile, or other three-dimensional art project that illustrates key concepts from the theme.

☆ Take a survey and present graphs and charts that explore questions related to the theme.

☆ Write journal entries for five to ten days about key concepts or ideas in the theme.

☆ Paste news clippings onto blank paper and write a short statement explaining how the article relates to the theme.

☆ Write a letter to the editor, the school government, City Hall, or the President of the United States about issues and ideas in the theme.

☆ Create maps that show the location of places mentioned in the theme.

☆ Create a time line that shows what happened in a story from the theme.

☆ Make a story chart that clearly labels the characters, plot, setting, climax, and ending of a story from the theme.

☆ Present a dramatic reading of one of the stories in the theme.

☆ Write a letter that gives advice or constructive criticism to a character in a story from the theme.

LESSON 1
THEME OPENER

STUDENT BOOK/SKILLS JOURNAL
PAGE 83

 KEY EXPERIENCES

- Discussing relocating
- Talking about previous homes
- Previewing theme content and titles
- Discovering the library
- Self-assessment

KEY LANGUAGE

- feelings and emotions
- *beads, Vietnam, Asia*

 MATERIALS

- index cards, wall map

1 ◆ INTRODUCE

Theme 5, New Faces, New Places, explores the feelings and emotions of being in a new place. Students will read and talk about the good and bad aspects of moving and living somewhere new. They will practice pronouns and learn about Asia and its languages.

Building background: Discussing relocating. Ask students if they have ever moved from one place to another. Encourage students to discuss how they felt about moving and what it was like to be in a new and strange place.

┌─ **MULTI-LEVEL TEACHING STRATEGIES** ─┐

You can include all students by asking questions appropriate to each student's language level.

Speech Emergence: *How did you feel when you knew you would be moving? How did you feel about your new home?*

Developing Fluency: *How did you make new friends? Tell how you feel about your new home now.*

└──────────────────────────┘

Talking about previous homes. Encourage students to talk about where they resided before they moved to their present homes. Ask multi-level questions such as *Where did you live before you came here? What was it like there? What things did you like most about where you used to live? Are there any things you didn't like about living there?*

2 ◆ EXPLORE

Activating prior knowledge. Open to page 83. To prompt discussion, ask multi-level questions such as *What does the photograph show? What do you think this theme will be about?*

Reading Corner. Have students read the titles, authors, and descriptions of the three books listed under Reading Corner. These are just a few selections from the Theme Booklist, chosen to help motivate students to want to read. Have the books available for students to look at. Prompt discussion about which book each student would like to read and why. Allow students to sign up for turns with the books. Use this experience to get your students excited about reading.

Previewing theme content and titles. Guide students as they look through the theme, inviting them to comment on titles, photos, and art. Ask for volunteers to read the selection titles aloud. Encourage students to predict what the selections will be about. (CALLA: Predicting)

 Activating prior knowledge; self-assessment. Students complete a chart before and after the lesson. Teaching suggestions are provided in the Skills Journal annotation.

3 ◆ EXTEND

Learning more about classmates. Ask each student to write the following information on an index card: name, place of origin, favorite food, favorite activity, favorite color. Working in pairs, students exchange cards and pretend they are the person

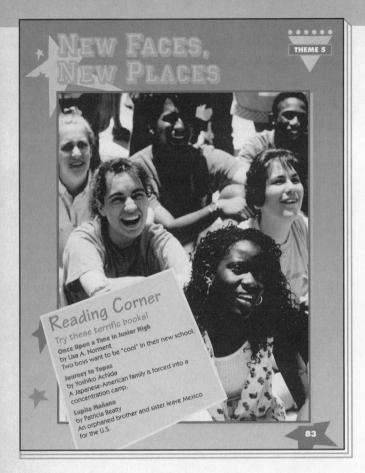

NEW FACES, NEW PLACES

THEME 5

Reading Corner
Try these terrific books!

Once Upon a Time in Junior High
by Lisa A. Norment
Two boys want to be "cool" in their new school.

Journey to Topaz
by Yoshiko Achida
A Japanese-American family is forced into a concentration camp.

Lupita Mañana
by Patricia Beatty
An orphaned brother and sister leave Mexico for the U.S.

83

in this search and, in so doing, will practice basic library and research skills. In the classroom, plan to read aloud to students each day. You may wish to record the books on tape and let students read the books as they listen to the tapes. Encourage students to read independently whenever possible.

ONGOING ASSESSMENT

PERFORMANCE **Written language.** Use the index cards that students prepared for the Extend activity to evaluate students' ability to record personal data.

BOOKBYTES

Have students use the BookBytes software as motivation for reading and writing about what they've read.

COMPUTER CONNECTION

Encourage students to use spreadsheet software to record, classify, correlate, and present information.

named on the card. Students then ask partners questions: *What is your name? Where are you from? What is your favorite...?* Extend this to a whole-class activity by putting all the cards in a pile and having students draw cards. Be sure no student has his or her own card. Students can pretend they are at a party and circulate about the room introducing themselves to others.

SOCIAL STUDIES/MATH Compiling information.
Have students compile information from the cards made for the previous activity. Encourage students to place pins on a wall map to show places of origin of class members. Students can also compile charts to show numbers of students from each place, numbers of favorite foods, and so on. Encourage students to analyze the date to see if there are correlations between place of origin and favorite foods or activities. (CALLA: Grouping)

Discovering the library. Lead students on a tour of your school or local library. With students, gather the books recommended for this theme in the Theme Booklist. Students will enjoy participating

LESSON 2
THE FAMILY FROM VIETNAM

 STUDENT BOOK/SKILLS JOURNAL PAGES 84–89

⭐ **KEY EXPERIENCES**

- Describing a sequence of events
- Reading/responding to a narrative story
- Making a story map
- Discussing cause and effect
- Writing a personal narrative
- Summarizing a story
- Using a chart

⭐ **KEY LANGUAGE**

- *I wonder if...*
- *I hope ....*
- modals
- past tense
- *ads, character, scene*
- *job application, newspaper*
- *city, village, war*

⭐ **MATERIALS**

- map of the world

The Family from Vietnam

ADAPTED FROM THE BOOK BY TANA REIFF

About the story

TIME: 1975, after the Vietnam War
PLACE: The United States

MAIN CHARACTERS:
Mai, a refugee woman from Vietnam
Set, Mai's husband
Bao and Thi, Mai and Set's children
Mr. and Mrs. Baker, sponsors for Mai and her children.

SETTING THE SCENE:
A family from Vietnam is separated after the war. The mother and children come to the United States.

——— Part 1 ———
The Job

Life in Lancaster was very difficult for Mai. She was poor. She had no husband. She had no job. She was living in an American city. It was a long way from her little village in Vietnam.

Mr. and Mrs. Baker were very good to Mai. They helped her a lot. Still, Mai wanted to be able to do things for herself. She didn't think she would ever see Set again.

Mai was a very smart woman. She did many things with her time. She went to school. She learned a lot. She put ads in the Vietnamese newspapers in the United States. She hoped the ads would help find her husband.

84

Theme 5

1 ♦ INTRODUCE

About this adaptation: "The Family From Vietnam" has been adapted from *The Family from Vietnam* by Tara Reiff. Copyright © 1979 by David S. Lake Publishers. Reprinted with permission of Globe Fearon.

Description of change: Some dialogue and narrative has been cut to advance the story. Occasionally vocabulary has been simplified.

Rationale: These changes were made for space reasons and to make the selection grade-level appropriate.

Building background: Discussing immigrant experiences. Show a map of the world. Have students point out their native countries or those of their parents on the map. Encourage students to use the map to trace and explain how their families came to the U.S.

MULTI-LEVEL TEACHING STRATEGIES

You can include all students by asking questions appropriate to each student's language level.

Speech Emergence: *Where are you from? Did you come to the U.S. in a plane, by boat, or in a car? Who came with you?*

Developing Fluency: *When did your family come to the U.S.? How did you feel when you got here? What things are different here?*

2 ♦ EXPLORE

Activating prior knowledge. Open to pages 84–85. Ask a volunteer to read the title of the story, "The Family from Vietnam." Use questions to elicit student ideas about difficulties the family might face in a new country. List ideas on the board.

Discussing Vietnam. Have a volunteer find Vietnam on the map of the world. Encourage students to

Soon she started to look for a job. In schools she had learned how to fill out a job application. She learned how to use a bus. And Mr. Baker sometimes took her in his car to look for jobs. But it was hard.

"Mr. Baker," she said. "I want to work. You are very good to me, but I should work. I will take any job."

She found an ad in the newspaper for a job at a chicken farm. She wanted to work, so Mr. Baker took her there.

"This is not very clean work," said the man at the chicken farm. "We kill chickens here. Then we get them ready to sell. But if you want a job helping us, you can have it."

"I want the job," said Mai.

"OK, then it's yours," the man answered.

Mai started work the next day.

New Faces, New Places   85

---

identify the continent and to share information about Vietnam, the war, and refugees.

Previewing a story. Have a volunteer read the section *About the story.* Ask questions about the setting and characters. Explain that there are three parts to the story. Ask students to find the titles and starting pages for each part. Then have students look at the pictures on pages 84–89. To prompt discussion, ask multi-level questions such as *Who do you think these people are? How many children are there in the family? What is the name of the farm? Why do you think they are at the farm? What is in Mai's mailbox? Who wrote the letter? Who is picking up the children? Are they happy or sad?*

GUIDED READING Reading a narrative story.
Read or play the tape for the story as students follow along in their books. Read the story again stopping to ask questions. You may wish to pose the following display/comprehension questions to prompt discussion of each page and monitor students' understanding.

Display/Comprehension Questions

Page 84

Does the story take place before or after the Vietnam War? (after the war)

How many characters are there? (6)

Where is Mai from? (Vietnam)

Who are Mai's sponsors? (Mr. and Mrs. Baker)

Where does Mai live in the U.S.? (Lancaster)

Was it easy or difficult for Mai in Lancaster? (difficult)

Why? (she was poor, missed her husband, had no job)

Who helped Mai? (Mr. and Mrs. Baker)

Who is Set? (Mai's husband)

What did Mai put in the Vietnamese newspapers? (ads)

Why did she put ads in the paper? (She hoped she would find her husband.)

Page 85

Who started to look for a job? (Mai)

Where did she learn to fill out a job application? (in school)

Does Mai drive a car or take the bus? (take the bus)

Who takes Mai to look for jobs? (Mr. Baker)

How did Mai find out about the job at the chicken farm? (an ad in the newspaper)

Does Mai want this job? (yes)

Page 86

Did Mai make enough money for her family? (yes)

Do you think she liked the work? (Answers will vary.)

What does Mai think of every day? (her home in Vietnam)

Who does she wonder about? (Set)

Does Mai know if Set is alive or not? (no)

What language did Mai's children learn? (English)

Who are their friends? (American children)

Do the children seem to be happy or sad? (happy)

How do you know? (Mai hears them laughing.)

What does Mai find in the mailbox? (a letter)

Who wrote the letter? (Set)

How do you think Mai feels? (Answers will vary.)

Page 87

Who does Mai call? (her children, Bao and Thi)
What does Mai read to the children? (the letter)
How long has it been since Mai has seen her husband? (a year)
Where is Set? (California)
How did Set find out about Mai and the children? (an ad in a Vietnamese newspaper)
How did Set feel when Mai and the children were on the plane? (very sad)
Who does Set live with now? (an American family)
Does Set miss his family? (yes)

Page 88

Why is Mai happy? (her husband is alive)
How many days have gone by since the letter? (8 days)
What did Mai do on Monday morning? (got up for work)
Who did Mai see on the street? (a small man)
What did Mai hear? (the doorbell ring)
Who got to the door first? (Bao and Thi)
Did the children recognize Set? (no)
What did Thi say? ("Daddy")
Why didn't Set say anything? (He was too happy.)

Page 89

Where was Mai? (at the top of the stairs)
How do you think Mai and Set felt? (Answers will vary.)
Who is hungry? (Thi)
Is Mai going to work? (no)
Why not? (she wanted to be with her family for the day)

Rereading. Reread the story in pairs or small groups. If possible, pair more proficient readers with less skilled readers.

Independent reading. Have students read the story silently. Then have volunteers read parts of the story aloud.

Your Turn. With the class, read the instructions under "Your Turn." Have students work with part-

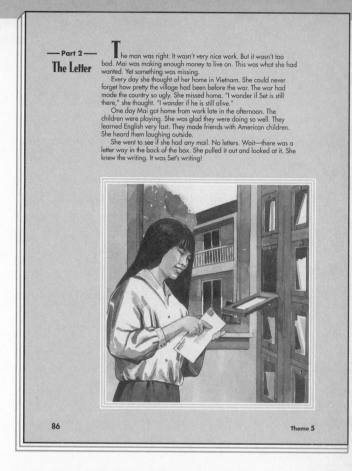

— Part 2 —
The Letter

The man was right. It wasn't very nice work. But it wasn't too bad. Mai was making enough money to live on. This was what she had wanted. Yet something was missing.

Every day she thought of her home in Vietnam. She could never forget how pretty the village had been before the war. The war had made the country so ugly. She missed home. "I wonder if Set is still there," she thought. "I wonder if he is still alive."

One day Mai got home from work late in the afternoon. The children were playing. She was glad they were doing so well. They learned English very fast. They made friends with American children. She heard them laughing outside.

She went to see if she had any mail. No letters. Wait—there was a letter way in the back of the box. She pulled it out and looked at it. She knew the writing. It was Set's writing!

86   Theme 5

ners as they discuss what the family talked about at breakfast. Students can write their conversations and then act them out for the class.

 **SKILLS JOURNAL PAGES 84-89** **Page 84: Using a chart; summarizing.** Students complete chart with information from the story. **Page 85: Reading comprehension.** Students write words from the story that mean the same as the sentences provided. **Page 86: Cloze exercise; writing.** Students complete a cloze of the letter from the story then write imaginary letters from longlost family members. **Page 87: Using learning strategies.** Students complete chart about the strategies they use to learn English then keep week-long diaries about how they learn English. **Page 88: Using a chart.** Students complete a chart about the story. **Page 89: Practicing conversations; writing.** Students read and practice a dialogue between story characters; ask and answer questions with a partner, then write about their new conversations. Teaching suggestions are provided in the Skills Journal annotations.

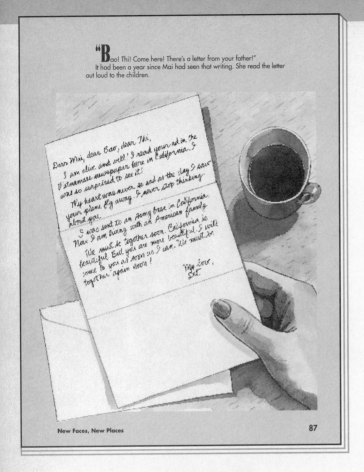

"**B**ao! Thi! Come here! There's a letter from your father!"
It had been a year since Mai had seen that writing. She read the letter
out loud to the children.

Dear Mai, dear Bao, dear Thi,
I am alive and well! I read your ad in the
Vietnamese newspaper here in California. I
was so surprised to see it!

My heart was never so sad as the day I saw
your plane fly away. I never stop thinking
about you.

I was sent to an Army base in California.
Now I am living with an American family.
We must be together soon. California is
beautiful. But you are more beautiful. I will
come to you as soon as I can. We must be
together again soon!

My love,
Set

New Faces, New Places   87

3 ◆ EXTEND

Making a story map. As a group, make a story map
to summarize the important events of the story.
Have students present an oral summary of the
story using the information on the story map.
(CALLA: Summarizing)

Discussing cause and effect. Use questions to help
elicit cause and effect statements about the story.
Write the sentences on the board. For example:

*Mai and her family came to the U.S. because of
the war.*

*Mr. Baker took Mai to the chicken farm because
Mai was looking for a job.*

Point out the word *because.* Provide additional
examples as needed. Use a chart or arrows to
show the relationship of the events in the sentences.

Writing a journal entry. Have students work together in small groups to write from Mai's point of view

about the day that Set arrived. What did the family
do together? What did they talk about? Did Set
plan to stay there or will the family move to
California? Did Set get there by bus, train, or
plane? Who was the happiest person?

Relating a story to personal experiences. Students
can discuss similarities and differences between
Mai's and their own experiences of being in a new
place. *What was difficult about coming to a new
place? How is life different? What things/people
do you miss from your homeland? What are your
hopes for the future?* As a class, you may want to
create a collage or display of things that are new
and different.

Home-School Connection. Suggest that students ask
parents and family members about their own immigrant experiences. Encourage students to write
about what they learn, or invite some of the families to share their stories with the class.

PROCESS WRITING PORTFOLIO See the list of ideas and writing
topics related to this theme.

ONGOING ASSESSMENT

PERFORMANCE Oral language. Have students
reread the part of the story that they like best.
Ask students to explain what difficulties Mai
faced in her new home and what is new for
them.

PORTFOLIO Writing. Save students' journal
entries or conversations as examples of independent writing. You may want to include both
the rough draft and the final copy to assess the
student's writing process.

LANGUAGE NOTES

Some students may not be aware of the difference between a *refugee* and an *immigrant*. An immigrant includes anyone who moves permanently to another country, usually by the person's own choice. A refugee is one who is forced to move because of fear of persecution or threats because of one's religion, ethnic group, or political beliefs. When a refugee is accepted for immigration to the U.S., a *sponsor* is arranged to help the refugee get settled in the new area.

MULTICULTURAL AWARENESS

Many ethnic groups have developed mutual assistance groups, newspapers, and radio/TV communications. Encourage students to talk about which means of communication their family uses to keep in contact with others of their language and cultural background.

PREDICTABLE PROBLEMS

Students may be confused with *It wasn't too bad*. Point out that the sentence implies that it wasn't good either. Make sure students understand that when the employer says, *Then it's yours*, he is offering the job to Mai.

— Part 2 —
Together Again

Mai was so happy. A year ago her world had fallen apart. Seeing Set again would be a dream come true.

Eight days went by. Still no Set. "I hope he is all right," thought Mai. It was Monday morning. Mai got up for work. She looked out the window. The sun was just coming up. The street was almost empty. But way down the street, a small man was walking slowly. Mai wondered if it could be Set.

She got dressed very quickly. She combed her long, dark hair. Then the doorbell rang. The man walking down the street *had* been Set!

Bao and Thi got to the door first. They were not sure who the man was. They were very small and had not seen their father for a year. Set picked up both of them.

"Daddy!" It was the first time little Thi had ever said that word. Set was so happy, he couldn't speak. Then he saw Mai.

88   Theme 5

♦ TEACHER'S NOTES ♦

Mai stood at the top of the steps. She watched the children and Set together again.

Then she walked down, one step at a time. Set just stood there. He smiled. Then he let the children down and ran to meet his wife.

They didn't say a word. They held each other close. They didn't want to let go ever again. They held each other to make up for every day of the year gone by.

Then little Thi said, "I'm hungry!"

The whole family went into the apartment. Mai called the chicken farm. She stayed home from work that day. The family ate a big breakfast together. They had so much to talk about. There was nothing but hope in everyone's heart.

 YOUR **T**URN What do you think the family talked about at breakfast? With a partner, write a short conversation. All the family members should say something. Read your conversation to a small group. The group can act it out.

New Faces, New Places 89

THEME 5: NEW PLACES, NEW FACES

LESSON 3
LANGUAGE POWER

STUDENT BOOK/SKILLS JOURNAL
PAGES 90–91

 KEY EXPERIENCES

- Reading for information
- Practicing pronouns and past tense verbs
- Writing about a past event
- Learning about U.S. history

 KEY LANGUAGE

- pronouns
- past tense verbs
- great-great-grandmother, grandchildren, right to vote, peace, computers, VCRs, bank machines

 MATERIALS

- index cards

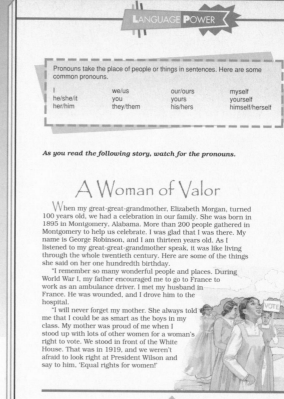

1 ♦ INTRODUCE

Building background: Discussing memories. Prompt a discussion of memories by modeling: *I remember a trip with my family when I was 10 years old. We had lots of fun.* Ask students to recount some of their memories.

> ### MULTI-LEVEL TEACHING STRATEGIES
>
> You can include all students by asking questions appropriate to each student's language level.
>
> **Speech Emergence:** *Do people in your family tell stories about things they remember? What do you remember about your last birthday?*
>
> **Developing Fluency:** *Tell a story about something that happened to you when you were younger.*

Exploring key vocabulary. Have students practice using pronouns and past tense verbs. Go around the room and ask each student to tell one thing they did yesterday or are doing today. Remind them to use complete sentences when they respond. Write the present and past tense forms of

the verbs students use on the chalkboard under the headings *Today/Present, Yesterday/Past.*

2 ♦ EXPLORE

Activating prior knowledge. Open to pages 90–91. Ask students to look at the pictures. To prompt discussion, ask multi-level questions such as *What do these pictures show? What do you think this story is about? How do you think the boy feels? Have you ever felt like the boy in the picture?* (CALLA: Previewing)

Grammar in context. Read the pronoun box at the top of page 90 aloud as students read along in their books. Instruct students to watch for the pronouns in the story as you read it aloud. Reread the story, stopping at each pronoun. Ask students what person or thing each pronoun refers to. Students who are able to should reread independently.

Recalling details from the story. Ask students to summarize the story. Prompt them by asking multi-

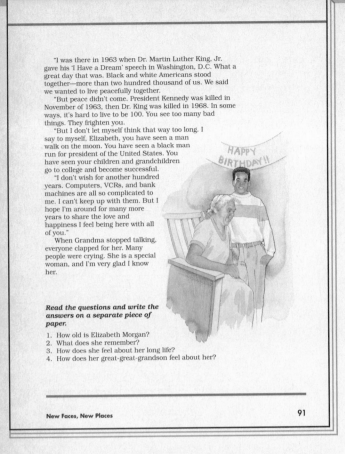

"I was there in 1963 when Dr. Martin Luther King, Jr. gave his 'I Have a Dream' speech in Washington, D.C. What a great day that was. Black and white Americans stood together—more than two hundred thousand of us. We said we wanted to live peacefully together.

"But peace didn't come. President Kennedy was killed in November of 1963, then Dr. King was killed in 1968. In some ways, it's hard to live to be 100. You see too many bad things. They frighten you.

"But I don't let myself think that way too long. I say to myself, Elizabeth, you have seen a man walk on the moon. You have seen a black man run for president of the United States. You have seen your children and grandchildren go to college and become successful.

"I don't wish for another hundred years. Computers, VCRs, and bank machines are all so complicated to me. I can't keep up with them. But I hope I'm around for many more years to share the love and happiness I feel being here with all of you."

When Grandma stopped talking, everyone clapped for her. Many people were crying. She is a special woman, and I'm very glad I know her.

Read the questions and write the answers on a separate piece of paper.

1. How old is Elizabeth Morgan?
2. What does she remember?
3. How does she feel about her long life?
4. How does her great-great-grandson feel about her?

New Faces, New Places   91

3 ♦ EXTEND

SOCIAL STUDIES Learning about U.S. history. Encourage students to do research to learn about how women won the right to vote in this country. Have students present their information to the class in the form of a written or oral report. (CALLA: Resourcing)

SOCIAL STUDIES Reading magazines and newspapers. Invite students to look through current magazines and newspapers for articles that interest them. Have students make a list of the articles they read and tabulate whether the article told about something that happened in the past, that is happening now, or that will happen in the future. (CALLA: Grouping)

Playing a past/present game. Write on separate index cards phrases indicating past or present time such as *yesterday, last week, last month, last year, in 1994; today, this week, this month, this year, now.* Place the cards in a pile, face down, and ask students to take one card each. Have students tell about something that happened or is happening during the time indicated by the phrase they drew.

ONGOING ASSESSMENT

PERFORMANCE Oral language. Evaluate students' abilities to use past tense verbs to describe a remembrance.

level questions such as *Whose birthday is it? Who is telling the story? What does Elizabeth remember first?* (CALLA: Summarizing)

Answering questions. Reread the story on pages 90–91 or play the tape again as students read along in their books. Then ask volunteers to read and answer the questions at the bottom of page 91. Have students work with partners to write answers to the questions.

Writing about remembrances. Invite students to write a paragraph describing a remembrance. Allow students to share their writing. Suggest that students who have a bad remembrance try to inject some humor in their writing.

Page 90: Pronouns. Students fill in cloze with correct pronouns. **Page 91: Antecedents.** Students read sentences from the story and write pronoun antecedents next to them. Teaching suggestions are provided in the Skills Journal annotations.

COMPUTER CONNECTION
Have students use a CD-ROM encyclopedia to research the events in U.S. history referred to in the story.

LESSON 4
EXPLORE...GEOGRAPHY

STUDENT BOOK/SKILLS JOURNAL
PAGES 92–93

⭐ KEY EXPERIENCES

- Discussing Asia

- Reading for information

- Reading/using a map

- Researching

⭐ KEY LANGUAGE

- *cultures, customs, populous, regions*

- *South, North, Southwest, East, Southeast, Central*

⭐ MATERIALS

- wall map, pictures from several Asian countries

1 ◆ INTRODUCE

Building background: Discussing Asia. Point out Asia on a large wall map. Write the words *continent* and *Asia* on the board. Have volunteers identify and locate the countries included in Asia. Encourage students to share what they know about Asia.

MULTI-LEVEL TEACHING STRATEGIES

You can include all students by asking questions appropriate to each student's language level.

Speech Emergence: *What is the largest continent? Where is Asia? Point to it on the map. Have you ever been to Asia?*

Developing Fluency: *What are some of the countries in Asia? What languages are spoken in these countries?*

Describing countries in Asia. Invite any students who have visited or lived in Asia to tell what they know about a country or region of the continent.

2 ◆ EXPLORE

Activating prior knowledge. Open to page 92. To prompt discussion, ask multi-level questions such as *What kinds of animals are these? Where do you think you might find these animals?*

Exploring key vocabulary. Write the following words on the chalkboard: *populous, cultures, customs, regions.* Have volunteers explain these words for classmates using synonyms or definitions. Provide context sentences.

GUIDED READING Reading for information. Have students read along in their books as you read aloud the text on page 92. To check students' comprehension, ask multi-level questions such as *Which is the largest continent? How many people live in Asia? How many regions is Asia divided into? What are these regions? How many languages are included in the chart? Do you think these are all the languages of Asia?*

Using a map. Direct students' attention to the map on page 93. Have them locate the six regions of

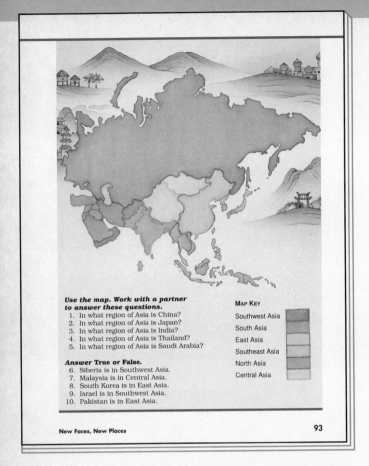

Use the map. Work with a partner
to answer these questions.
1. In what region of Asia is China?
2. In what region of Asia is Japan?
3. In what region of Asia is India?
4. In what region of Asia is Thailand?
5. In what region of Asia is Saudi Arabia?

Answer True or False.
6. Siberia is in Southwest Asia.
7. Malaysia is in Central Asia.
8. South Korea is in East Asia.
9. Israel is in Southwest Asia.
10. Pakistan is in East Asia.

MAP KEY

Southwest Asia
South Asia
East Asia
Southeast Asia
North Asia
Central Asia

New Faces, New Places   93

---

they know about that country with the class.
(CALLA: Resourcing)

SCIENCE/SOCIAL STUDIES Learning about animals of Asia. Have students research the animals of Asia. Ask students to present their information graphically. (CALLA: Resourcing/Grouping)

SOCIAL STUDIES Learning about current events. Have students find articles in newspapers and magazines about something that is happening in Asia now. Ask students to summarize the article for the class. (CALLA: Summarizing)

 **PROCESS WRITING PORTFOLIO** See the list of ideas and writing topics related to this theme.

ONGOING ASSESSMENT

PERFORMANCE Oral language. Ask students to tell the most interesting thing they learned about Asia in this lesson.

Asia on the map. Ask multi-level questions such as *How many regions are shown on this map? What region is shown in red? What color is used to show the region of Southeast Asia? What region is Iran in?*

Reading and answering questions. Have volunteers read and answer the questions. After going over all the questions and answers as a whole class activity, have students work in pairs to write answers to the questions.

SKILLS JOURNAL PAGES 92-93 **Reading a map.** Students answer questions about a map of the United States. Teaching suggestions are provided in the Skills Journal annotation.

3 ◆ EXTEND

SOCIAL STUDIES Learning about an Asian country. Encourage students to use the library and other resources to learn more about one Asian country. Invite students to give an oral report to share what

COMPUTER CONNECTION
Have students use a multimedia CD-ROM encyclopedia to research more information about Asia. If available, have students use graphics software to present their reports on the animals of Asia.

LESSON 5
FLIGHT SONG

**STUDENT BOOK/SKILLS JOURNAL
PAGES 94–95**

⭐ **KEY EXPERIENCES**

- Reading/responding to a poem
- Understanding creative language
- Writing a poem

⭐ **KEY LANGUAGE**

- *beauty, ripening grain, sorrow, joy, courage, strength, pain, hope, gain*

⭐ **MATERIALS**

- pictures of nature scenes, city homes, country homes

1 ◆ INTRODUCE

Building background: Discussing the U.S. Show pictures of nature scenes in the U.S. (mountains, prairies, forests, fields of grain, etc.) and pictures of city homes and country homes. Invite students to comment on the pictures. Stress that all of these different places are in the United States.

MULTI-LEVEL TEACHING STRATEGIES

You can include all students by asking questions appropriate to each student's language level.

Speech Emergence: *Where do you think this picture was taken? Have you seen places like this? Which picture looks like where you live?*

Developing Fluency: *Describe the city or countryside where you live. How is it different from these pictures? How is it similar to these pictures?*

2 ◆ EXPLORE

Activating prior knowledge. Open to pages 94 and 95. Ask a volunteer to read the title of the poem, "Flight Song." Encourage students to comment on

the title of the poem. To prompt discussion, ask multi-level questions such as *What do you see in the picture? What do you think this poem is about? What does the title mean?*

GUIDED READING Reading a poem. Read or play the tape for the poem as students follow along in their books. Read the poem again. You may want to pose the following display/comprehension questions to prompt discussion and monitor students' understanding.

Display/Comprehension Questions

What word does the poet use to describe mountains? (lovely)
Where would you see ripening grain? (on a farm; in a field)
What are the different parts of nature in the poem? (mountains, river, grass, tree, forest, hill, plain)
How are cars and trains alike? What do they do? (kinds of transportation; run)
What is in the city? (tall buildings)
How are the city and country alike? (both have

Sing of the people of many a race,
Sing of the sorrow and joy on each face;
Sing of their courage, their strength and their pain,
Sing of their children, their hope and their gain.

Sing of America, the land of the free,
Sing of her beauty and greatness-to-be;
Sing of America, the land of the free,
Sing of her beauty and greatness-to-be.

YOUR TURN What would you like to sing about? What makes you feel happy or proud about where you live? Talk about it with a small group.

New Faces, New Places   95

large and small homes)

What emotions show on people's faces? (sorrow and joy)

What does the poet admire about people? (their courage, strength, and hope)

Why is America the land of the free? (Answers will vary.)

What does greatness-to-be mean? (Answers will vary.)

Why is the poet singing of these things? (She feels proud of her country; encourage various answers)

Rereading. Arrange students in pairs or small groups and have them read the poem together. Go around the room helping students as needed.

Independent reading. Have students read the poem silently. Then ask volunteers to read parts of it aloud.

Your Turn. With the class, read the instructions under "Your Turn." Have students work with partners as they discuss their feelings of pride in where they live.

**SKILLS
JOURNAL
PAGES 94-95** **Page 94: Discussing emotions; note-taking.** Students discuss the poem with a partner, taking notes about their conversation. **Page 95: Using a chart; writing.** Students complete a chart about the poem then write a paragraph on the topic. Teaching suggestions are provided in the Skills Journal annotations.

3 ◆ EXTEND

Understanding poetic language. Point out the use of rhyme in the poem. Ask students to read the rhyming words aloud and consider how these rhyming words help the poet express her ideas.

Creative writing/Writing a poem. Encourage students to write a poem about a feeling. Encourage students to describe the feeling and compare it to something else. Invite students to share their poems with the class. Have students make drawings based on their poems. Save student work in their portfolios.

ART Making a collage/display. Have students look through magazines or make their own illustrations for different feelings. Students can make collages of the pictures and their poems about feelings.

ONGOING ASSESSMENT

PERFORMANCE Oral language. With books closed, have students talk about their feelings about this country or their country of origin.

PORTFOLIO Writing. Save Skills Journal page 95 as an example of independent writing.

★ **LANGUAGE NOTE**
Point out the word *greatness-to-be*. Explain that this is a word that the poet made up by combining other words. Brainstorm other ways to express the same idea as "greatness-to-be." Ask students why they think the poet used this new word.

LESSON 6
ALL STAR NEWS

📖 STUDENT BOOK/SKILLS JOURNAL
PAGES 96–97

⭐ **KEY EXPERIENCES**

- Discussing "being cool"/peer pressure

- Reading for information and pleasure

- Understanding/making charts and graphs

- Taking a poll

- Calculating percentages

- Process writing

⭐ **KEY LANGUAGE**

- *foreign-born, immigrants, languages, population*

⭐ **MATERIALS**

- magazines with pictures of teens, clothing, music, movies; maps of the world and the U.S.

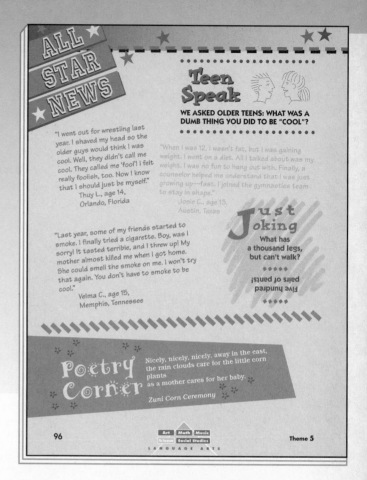

1 ◆ INTRODUCE

Building background: Discussing "being cool." Bring in magazines for students to look through. Ask students to find examples of "cool" or popular items. You may want to suggest that students look at clothing, activities, hair styles. Students can also give examples of musicians, movie stars, or athletes that they think are "cool."

MULTI-LEVEL TEACHING STRATEGIES

You can include all students by asking questions appropriate to each student's language level.

Speech Emergence: *What kinds of clothing do kids like to wear? Do parents like these clothes? What kind of music do you like to listen to?*

Developing Fluency: *Why do kids want to be "cool"? How do you choose your friends? How important is it to be "cool"?*

2 ◆ EXPLORE

Activating prior knowledge. Open to pages 96 and 97. Have students find and read the article headings and chart titles. Ask students to guess what the articles will be about. You may want to have students use headings and chart titles to form questions about the content. For example, *What countries do immigrants come from?* (CALLA: Predicting)

Scanning for information. Do rapid scanning practice by asking questions, such as *How many countries are on the first chart on page 97? What's the largest percentage on the second chart?* (CALLA: Selective attention)

📖 **GUIDED READING Reading for information.** Play the tape or read the selections, pausing occasionally to ask multi-level questions. Students who are able to should read the pages independently.

Understanding humor. Read the joke on page 96 as students follow along in their books. Be prepared

News From All Over

Families from many countries come to live in the USA.

TOP TEN COUNTRIES FOR IMMIGRANTS IN THE 1990s:	
Mexico	22.0%
Vietnam	8.0%
Philippines	6.3%
Dominican Republic	4.3%
China	4.0%
India	3.8%
El Salvador	2.7%
Poland	2.6%
United Kingdom	2.1%

AMAZING FACTS!

● 32 million people in the U.S. (13%) speak languages other than English at home.

● Since 1901, 30% of the U.S. Nobel Prize winners have been immigrants.

● More than 100 languages are spoken in the school systems of New York City, Chicago, Los Angeles, and Fairfax, VA.

CITIES WHERE MORE THAN HALF THE POPULATION IS FOREIGN-BORN:	
Miami, FL	60%
Huntington Park, CA	59%
Union City, NJ	55%
Monterey Park, CA	52%
Miami Beach, FL	51%
Santa Ana, CA	51%

New Faces, New Places   97

to explain the answer. Invite students to share other jokes that they know.

Taking a poll. Have students prepare and conduct a poll of the number of languages spoken in the school. Students can prepare questions or a survey questionnaire to give to others in the school. Then students can work in groups to compile the results and prepare graphs or charts. If there is a school newspaper, encourage students to write an article sharing the results of their polls.

SKILLS JOURNAL PAGES 96-97   **Process writing.** Students read a sample newspaper article then write an article of their own on the same topic. Teaching suggestions are provided in the Skills Journal annotation.

3 ◆ EXTEND

MATH Calculating percentages. Use the charts on page 97 to calculate other information. For example, What is the percentage of immigrants from other countries? What percentage of the residents

in each of the cities is native-born? What percentage of people speak English at home? How many people is that?

SOCIAL STUDIES Learning about immigration. Students can look for reference materials in the library or on computer to research immigration throughout U.S. history. Students may want to find the actual numbers of immigrants for the chart on page 97, the ten countries for immigrants for different periods of U.S. history, and current immigration policy. Interested students may want to explore why immigrants came from specific countries at different points in history. Students can prepare a short oral or written report to share with the class. (CALLA: Resourcing)

SOCIAL STUDIES Researching famous immigrants. Encourage students to find out about a famous person of their ethnic group who was an immigrant. Suggest that students make a timeline to trace the person's life.

Discussing peer pressure. Encourage students to talk about how friends can influence others for good or bad. Invite students to share ideas on how to say no to things they believe are wrong. You may want to have students role-play situations dealing with smoking and other issues relevant to kids.

ONGOING ASSESSMENT

PERFORMANCE Reading. Check student responses for ability to scan for information.

PORTFOLIO Writing. Save Skills Journal pages 96–97 as an example of independent writing.

★ **TEACHER TO TEACHER**
You may want to work with a math teacher to make sure students understand and can calculate percentages.

LESSON 7
ALL STAR NEWS

STUDENT BOOK/SKILLS JOURNAL PAGES 98–99

 KEY EXPERIENCES

- Reading for information
- Reading and following directions
- Responding to a letter
- Working in collaborative groups:
  - photo essay
  - collage
  - research
- Practicing science process skills

 KEY LANGUAGE

- *craft, quilling, roll, strips, wrapping paper*

MATERIALS

- examples of crafts; pencil, ruler, scissors, glue, magazines, wrapping paper, Q-tips, waxed paper, juice-box straws, string

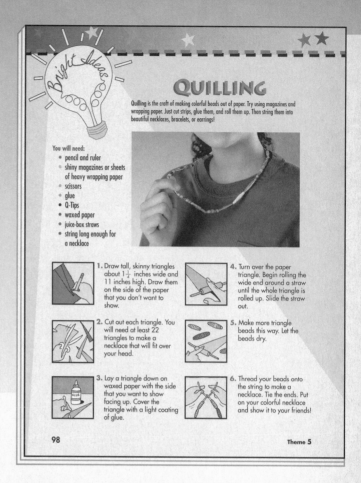

1 ♦ INTRODUCE

Building background: Discussing crafts. Display several types of crafts and use these as a prompt to encourage student discussion. Encourage students to tell about any craft hobbies they have. Ask students what crafts are done in their countries of origin.

┌─ **MULTI-LEVEL TEACHING STRATEGIES** ─┐

You can include all students by asking questions appropriate to each student's language level.

Speech Emergence: *What crafts do you know about? What crafts are made in (country)?*

Developing Fluency: *Do you, or anyone you know, sew, knit, or work with wood or clay? Tell us about it.*
└─────────────────────────────────────┘

2 ♦ EXPLORE

Activating prior knowledge. Open to page 98. To prompt discussion, ask multi-level questions such as *What do you think this activity is about? What are we going to make? What materials will we need? Have you ever done anything like this?*

Bright Ideas. Call on volunteers to read the paragraph, list of materials, and directions on page 98 as students follow along in their books. Use TPR as you demonstrate actions such as rolling up paper and sliding a straw through. Check comprehension by asking multi-level questions such as *What are we going to make? What do we do first?*

Following directions: Making a necklace. Have students work in small groups to make their beads and necklaces. Encourage interested students to experiment by making bracelets and earrings as well as necklaces and to try varying the size of the paper triangles to get beads of different shapes. Suggest that boys in the class can make jewelry as gifts for their mothers, sisters, or female friends.

Mailbox. Direct students' attention to the Mailbox on page 99. Have a volunteer read aloud the letter to All Star News. If any students are unfamiliar with rap music, play some or encourage students who know some rap songs to perform for the class. Ask students to raise their hands to show whether they like rap music. Then have students discuss the

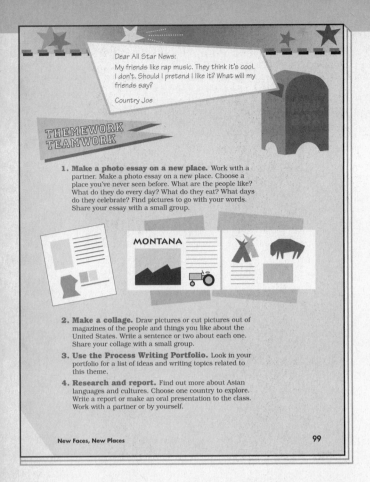

Dear All Star News:
My friends like rap music. They think it's cool. I don't. Should I pretend I like it? What will my friends say?

Country Joe

THEMEWORK TEAMWORK

1. **Make a photo essay on a new place.** Work with a partner. Make a photo essay on a new place. Choose a place you've never seen before. What are the people like? What do they do every day? What do they eat? What days do they celebrate? Find pictures to go with your words. Share your essay with a small group.

MONTANA

2. **Make a collage.** Draw pictures or cut pictures out of magazines of the people and things you like about the United States. Write a sentence or two about each one. Share your collage with a small group.

3. **Use the Process Writing Portfolio.** Look in your portfolio for a list of ideas and writing topics related to this theme.

4. **Research and report.** Find out more about Asian languages and cultures. Choose one country to explore. Write a report or make an oral presentation to the class. Work with a partner or by yourself.

New Faces, New Places   99

---

dents to demonstrate their hobby to the class.

SOCIAL STUDIES/ART Displaying craft objects. Invite students to bring to class examples of crafts from other cultures. Students can prepare a craft display with labels and descriptions.

MUSIC Composing a rap song. Have students work independently or in small groups to compose rap songs. Allow them to perform the songs for the class and record their performances on video or audiotape.

PROCESS WRITING PORTFOLIO See the list of ideas and writing topics related to this theme.

ONGOING ASSESSMENT

PERFORMANCE Oral language. Ask students to tell why they selected a certain project for the Themework/Teamwork activity.

PORTFOLIO Writing. Save Skills Journal page 98 as an example of independent writing.

---

letter and tell what they think the writer should do. Students can write a letter to Country Joe on Skills Journal page 99.

Themework/Teamwork. Ask volunteers to read aloud the list of projects as students follow along in their books. Students can select one or more projects. They can work independently or collaboratively to complete the projects. Encourage students to share finished projects with the class.

SKILLS JOURNAL PAGES 98-99 **Page 98: Expressing opinions; letter writing.** Students answer the letter in Mailbox on student book page 98. **Page 99: Science skills; comparing/contrasting.** Students read a cartoon science experiment then try it themselves. Teaching suggestions are provided in the Skills Journal annotations.

3 ◆ EXTEND

ART Writing directions for a craft. Encourage students who have a craft hobby to write directions for using their craft to make something. Ask stu-

⭐ **PREDICTABLE PROBLEM**
It is sometimes difficult for learners to hear and understand lyrics in another language. You may find that you need to address the question of appropriateness of lyrics before inviting students to play or perform rap songs they may have heard outside the classroom.

⭐ **TEACHER TO TEACHER**
Invite other classes to enjoy your class craft display, or arrange to exhibit the crafts in a school display case.

LESSON 8
HOLISTIC ASSESSMENT

 STUDENT BOOK/SKILLS JOURNAL PAGES 100–101

⭐ **KEY EXPERIENCES**

■ Demonstrating comprehension

■ Summarizing the story

■ Thinking critically

■ Self-assessment

■ Writing about oneself

⭐ **KEY LANGUAGE**

■ upset, laughed at, smiled

> **LISTEN** | **SPEAK**

A Bad Day for Abdul
• • • • • • • • • • • • • •

> ▶ **LISTEN**
> Listen to the beginning of the story. Tell whether each sentence is **True** or **False**.
>
> 1. The students all smiled at Abdul.
> 2. Abdul understood what the teacher said to him.
> 3. Abdul opened his science book.
> 4. The teacher wanted Abdul to read his book.
> 5. The students laughed at Abdul.
> 6. Abdul had three more classes to go.
>
> ▶ **SPEAK**
> Tell about Abdul's first class. What class was it? Why did he hate the class?
>
> 100   Art Math Music Science **Social Studies** **Theme 5**
> L A N G U A G E   A R T S

1 ◆ INTRODUCE

These two pages offer a variety of assessment opportunities. The left-hand page consists of listening and speaking activities that follow a taped presentation. In the speaking activity, students are asked to summarize what they have heard. The right-hand page consists of writing and critical thinking activities. These follow a reading passage that completes the listening component. You can use the activities to assess listening, speaking, reading, writing, and critical thinking skills. Have students work as a class or in small groups as you circulate and record observations on the **Anecdotal Record Form**, the **Reading Checklist**, and the **Writing Checklist** in the *All Star Assessment Package*.

Observing and recording student performance. Note the level of participation and the particular abilities of each student. How much do students understand? How well can they express themselves orally? What language structures do they use? What new words and concepts do they use? How actively do they participate? Use the **Anecdotal Record Form** in the *All Star Assessment Package* to record your observations and note areas for further development. Place in students' **portfolios.**

2 ◆ EXPLORE

Previewing. Open to pages 100 and 101 and let the students comment on the illustrations. Read the title "A Bad Day for Abdul" or call on a volunteer to do so. Give students time to read the listening questions.

 Listening. Read or play the tape for the first part of "A Bad Day for Abdul." You will find the tapescript in the Appendix. Have students work independently to answer the listening questions. Read or play the tape again for students to check their work.

Speaking. Discuss what students have heard up to this point. Ask multi-level questions such as *What happened when Abdul walked into the classroom? Did Abdul understand what the teacher said?* If some students are struggling, play the tape again and summarize the story once yourself. Ask questions again. When you are satisfied with this stage, go on to the next.

READ · WRITE · THINK!

READ

At last, the day was over. Abdul hurried home. His mother said, "You look upset, Abdul. What happened at school?"

Abdul answered, "Mom, I hate school. I don't understand what anyone says to me. The other kids laugh at me. I don't want to go back." His mother said, "I know. It's going to be okay. Your teacher called your uncle this afternoon and told him about some new classes at school to help students learn English. She said the classes would help you understand and be able to talk to the other students."

A smile came to Abdul's face, "You mean they will help me learn English?" "Yes," his mother replied. "They'll teach you English and help you with your other classes, too."

"When can I go to these classes?" asked Abdul.

"Next week," said his mother. "You will go to them part of every day at school. Mrs. Nunez will show you where to go. You can ask her for help when you need it."

Abdul smiled. Suddenly his bad day was looking better.

WRITE
Write about your first day in a new school. What happened? How did you feel?

THINK
Why didn't Abdul want to go back to school?

New Faces, New Places   101

Reading. Read the story on page 101 or play the tape as the students listen and follow along in their books. Pause occasionally to ask multi-level questions. Then have the students do partner reading, alternating paragraphs.

Writing. Encourage students to tell you what they have heard and read. Do not look for word-for-word retelling, even from your best students. Have students write their summaries. (CALLA: Summarizing)

Thinking. Ask students questions such as *What do you think was on the slip of paper? Do you think the teacher was really angry? Why do you think the school called Abdul's uncle?*

SKILLS JOURNAL PAGES 100-101 **Page 100: Assessment; reinforcing key vocabulary.** Students circle the words that don't belong in vocabulary groups. **Page 101: Self-assessment; Home-School connection.** Students check things they can do and words they know. Teaching suggestions are provided in the Skills Journal annotation.

3 · EXTEND

Writing a letter of advice. Have students work in pairs or small groups to write a letter of advice to Abdul. Students begin by brainstorming some of the suggestions they would make based on their own experiences. You may want to provide a model letter for students to follow. Later, students share their ideas with the class.

Home-School Connection. In the story, Abdul's uncle gets the call from the school. Ask students if a family member helped them settle into their new community. Have their parents helped other family members? In what ways have they helped or been helped?

★ **PREDICTABLE PROBLEM**

Students may have some difficulty following the pronouns in the story. As you replay the tape, pause to ask students who the person referred to is. You might draw pictures on the board to represent Abdul or his teacher.

LESSON 9
FEELINGS AND EMOTIONS

 **STUDENT BOOK/SKILLS JOURNAL PAGE 102**

★ **KEY EXPERIENCES**

■ Reviewing the theme

■ Singing a song

■ Writing new verses

★ **KEY LANGUAGE**

■ *emotions, feelings, ocean, waves*

■ *happy, angry, sad, shy*

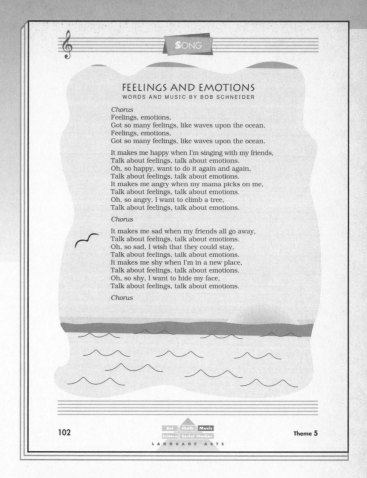

1 ◆ INTRODUCE

Activating prior knowledge: Reviewing the theme.
Engage students in a discussion and review of the things they learned in this theme.

┌─ **MULTI-LEVEL TEACHING STRATEGIES** ─┐

You can include all students by asking questions appropriate to each student's language level.

Speech Emergence: *What did you learn about in this theme? What was your favorite selection?*

Developing Fluency: *How does (selection title) relate to the theme "New Places, New Faces"?*

2 ◆ EXPLORE

Activating prior knowledge. Open to page 102. Read the song title. To prompt discussion, ask multi-level questions such as *What do you see on this page? How do you think the illustration relates to the song?* (CALLA: Predicting)

 **MUSIC Singing the song.** Ask volunteers to read through the song as students follow along in their books. Help students identify and pronounce the pairs of rhyming words. Play the tape of the song several times, inviting students to join in singing as soon as they are ready.

Writing new verses. List students' responses to what makes them sad, angry, and happy on the

board. Encourage students to use this list to write their own new verses for the song.

SKILLS JOURNAL PAGE 102 **Cloze exercise; learning language through song.** Students complete a cloze of the song. Teaching suggestions are provided in the Skills Journal annotation.

3 ◆ EXTEND

Home-School Connection: Sharing the book.
Encourage students to take the book home to share with family and friends. They can read the stories in the theme to a younger sibling, a parent, or a friend.

★ **LANGUAGE NOTES**

Ask a volunteer to explain the meaning of *picks on* in this context. Also make sure students understand that the *b* in *climb* is silent.

WRAP UP

ASSESSMENT

You have been collecting assessment data through the ongoing and holistic assessment options (Oral Language Checklist, Reading Checklist, Anecdotal Record Form) in this theme. Following are some additional assessment strategies that will help you evaluate your students' progress as well as adapt your instruction to meet their needs.

Student Self-Assessment. Self-assessment surveys are a means for students to have input into their own learning process. Students can use them to reflect on the work they have done and the learning strategies they have used during this theme. Be sure to check students' self-assessment pages for each theme in the Skills Journal.

Informed Instruction. Evaluate the checklists, anecdotal records, and Process Writing Portfolio collections from this theme as a means of informing your instruction.
• In which areas are students showing confidence and enthusiasm?
• In which areas are they hesitant or confused?
• Should you provide more classroom opportunities for oral language or writing?
• Would certain students (or the whole class) benefit from a focused mini-lesson on a certain area or skill?
• Remember to recycle skills as you teach the next theme and provide students with many opportunities to gain competence.

READING

Don't forget to check on and encourage students' independent reading. Students who weren't ready for independent reading in English at the beginning of this theme may be ready now. Students who continue to read in their first language should be encouraged to do first language book reviews and be an attentive audience for other students' reviews in English.

BOOKBYTES

Have students been able to use the *All Star BookBytes* CD-ROM software? The BookBytes' book list includes the titles on the Theme Booklists for all levels of *All Star English*. BookBytes helps students choose a book to read based on their responses to a short questionnaire, then prompts students to think about and respond to what they've read through writing, drawing, and drama. Students can print out their work and share it with others. They can also choose to see other students' work on-screen in a gallery presentation.

THEME CELEBRATION

If your class is participating as an All Star Team, the end of theme is a good time to review students' accomplishments with the Theme Booklist and Theme Projects. Consider posting a chart in the classroom where students may check off their accomplishments and, if you are using a point system, total their points for the theme. Students should strive to do their best and outdo their *own* scores, not compete with each other. Encourage students to present their All Star projects to the class to allow more oral practice and to sharpen students' presentation skills. You might invite other classes or families to attend the presentations.

PREVIEW
STUDENT BOOK/SKILLS JOURNAL, PAGES 103–122
IN THE WILD•••••••••••••••••••••••

CONCEPTS
- the environment
- endangered animals
- rain forests
- rescuing endangered animals
- appreciating nature

LITERATURE

- Animals in Danger *(nonfiction article)*
- Animal Rescue Success Stories *(nonfiction article)*
- In My Mountains *(poem)*
- All Star News *(short nonfiction articles)*
- Listen to the Water *(song)*

READING/WRITING SKILLS

- summarizing a story
- reading for information and pleasure
- classifying information
- making comparisons
- critical thinking
- reading comprehension
- process writing
- reading/responding to nonfiction
- writing a description of an animal
- writing a letter requesting information
- reading/responding to a nonfiction article
- reading/responding to a poem
- writing a poem
- writing about oneself
- writing new song verses

CONTENT

- **Social Studies:** reporting the news, making a world map of dangerous weather, learning about protected species, debating environmental laws, starting a recycling campaign, learning about national parks
- **Art/Music:** depicting an animal, making posters, describing a scene, making a display, singing a song, writing another song version
- **Science:** categorizing animals, observing animals, keeping a weather diary, adopting a rain forest, researching global warming, interpreting animal tracks

KEY LANGUAGE/KEY EXPERIENCES

- simple future tense
- review of simple present
- present conditional tense
- contrasting night and day
- understanding graphs and charts
- understanding humor
- taking a poll
- self-assessment
- categorizing animals
- using a chart
- working in collaborative groups
- practicing science process skills
- researching
- vocabulary development
- completing analogies
- expressing opinions
- brainstorming

THEME BOOKLIST/ THEME PROJECTS

As this new theme begins, photocopy the Theme Booklist/Theme Projects pages (following spread) for students. Encourage students to read as many books as they like from the Booklist, and to complete any of the assignments on the Project list as homework for this theme.

AWARDING POINTS FOR ALL STAR TEAMS

This is a good opportunity to motivate students through an All Star Team approach. Consider assigning point values to each project, including reading books from the booklist. Explain to students that they will accumulate points for each book they read or project they complete during the theme. Students will try to top their own scores as they work through each theme, competing against themselves, not each other. Remind students that they will have the opportunity to present their *All Star* projects to the class at the end of the theme.

BOOKBYTES

If you have a computer with a CD-ROM drive available, introduce students to the *All Star BookBytes* software which is correlated to the Theme Booklists throughout *All Star English. BookBytes* categorizes the books by genre and helps students choose a book to read based on their answers to a short questionnaire. It then prompts students to think about and respond to what they've read through writing, drawing, and drama activities. Students can print out their work and share it with others or view work on-screen in a gallery presentation.

THEME BOOKLIST

HERE ARE SOME BOOKS YOU MIGHT LIKE TO READ.
LOOK FOR THEM IN YOUR LIBRARY.

All Creatures Great and Small, by James Herriot. St. Martin's Press, 1972. The classic about a young veterinarian in Yorkshire, England.

The Animal Family, by Randall Jarrell. Random House, 1965. A lonely hunter befriend's a mermaid...and other unlikely creatures.

As Dead as a Dodo, by Paul Rice and Peter Mayle. David Godine, 1980. Extinct animals—how they got that way.

Kid Heroes of the Environment: Simple Things Real Kids Are Doing to Save the Earth, by The Earth Works Group. Earthworks Press, 1991.

The Lampfish of Twill, by Janet T. Lisle. Scholastic, Inc., 1993. An environmental fantasy you won't forget.

The Landing: A Night of Birds, by Katherine Scholes. Doubleday, 1989. A girl communicates with a flock of birds; story set on a remote Australian coast.

Life in the Rainforests, by Lucy Baker. Watts, 1990. Animals, plants and people in a unique habitat.

The Night the White Deer Died, by Gary Paulson. Delicorte Press, 1990. A good adventure.

My Side of the Mountain, Jean Craighead George. E.P. Dutton, 1990. A boy survives a winter in the woods alone.

A Stranger Came Ashore, by Mollie Hunter. Harper Junior Books, 1975. A haunting tale based on Shetland Island folklore.

Swimming with the Sea Lions, by Ann McGovern. Scholastic, 1992. Adventures in the Galápagos Islands.

BOOKS IN LANGUAGES OTHER THAN ENGLISH

Cuentos de la selva (Stories from the Jungle), by Horacio Quiroga. México: Editorial Grijalbo/EDUCAL.

The Painter and the Wild Swans, by C. Clement (English/Japanese). Arcadia, CA: Shen's Books and Supplies.

Story of the Chinese Zodiac, by Monica Chang (English/Chinese; English/Spanish; English/Hmong; English/Khmer; English/Korean; English/Vietnamese; English/Lao; English/Tagalog; English/Thai). Arcadia, CA: Shen's Books and Supplies.

THEME PROJECTS

YOU MAY WANT TO WORK ON THESE PROJECTS ALONE OR WITH A PARTNER OR SMALL GROUP.

☆ Make a set of vocabulary cards that show vocabulary words learned in the theme on one side and illustrations of the words on the other.

☆ Write dialogues that use vocabulary or grammatical structures learned in the theme.

☆ Write original sentences or stories using key vocabulary words.

☆ Create a word search or crossword puzzle that uses vocabulary from the theme.

☆ Translate a song, poem, or prose selection from your native language into English.

☆ Create paintings, drawings, or dioramas of stories or readings within the theme.

☆ Produce scripts or dramatizations of information presented in the theme.

☆ Create a collage, mobile, or other three-dimensional art project that illustrates key concepts from the theme.

☆ Take a survey and present graphs and charts that explore questions related to the theme.

☆ Write journal entries for five to ten days about key concepts or ideas in the theme.

☆ Paste news clippings onto blank paper and write a short statement explaining how the article relates to the theme.

☆ Write a letter to the editor, the school government, City Hall, or the President of the United States about issues and ideas in the theme.

☆ Create maps that show the location of places mentioned in the theme.

☆ Create a time line that shows what happened in a story from the theme.

☆ Make a story chart that clearly labels the characters, plot, setting, climax, and ending of a story from the theme.

☆ Present a dramatic reading of one of the stories in the theme.

☆ Write a letter that gives advice or constructive criticism to a character in a story from the theme.

LESSON 1
THEME OPENER

STUDENT BOOK/SKILLS JOURNAL PAGE 103

 KEY EXPERIENCES

- Discussing the environment
- Previewing theme content and titles
- Making a poster
- Self-assessment
- Discovering the library

 KEY LANGUAGE

- *environment, recycle, the wild*

 MATERIALS

- poster board, markers

1 ◆ INTRODUCE

Theme 6, In the Wild, looks at endangered animals around the world. Students will read about endangered animals and what they can do to help. They will practice the future tense and learn about weather maps and extreme weather situations.

Building background: Discussing the environment. Encourage students to share what they know about environmental issues, such as depletion of natural resources and endangered animals. Start the discussion by eliciting a definition of *environment* as air, water, minerals, plants, and animals.

MULTI-LEVEL TEACHING STRATEGIES

You can include all students by asking questions appropriate to each student's language level.

Speech Emergence: *What might happen if all our water was unsafe for people or animals to drink? What would our world be like if all the trees were cut down to make paper? Why should we recycle these things?*

Developing Fluency: *What are some ways we can protect our environment?*

---

2 ◆ EXPLORE

Activating prior knowledge. Open to page 103. To prompt discussion, ask multi-level questions such as *What does the photo show? What's the title of the theme? What do you think this theme will be about?*

Reading Corner. Have students read the titles, authors, and descriptions of the three books listed under Reading Corner. These are just a few selections from the Theme Booklist, chosen to help motivate students to want to read. Have the books available for students to look at. Prompt discussion about which book each student would like to read and why. Allow students to sign up for turns with the books. Use this experience to get your students excited about reading.

Previewing theme content and titles. Guide students as they look through the theme, inviting them to comment on titles, photos, and art. Ask for volunteers to read the selection titles aloud. Encourage students to discuss what they think the stories will be about. (CALLA: Predicting)

 Activating prior knowledge; self-assessment. Students complete a chart before and after the lesson. Teaching suggestions are provided in the Skills Journal annotation.

3 ◆ EXTEND

SCIENCE Making a chart. Encourage students to make a chart listing environmental danger signs and things we can do to help eliminate the dangers. (CALLA: Grouping)

SCIENCE/ART Making a poster. Have students make a poster promoting recycling or some other environmental issue.

Making "New Day's" resolutions. Remind students of our custom of making New Year's resolutions, which are often promises to ourselves to change bad habits. Encourage students to think of some

THEME 6

★ **In The Wild**

Reading Corner
Try these terrific books!

The Lampfish of Twill
by Janet T. Lisle
An environmental fantasy you won't forget.

Life In the Rainforests
by Lucy Baker
Animals, plants, and people in a unique habitat.

As Dead As A Dodo
by Paul Rice and Peter Mayle
Extinct animals—and how they got that way!

103

★ **BOOKBYTES**
Have students use the BookBytes software as motivation for reading and writing about what they've read.

★ **LANGUAGE NOTE**
Make sure students understand that *wild* in the title is used as a noun. Elicit that the preposition helps them know that it is a place. Contrast this with the more familiar use of *wild* as an adjective.

★ **TEACHER TO TEACHER**
Display students' posters in the hallway so they can be appreciated by others in your school.

thing they could change about their habits that would help the environment. Students write down their resolutions. Invite students to share their resolutions with the class.

Discovering the library. Lead students on a tour of your school or local library. With students, gather the books recommended for this theme in the Theme Booklist. In the classroom, read aloud to students when appropriate. You may wish to record the books on tape and let students read the books as they listen to the tapes. Encourage students to read independently whenever possible.

┌ **ONGOING ASSESSMENT**
PERFORMANCE Written language. Use students' resolutions to evaluate their proficiency with written language.

LESSON 2
ANIMALS IN DANGER

📷 **STUDENT BOOK/SKILLS JOURNAL PAGES 104–107**

⭐ **KEY EXPERIENCES**

- Discussing endangered species
- Reading/responding to nonfiction
- Making an outline of a story
- Writing a description of an animal
- Categorizing animals
- Using a chart

⭐ **KEY LANGUAGE**

- *danger, pollution, dying out, tusks, ivory, bamboo, livestock*
- *quetzal, macaw, jaguar, chimpanzee, elephant, giant panda, gray wolf,*

⭐ **MATERIALS**

- pictures of animals, especially endangered species; map of the world

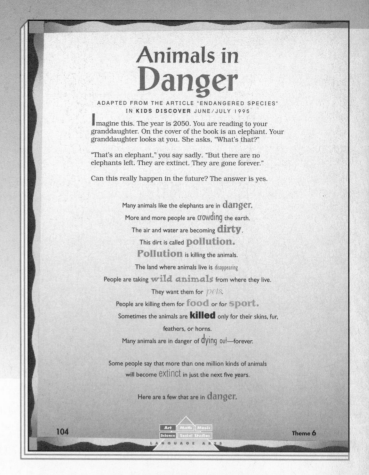

1 ◆ INTRODUCE

Building background: Discussing endangered species. Show pictures of animals. Ask students to describe the animals and point out where they live on a map. Students can discuss characteristics of each of the animals: types of food, habitats, homes or nests, natural enemies, behavior. Explain the meaning of *endangered*.

┌─ **MULTI-LEVEL TEACHING STRATEGIES** ─┐

You can include all students by asking questions appropriate to each student's language level.

Speech Emergence: *Name an endangered animal. Why is it endangered?*

Developing Fluency: *Do people put animals in danger? Why? How can we help?*

└──────────────────────────────────┘

Making an animal word web. With students, brainstorm a list of animals and show them in the form of a word web. You may also want to have students categorize the animals as pets, wild, or endangered.

2 ◆ EXPLORE

Activating prior knowledge. Open to page 104. Ask a volunteer to read the title, "Animals in Danger." Have students look at the pictures on pages 104–107. To prompt discussion, ask multi-level questions such as *Why are animals in danger? Which animals are in danger? Which animals have you seen? Where do these animals live? Who would want to hurt these animals?*

Previewing the selection. Have students find and read the subtitles in the story. Ask volunteers to find the different countries and areas that are mentioned on the map. Encourage students to use the subtitles as they read to organize details and important information about the different species.

📷 **GUIDED READING Reading nonfiction.** Read or play the tape for the story as students follow along in their books. Ask students how they know what they are reading is based on fact and not just a story to entertain. List student ideas on the board.

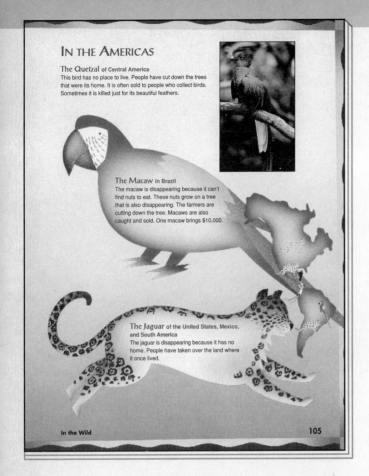

IN THE AMERICAS

The Quetzal of Central America
This bird has no place to live. People have cut down the trees
that were its home. It is often sold to people who collect birds.
Sometimes it is killed just for its beautiful feathers.

The Macaw in Brazil
The macaw is disappearing because it can't
find nuts to eat. These nuts grow on a tree
that is also disappearing. The farmers are
cutting down the tree. Macaws are also
caught and sold. One macaw brings $10,000.

The Jaguar of the United States, Mexico,
and South America
The jaguar is disappearing because it has no
home. People have taken over the land where
it once lived.

In the Wild   105

Read the story again stopping to ask multi-level questions. You may wish to pose the following display/comprehension questions to prompt discussion of each page and monitor students' understanding.

Display/Comprehension Questions

Page 104

Are there many animals or few animals in danger? (many)
What is pollution? (dirt in the air and water)
Does the pollution hurt animals? (yes)
Why is there less land for the animals? (more people are crowding the earth)
What are some reasons for people taking animals? (for pets, killing for food or sport)
What parts of animals are collected? (skins, fur, feathers, horns)
How many kinds of animals might become extinct in the next five years? (more than one million; make sure students know this includes insects)

Page 105

Where does the macaw live? (Brazil)
What do macaws like to eat? (nuts)
Who is cutting down the nut trees? (farmers)
Are macaws expensive or cheap? (expensive)
How much can a macaw cost? ($10,000)
Where do jaguars live? (in the United States, Mexico, and South America)
Why are jaguars disappearing? (People are taking over the land where they live.)
Is the quetzal a bird or a fish? (bird)
Why do some people kill quetzals? (for their beautiful feathers)

Page 106

Why do some people kill elephants? (for their white tusks)
What is ivory? (the white tusks)
How is ivory used? (to make jewelry and other things)
What other animal in Africa is disappearing? (chimpanzee)
Who are chimps sold to? (zoos and people for pets)

Page 107

Does the giant panda live in Africa or in Asia? (Asia)
What can't the panda find? (food and safety)
What animal sometimes kills livestock? (wolves)
Who kills the wolves? (farmers)
What other animals do wolves hunt? (deer and bison)

Rereading. Have students reread the story in pairs or small groups. Pair more proficient readers with less proficient students.

Independent reading. Have students read the story silently. Then call on different volunteers to read parts of the story aloud.

Making a story outline. As a group, make an outline on the board for the reading selection. Point out that the subtitles can be used to help write the outline. Encourage students to restate the important details for each of the animals mentioned in the selection, using their own words.

SKILLS JOURNAL
PAGES 104-107

Page 104: Vocabulary development; analogies. Students finish analogies with names of body parts. **Page 105: Using a chart; categorizing.** Students categorize animals by their body parts. **Page 106: Using a chart; distinguishing true-false statements.** Students fill in chart with information from the text. **Page 107: Reading comprehension.** Students match sentences for meaning. Teaching suggestions are provided in the Skills Journal annotations.

3 ♦ EXTEND

Writing a description of an animal. Students work in groups of three to take turns telling about their favorite animals. Students help each other as needed. Then each student independently writes a paragraph about the animal. Remind students to check paragraph form, punctuation, and capitalization. Then have students regroup and share their descriptions. Students help each other correct, clarify, and, if necessary, expand what they have written. Students make corrections to their drafts. When finished, have students recopy their descriptions, making corrections and revisions.

ART Depicting an animal. Students can illustrate their descriptions of animals. Alternatively, students can draw an animal and label the body parts, make a model of an animal, create a diorama showing the animal in its habitat, or make a more artistic rendition using paints or other media.

SCIENCE Categorizing animals. Have students brainstorm a list of animals. Then introduce the categories: birds, mammals, reptiles, fish, amphibians. Students list the animals in the proper categories. Ask students to circle or highlight endangered species that are on the chart. (CALLA: Comparing)

SCIENCE Observing animals. Arrange for the class to take a trip to a local zoo or park. Have students look for animal life. Encourage students to choose an animal to watch and take notes on their observations. What was the animal doing? Where was it? What did it look like? How did it act? Did it make any sounds? Have students share their observations with the class.

IN AFRICA

The Chimpanzee
The chimpanzee is dying out because the land where it lives is disappearing. It is also being hunted for sport. Chimps are sold to zoos and to people who want them for pets.

The Elephant
The elephant is killed for its white tusks made of ivory. Ivory is used to make jewelry and other things.

106   Theme 6

PROCESS WRITING PORTFOLIO

See the list of ideas and writing topics related to this theme.

Learning about extinct animals. Interested students may want to research and report on some species that are already extinct. Suggest that students find out when, where, and why the animal became extinct. In some cases the date of the death of the last known specimen is known. Some possibilities include the great auk, the passenger pigeon, the dodo—all bird species—and the Tasmanian devil. Encourage students to look for illustrations of these animals that they can photocopy or redraw. Also encourage students to make some generalizations about causes for animal extinction based on what they have read.

Making an endangered species map. Use a world map to create a classroom display or bulletin board showing endangered species. Have each student draw a picture of an endangered species and write a brief description of the animal.

IN ASIA

The Giant Panda in Southern China
The land where the panda lives is disappearing. People are taking the pandas' land for farming. They cut down the bamboo trees that the pandas eat. Now it is hard for the pandas to find food and shelter.

The Gray Wolf
Farmers kill gray wolves because they eat livestock. In some places, gray wolves hunt large, hoofed animals like deer and bison.

In the Wild   107

★ PREDICTABLE PROBLEM

The passive voice is often used in content area readings. Students often confuse the passive voice with the past tense. Make sure students understand who did the action as they read the passive voice sentences in the selection.

★ COMPUTER CONNECTION

Have students use a multimedia CD-ROM encyclopedia to find pictures and information about the different endangered animals as well as animals that are extinct.

Developing vocabulary. Use magazine pictures or photos of animals to introduce and practice additional vocabulary related to animals. You may want to introduce words for body parts such as *hoof, antler, horn, tail, flipper;* verbs used to describe movements such as *swim, dive, pounce, leap* or sound words such as *grunt, roar, squeal, growl.*

- - - **ONGOING ASSESSMENT** - - -

PERFORMANCE Oral language. Have students reread the part about the animal that they like the best. Ask students to explain why the animal is endangered.

PORTFOLIO Writing. Save students' descriptions of animals as an example of independent writing. You may want to include both the rough draft and the final copy to assess the student's writing process.

LESSON 3
LANGUAGE POWER

STUDENT BOOK/SKILLS JOURNAL
PAGES 108–109

★ KEY EXPERIENCES

- Discussing weather
- Reading for information
- Reporting the news
- Making a world weather map
- Keeping a weather diary

★ KEY LANGUAGE

- simple future tense
- review of simple present tense
- *blizzard, drought, flood, hurricane, tornado*

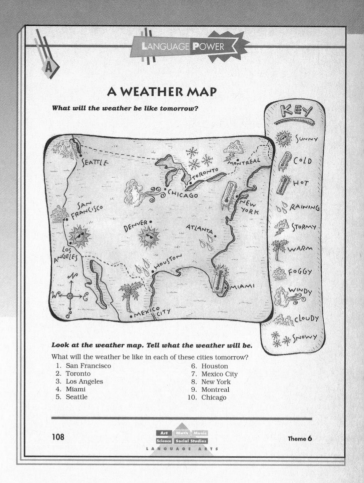

1 ♦ INTRODUCE

Building background: Discussing the weather.
Encourage students to discuss what the weather is like today and what they predict it will be like tomorrow. Invite them to describe any violent weather they have experienced.

⌐ MULTI-LEVEL TEACHING STRATEGIES ¬

You can include all students by asking questions appropriate to each student's language level.

Speech Emergence: *Is it hot/rainy/cold/sunny/cloudy today? Do you think it will snow tomorrow? Have you ever been in a (type of dangerous weather)?*

Developing Fluency: *What is the weather like today? What do you think it will be like tomorrow?*

2 ♦ EXPLORE

Activating prior knowledge. Open to page 108. To prompt discussion, ask multi-level questions such as *Have you ever seen a map like this before? Where did you see the map? What does the map tell you?*

GUIDED READING Reading a weather map. Ask volunteers to read the sentence and map titles.

Prompt students to examine the map by asking questions: *What does the "sun face" by Los Angeles tell us? What symbol shows that the weather will be rainy in Houston? What will the weather be like in San Francisco? Which city do you think will be coldest/warmest tomorrow?*

Grammar in context. Students practice the simple future tense as they predict tomorrow's weather in cities across the country. Ask volunteers to read the sentences and list of cities under the map. Ask other volunteers to tell what the weather prediction is for each of the cities listed. Then have students work with partners to write each city's weather prediction.

Reading "Wild Weather." Ask students to follow along in their books as you read the article about dangerous weather. Ask multi-level questions to check students' comprehension: *What is a flood? What causes floods? Why are floods dangerous? What kind of storm is a hurricane?*

Asking and answering questions about weather. Have students work with partners to ask and

ALL STAR ENGLISH LEVEL 2

WILD WEATHER

Sometimes the weather is warm and friendly. Sometimes the weather is wild and dangerous.

A flood is the result of too much rain. When it rains for many days, rivers and lakes overflow. Flood waters cause a lot of damage to houses, buildings, roads, and crops.

A drought is the opposite problem from a flood. A drought is the result of little or no rain. If it doesn't rain, plants and animals will die. A drought is a dangerous condition for farmers and ranchers.

A hurricane is an extremely dangerous storm with high winds and torrential rain. Hurricanes form over the ocean. They roar up the east coast of the U.S. from the Caribbean. Many hurricanes remain at sea, but hurricanes often travel inland. When a hurricane hits land, it can destroy everything for miles around.

A tornado is another kind of wind storm. States in the middle of the U.S. experience many tornadoes. Tornadoes are very dangerous. They can destroy anything in their path. Tornadoes make a loud, roaring sound like a speeding train.

A big winter snowstorm is called a blizzard. A blizzard has a lot of snow and high wind. The wind blows the snow into huge snowdrifts. Airports close; roads close. People can lose electricity, heat, and phones. A snowfall can be pretty, but a blizzard is a winter storm you don't want to be caught in!

Tornado in the midwest

In the Wild 109

answer questions about the storms they have read about. Then have them ask and answer questions about what the weather will be like tomorrow.

SKILLS JOURNAL PAGES 108-109

Page 108: Present conditional tense; comparing. Students practice present conditional tense with "if" clauses. **Page 109: Reading a chart; weather vocabulary.** Students read a chart about weather emergencies and answer questions. Teaching suggestions are provided in the Skills Journal annotations.

3 ◆ EXTEND

SOCIAL STUDIES Reporting the news. As a small group activity, encourage students to stage a TV newscast. If you have a video camera available, they will enjoy recording their production for viewing by families and other classes. Suggest that students use a current newspaper to find stories to report on. Have students in each group select tasks to perform during the activity: the parts of news anchors, on-the-scene reporters, weather

reporters, camera people, director, script writer; others can gather and make props such as maps and microphones.

SOCIAL STUDIES/ART Making a world map of dangerous weather. Have students research where various types of dangerous weather occur in the world. Challenge students to make a world weather map showing the typical locations of each type of weather. Students can design icons to stand for different types of storms. (CALLA: Resourcing/ Grouping)

SCIENCE Keeping a weather diary. Encourage students to keep a weather diary for a specific period, such as two weeks. Each day students write one sentence to describe the current weather and a second sentence to predict what they think the weather will be like the next day. At the end of the activity, have students check to see how many correct weather predictions they made.

ONGOING ASSESSMENT

PERFORMANCE Oral language. Ask students to describe the weather today and what they predict it will be tomorrow.

MULTICULTURAL AWARENESS

Encourage students to describe the typical climate and weather patterns in other countries or states where they have lived.

COMPUTER CONNECTION

Students can use graphics software to create title frames, weather maps, and other props for their videotaped newscast.

LESSON 4
EXPLORE...SCIENCE

STUDENT BOOK/SKILLS JOURNAL
PAGES 110–111

 KEY EXPERIENCES

- Discussing rain forests
- Reading for information
- Writing a letter requesting information
- Researching

KEY LANGUAGE

- *carbon dioxide, evaporates, global warming, moisture, rain forest, temperature, tropical*

EXPLORE...
SCIENCE

The Amazing Rain Forest

A tropical rain forest is an amazing place. Most rain forests are in South America, Africa, and Asia. More than half of the plants and animals in the world live in rain forests. The trees grow straight up to 100 feet or more. At the top, the leaves and branches make a tent that shades the forest floor.

These forests are called rain forests because they actually help create rain.
1. The rain falls on the leaves at the top.
2. The water drips down to the forest floor.
3. Some of this water drains into the streams and rivers. Some water goes into the soil and back up the tree trunk through the roots.
4. Lots of moisture stays at the top in the leaves. This moisture evaporates and forms clouds.
5. The water in the clouds falls again as rain.

Do you remember how much rain falls each year in the Puerto Rican rain forest?

110   Theme 6

1 ◆ INTRODUCE

Building background: Discussing rain forests. Begin your discussion of rain forests by having students recall the model rain forest they built in Theme 1 and the associated activities they completed for that lesson. Encourage students to share what they already know about rain forests.

┌─ **MULTI-LEVEL TEACHING STRATEGIES** ─┐

You can include all students by asking questions appropriate to each student's language level.

Speech Emergence: *Which countries have you read about that have rain forests? What kinds of plants grow in rain forests?*

Developing Fluency: *Why are some forests called rain forests? Why do you think there is so much moisture in rain forests?*

└──────────────────────────────────┘

2 ◆ EXPLORE

Activating prior knowledge. Open to pages 110–111. To prompt discussion, ask multi-level questions such as *What does the picture show? What kinds of plants and animals are shown? Where might you find plants and animals like these?*

GUIDED READING Reading for information. Ask students to follow along in their books as you read

aloud the article. Then have students reread the story independently. Call on volunteers to reread page 110. Check students' comprehension by having them respond *true* or *false* to the following statements:

Most rain forests are in the United States? (false)
Very few animals live in rain forests. (false)
Rain forests help create rain. (true)
Moisture from trees in the rain forest evaporates and forms clouds. (true)

Call on volunteers to reread page 111. Then continue the true/false comprehension check:

People do not destroy rain forests. (false)
It only takes a short time to replace trees that have been destroyed. (false)
Trees absorb carbon dioxide. (true)
Too much carbon dioxide causes global warming? (true)

Summarizing. Ask for volunteers to explain how rain forests help create rain. Ask other volunteers to summarize the information on page 111.

Requesting information. Ask students what they

People are destroying an area of rain forest as big as Pennsylvania every year. All the rain forests in the world may be gone in 50 years! People cut down rain forest trees to build furniture and houses. People cut down the trees to clear land for cattle. Then they sell the beef to other countries.

It takes several hundred years for trees to grow back as big as they were. When the trees are gone, the soil washes away. Plants and animals die. Carbon dioxide in the air increases because there aren't enough trees to absorb it. Too much carbon dioxide traps the sun's heat on the earth. This global warming makes temperatures rise. Floods and droughts are the result.

Rain forests are important to the health of the whole planet. You can help protect the rain forest. Write to:

Tree Amigos Project
143 Bostwick, NE
Grand Rapids, MI 49503

Find out how you can "adopt" acres of rain forest.

In the Wild   111

forest. Give students wide range in selecting methods for completing this activity. Small groups might want to select specific tasks to complete for the project; for example, making posters, making a "thermometer" to record fund raising success, writing bulletins for the school paper, canvassing other classes. When the campaign is completed, ask students to discuss the results. (CALLA: Cooperation)

SCIENCE Researching global warming. Encourage students to research global warming. Has the earth already begun warming? How much have temperatures risen? What predictions have scientists made for rates of warming? Can global warming be reversed? Ask students to share their information in the form of oral or written reports. (CALLA: Resourcing)

ONGOING ASSESSMENT

PERFORMANCE Oral language. Ask students to describe the tasks they completed for the adopt-a-rain-forest activity.

think it means to "adopt" a rain forest. Help them compose a sample letter to the Tree Amigos Project requesting more information. Have students work with partners to write letters. Hold a drawing to select one letter to mail. Use this opportunity to review with students the proper form for addressing an envelope.

Page 110: Reading comprehension; vocabulary development. Students read about deserts and answer questions. **Page 111: Research; classifying.** Students complete a Venn diagram and classify statements by topic. Teaching suggestions are provided in the Skills Journal annotations.

3 ◆ EXTEND

SCIENCE Adopting a rain forest. When you receive a response to the letter to the Tree Amigos Project, share it with students. Encourage interested students to stage a campaign to enlist others in the school and community to join in adopting the rain

TEACHER TO TEACHER
When asking true/false questions, be sure to include questions that involve higher level thinking skills such as inferencing.

LANGUAGE NOTE
Elicit from students that *amigos* is the Spanish word for *friends*.

LESSON 5
ANIMAL RESCUE SUCCESS STORIES

 STUDENT BOOK/SKILLS JOURNAL PAGES 112–114

⭐ **KEY EXPERIENCES**

- Discussing animal protection
- Reading/responding to a nonfiction article
- Classifying animals
- Writing a letter requesting information
- Making posters

⭐ **KEY LANGUAGE**

- *rescue, extinct, success*
- *manatee, koala, loggerhead turtle, bluebirds, humpback whale*
- *oxygen, poisons, insulation*

⭐ **MATERIALS**

- pictures or videos of animals, including endangered species

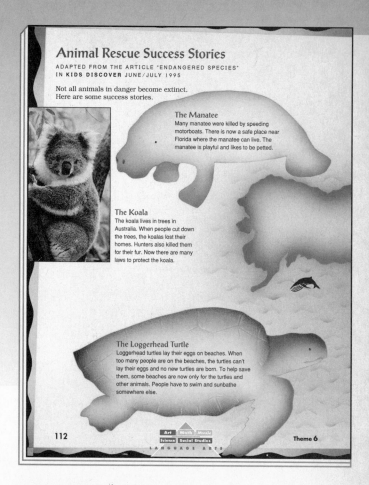

1 ◆ INTRODUCE

Building background: Discussing animals. Show pictures or videos of animals, including some of those mentioned in the lesson. Encourage students to talk about where the animals might live and eat. Students can suggest how to protect different species.

┌─ **MULTI-LEVEL TEACHING STRATEGIES** ─┐

You can include all students by asking questions appropriate to each student's language level.

Speech Emergence: *Where do turtles live? What do they eat? Do you think they are in danger?*

Developing Fluency: *What are some dangers for animals? Can animals protect themselves from pollution? How do you think people can help protect animals?*

└──────────────────────────────┘

SCIENCE Classifying animals. Create a chart on animals. Make columns with the headings: On the Land, In the Water, In the Air. Have students list as many animals as they can for each of the categories. (CALLA: Grouping)

2 ◆ EXPLORE

Activating prior knowledge. Open to pages 112 and 113. Have students look at the pictures. To prompt discussion, ask multi-level questions such as *Point to the bluebird. Which animals live in the water? Do you think a manatee can fly? Where do koalas live?*

Previewing a story. Ask a volunteer to read the title of the selection, "Animal Rescue Success Stories." Have students look at the pictures on pages 112–113 and identify the animals. Point out the subtitles/headings in the selection. Encourage students to predict what information they will learn from reading the selection. You may want to write student ideas on the board to guide their reading. (CALLA: Predicting)

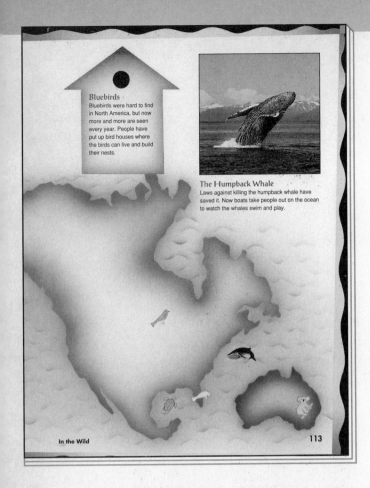

Bluebirds
Bluebirds were hard to find in North America, but now more and more are seen every year. People have put up bird houses where the birds can live and build their nests.

The Humpback Whale
Laws against killing the humpback whale have saved it. Now boats take people out on the ocean to watch the whales swim and play.

In the Wild   113

GUIDED READING Reading a nonfiction article.

Read or play the tape for the selection as students follow along in their books. Read the selection again. Students who are able to should read independently. You may wish to pose the following display/comprehension questions to prompt discussion of each page and monitor students' understanding.

Display Comprehension Questions

Page 112

Are these animals extinct? (no)
Why were hunters killing the koalas? (for their fur)
What protects the koalas now? (laws)
Who uses the beaches where the loggerhead turtles live? (swimmers)
Did the swimmers or the turtles move? (swimmers)
Where do manatees live? (Florida)
How were some of the manatees killed? (speed boats running over them)
Are manatees playful? (yes)

Page 113

What kind of birds are coming back to North America? (bluebirds)
How do people help the birds? (put up bird houses)
Where do bluebirds build their nests? (in the bird houses)
What has saved the humpback whales? (laws)
Which animal do people like to watch swim? (humpback whales)

Page 114

How do bird houses help birds? (give them protection)
Why should you cut up plastic rings? (so birds don't get caught in them)
What do trees put in the air? (oxygen)
Who needs the oxygen? (animals and people)
What is another way that animals use trees? (for homes)
How can you help stop pollution? (walk, ride a bike, take a bus)
What is acid rain? (pollution from the air that goes into the land and water)
What can be recycled? (cans, newspapers, plastic bottles)

Rereading. Arrange students in pairs or small groups and have them read the selection together. Go around the room helping students as needed.

Independent reading. Have students read the selection silently. Then ask volunteers to read parts of it aloud.

Your Turn. With the class, read the instructions under "Your Turn." Have students work with partners as they talk about and write a letter requesting information about ways to help animals and the earth. Have students read their letters aloud to others and get suggestions for improvements. Students then revise their letters and make clean copies.

SKILLS JOURNAL PAGES 112–114

Page 112: Reading comprehension; writing. Students match correct answers with sentences. **Page 113: Research; using a chart; writing.** Students choose an animal to research, complete a chart, then write about their animal. **Page 114: Reading comprehension; brainstorming; note-taking.** Students complete a check list, discuss the topic with a partner, and write their ideas. Teaching suggestions are provided in the Skills Journal annotation.

3 ◆ EXTEND

Writing a letter. You may want to have the class write a letter as a group to one of the organizations listed on page 114. Brainstorm what to include and discuss how to organize the letter: date, address, greeting, body of the letter, closing, signature. Practice writing addresses and dates as needed. Provide a model for students to follow.

ART Making posters. Students can make illustrations and slogans to encourage others to help save animals and the environment. Display posters around the room or in the halls.

SOCIAL STUDIES Learning about protected species. Students can research additional information about protected species. What laws protect them? Are the animals protected everywhere or just in certain areas? Does everyone agree with the laws? What are the different views of the law? Invite students to share their findings with the class.

SOCIAL STUDIES Debating laws. Depending on the level of the students, you may want to bring in recent newspaper and magazine articles that present different sides of controversial animal protection cases such as the wolves in Wyoming and the spotted owl on the West Coast. Have students choose sides and debate the issues.

SOCIAL STUDIES Starting a recycling campaign. Students can find out what other materials can be recycled and where they can be recycled. Students can make posters or flyers to distribute to encourage others in the school and community to recycle.

 **PROCESS WRITING PORTFOLIO** See the list of ideas and writing topics related to this theme.

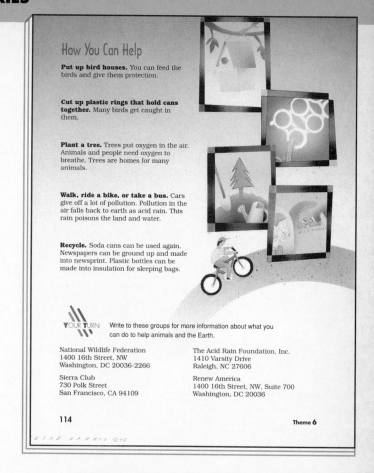

How You Can Help

Put up bird houses. You can feed the birds and give them protection.

Cut up plastic rings that hold cans together. Many birds get caught in them.

Plant a tree. Trees put oxygen in the air. Animals and people need oxygen to breathe. Trees are homes for many animals.

Walk, ride a bike, or take a bus. Cars give off a lot of pollution. Pollution in the air falls back to earth as acid rain. This rain poisons the land and water.

Recycle. Soda cans can be used again. Newspapers can be ground up and made into newsprint. Plastic bottles can be made into insulation for sleeping bags.

YOUR TURN Write to these groups for more information about what you can do to help animals and the Earth.

National Wildlife Federation
1400 16th Street, NW
Washington, DC 20036-2266

The Acid Rain Foundation, Inc.
1410 Varsity Drive
Raleigh, NC 27606

Sierra Club
730 Polk Street
San Francisco, CA 94109

Renew America
1400 16th Street, NW, Suite 700
Washington, DC 20036

114   Theme 6

- - - **ONGOING ASSESSMENT** - - -

PERFORMANCE Oral language. With books closed, have students talk about ways that animals are being protected and how people in the local area can help.

PORTFOLIO Writing. Save Skills Journal page 113 as an example of independent writing.

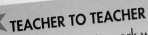

◆ TEACHER'S NOTES ◆

★ **TEACHER TO TEACHER**
You may want to work with a science teacher or invite a guest speaker in to share some local success stories with students.

★ **MULTICULTURAL AWARENESS**
Ask students about laws and opinions about animal protection laws around the world. What animals are special in other countries? Why are they special? Are they protected? If so, how?

★ **COMPUTER CONNECTION**
Encourage students to use the computer as they make notes and plan presentations. Students can also use on-line/internet services to access information relating to conservation issues and controversies.

LESSON 6
IN MY MOUNTAINS

 **STUDENT BOOK/SKILLS JOURNAL PAGE 115**

⭐ **KEY EXPERIENCES**

- Discussing nature
- Reading a poem
- Describing a scene
- Creative writing of a poem
- Contrasting night and day

⭐ **KEY LANGUAGE**

- *scent, stream, gurgling, creeping, breeze, floats, campfire, dying*

⭐ **MATERIALS**

- pictures of mountain scenes

1 ◆ INTRODUCE

Building background: Discussing nature. Show pictures of mountain scenes. Have students name the natural features and living things in the scenes. Make a list on the board. Classify these things under the headings: plants, animals, water, land, air. Encourage students to think about the sights, sounds, and smells associated with these places. (CALLA: Grouping)

MULTI-LEVEL TEACHING STRATEGIES

You can include all students by asking questions appropriate to each student's language level.

Speech Emergence: *Are there any animals in this picture? Is it quiet or noisy here? What animals live here? Do many people live here?*

Developing Fluency: *Why might people come here? What could you see at night in the sky? Do you like to be in places like this? How does it make you feel?*

2 ◆ EXPLORE

Activating prior knowledge. Open to page 115. Ask a volunteer to read the title of the poem, "In My Mountains." To prompt discussion, ask multi-level questions about the picture such as *Are there any*

trees? Where is the stream? Do you think the poet lives here? What can she see in the mountains?

🖪 **GUIDED READING** **Reading a poem.** Read or play the tape for the poem. Encourage students to listen with their eyes closed the first time and to imagine the scenes as the poet describes them. Read the poem again as students follow along in their books. Ask multi-level questions to check understanding. *Is the wind hot or cold? What can you smell in the mountains? Are there many animals? Where are the fish? How does the water feel? What can you see at night? What sounds can you hear? Does this poem make you feel happy or afraid? Why does the writer like the mountains?*

Rereading. Help students with the pronunciation of any problematic words. Then reread the poem chorally.

Independent reading. Have students read the poem silently. Then ask volunteers to read the poem aloud.

📖 **SKILLS JOURNAL PAGE 115** **Brainstorming; using a chart; writing.** Students fill in a graphic organizer before writing their own poems. Teaching suggestions are provided in the Skills Journal annotation.

3 ◆ EXTEND

ART Describing a scene. Ask students to describe a natural area that they like. It could be a park or other natural area. Invite students to close their eyes and visualize the sights, sounds, and smells associated with the place. Then have them write their ideas. Students can write a description of the scene and then draw pictures to illustrate it.

Writing a poem/Contrasting day and night. Have students look back at the poem and compare the sights and sounds of the daytime to those of the nighttime. Are they the same or different? Have students consider what is different between the daytime and nighttime in their town or city. Then invite students to compose a poem of their own.

In My Mountains

In my mountains,
Where the wind blows cold and fresh,
The scent of wild flowers floats on the breeze,
Animals are roaming everywhere,
Fish are swimming in the streams,
Streams that are pure and clear,
Streams that are cold.

The sound of night
With stars shining bright,
Of the stream gurgling on its way,
The animals creeping in the distance,
And the smell of the dying campfire,
Yes, I love my mountains.

Jill Yokomizo
Cleveland School
Oakland, CA

In the Wild   115

◆ TEACHER'S NOTES ◆

ONGOING ASSESSMENT

PERFORMANCE Oral language. With books closed, have students talk about the mountain scene and one of the senses that is described in the poem.

PORTFOLIO Writing. Save Skills Journal page 115 as an example of independent writing.

LANGUAGE NOTE
Point out the word *gurgling* as an example of onomatopoeia. Provide students with other examples such as *buzzing*.

TEACHER TO TEACHER
Choral reading is a good way to have students practice pronunciation and intonation.

LESSON 7
ALL STAR NEWS

 STUDENT BOOK/SKILLS JOURNAL
PAGES 116–117

⭐ KEY EXPERIENCES

- Discussing the environment
- Reading for information and pleasure
- Understanding graphs and charts
- Understanding humor
- Taking a poll
- Making a display
- Process writing

⭐ KEY LANGUAGE

- *chemical fertilizers, garbage, landfills, pesticides*
- *preserve, reservation, respect*
- *vacation, ancestors, canoes, hand-harvesting, stalks, wild rice*
- *lizard, mosquito, snow leopard*

⭐ MATERIALS

- pictures of environmental problems; samples of wild rice, brown rice, white rice

1 ◆ INTRODUCE

Building background: Discussing environment. Have students look back through the theme for different things that make up the environment. Encourage students to point out things that are problems and dangers to animals and other forms of wildlife. Show additional pictures to prompt discussion.

MULTI-LEVEL TEACHING STRATEGIES

You can include all students by asking questions appropriate to each student's language level.

Speech Emergence: *What makes up our environment? What are some problems with the environment?*

Developing Fluency: *What are some ways that people protect the environment? What will happen if people don't protect the environment?*

---

2 ◆ EXPLORE

Activating prior knowledge. Open to pages 116 and 117. Have students find and read the article headings on pages 116 and 117. Ask students to guess what the articles will be about. You may want to have students use article titles to form questions about the content. For example, for "Native Americans Protect Wild Rice": *What is wild rice? Where does it grow? How do Native Americans protect it?* (CALLA: Predicting)

Scanning for information. Do rapid scanning practice by asking questions such as *Which selection is about Native Americans? How many kids were asked the question in* Teen Talk? *How many places are on the chart?* (CALLA: Selective attention)

 Reading for information. Play the tape or read the selections, pausing occasionally to ask multi-level questions. Students who are able to should read the pages independently. **Understanding humor.** Read the joke on page 116 as students follow along

News From All Over

Native Americans Protect Wild Rice

AMAZING FACTS!

- The Komodo dragon is the world's largest lizard. It can stretch out the length of a compact car!

- A snow leopard can jump 50 feet. The record for a human jump is 29 feet, 2 1/2 inches.

- After a good drink of your blood, a mosquito's weight can increase up to four times.

- A future Hawaiian island is forming about a half mile under the ocean. It will take around 30,000 years for it to rise to the surface.

The Chippewa people live on the White Earth Reservation in Minnesota.

They are hand-harvesting wild rice like their ancestors did. Hand-harvesting protects the water. It preserves surrounding plant life. it uses no pesticides or chemical fertilizers.

The Chippewa float through the rice beds in canoes. They use 28-inch long ricing sticks to knock the ripe rice off the stalks. "I have harvested rice for 35 years," says Margaret Smith. "It's hard work."

Margaret Smith and Winona LaDuke started to sell the hand-harvested rice in 1985. The response was terrific. People told them that the pure, natural rice was just what they wanted.

"Instead of trying to tame the wild, we're showing people how to respect it," says LaDuke. "This helps both the Chippewa and the environment."

In the Wild   117

strongly about. Students can use the Teen Speak selections as models. Encourage students to draw illustrations or make collages from magazine pictures to accompany the writing. Display writing and pictures on a bulletin board titled *Save the Environment.*

SOCIAL STUDIES/ART Learning about national parks. If students are interested, have them find the names of some national parks and where they are located. Students can find pictures of popular sights and attractions in these parks. Alternatively, students can share information about a favorite vacation spot in their native countries. Students can also create vacation travel posters for a national park or vacation spot of their choice.

ONGOING ASSESSMENT

PERFORMANCE Reading. Check student responses for ability to scan for information.

PORTFOLIO Writing. Save Skills Journal pages 116–117 as an example of independent writing.

in their books. Be prepared to explain the answer. Invite students to share other jokes that they know.

MATH/SOCIAL STUDIES Taking a poll. Have students conduct a poll of favorite vacation places, environmental problems, or another idea from the All Star News pages. Students can prepare questions for oral interviews or a survey questionnaire to give to others in the school. Later students work in groups to compile the results and prepare graphs or charts. If there is a school newspaper, encourage students to write an article to share the results of their polls.

SKILLS JOURNAL PAGES 116-117

Process writing. Students read a sample newspaper article then write their own article on the same topic. Teaching suggestions are provided in the Skills Journal annotation.

3 ◆ EXTEND

SCIENCE/ART Making a display. Have students write about an environmental problem they feel

COMPUTER CONNECTION
Have students use a multimedia CD-ROM encyclopedia to find pictures and information about the following subjects: Chippewa Indians, Minnesota wild rice, komodo dragons, snow leopards, mosquitoes, Hawaii.

LESSON 8
ALL STAR NEWS

STUDENT BOOK/SKILLS JOURNAL
PAGES 118–119

⭐ **KEY EXPERIENCES**

- Talking about recycling
- Reading for information
- Making a trash graph
- Writing letters of request
- Working in collaborative groups:
  - project
  - research
  - letter-writing
- Planning a recycling campaign
- Practicing science process skills

⭐ **KEY LANGUAGE**

- *expensive, waste, steal, trash*

⭐ **MATERIALS**

- envelopes, postage stamps, poster board, markers, trash receptacles

1 ◆ INTRODUCE

Building background: Discussing recycling. Prompt a discussion of recycling by asking students to think about the things they throw away every day, what in our environment was used to make these discarded objects, what happens to the trash, and what they can do to make less trash.

┌─ **MULTI-LEVEL TEACHING STRATEGIES** ─┐

You can include all students by asking questions appropriate to each student's language level.

Speech Emergence: *What things did you throw in the trash today? Do you think any of those things could have been reused? Do you recycle trash?*

Developing Fluency: *What do you think would happen if all the forests were cut down to make paper? Have you ever seen a trash dump? What would happen if we ran out of trash dump space? How does recycling help the environment?*

Making a chart. During the discussion of recycling, write students' ideas on the board under the following headings: Things We Throw Away, What Was Used to Make Them, How We Can Make Less Trash. When the discussion is over, have students work in small groups to organize their ideas in a chart.

2 ◆ EXPLORE

Activating prior knowledge. Open to pages 118–119. To prompt discussion, ask multi-level questions such as *What do the pictures show? What do you think this lesson will be about? Do you know what Earth Day is?*

Bright Ideas. Have students follow along in their books as volunteers read the information in "Earth Day." Ask, *What types of organizations are these? Which organization interests you most?* Then call on other volunteers to read "Track Your Trash." Ask students to predict how much trash they throw away in one week. Students who are able to should read independently.

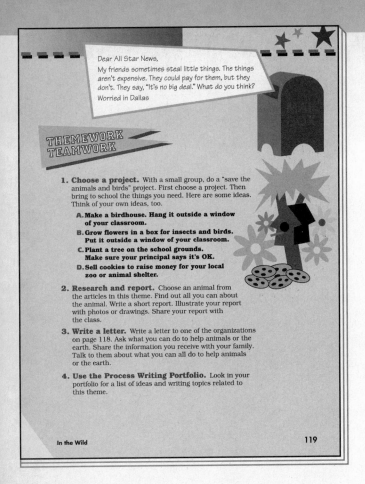

Dear All Star News,
My friends sometimes steal little things. The things aren't expensive. They could pay for them, but they don't. They say, "It's no big deal." What do you think?
Worried in Dallas

THEMEWORK TEAMWORK

1. **Choose a project.** With a small group, do a "save the animals and birds" project. First choose a project. Then bring to school the things you need. Here are some ideas. Think of your own ideas, too.

   A. **Make a birdhouse.** Hang it outside a window of your classroom.
   B. **Grow flowers in a box for insects and birds.** Put it outside a window of your classroom.
   C. **Plant a tree on the school grounds.** Make sure your principal says it's OK.
   D. **Sell cookies to raise money for your local zoo or animal shelter.**

2. **Research and report.** Choose an animal from the articles in this theme. Find out all you can about the animal. Write a short report. Illustrate your report with photos or drawings. Share your report with the class.

3. **Write a letter.** Write a letter to one of the organizations on page 118. Ask what you can do to help animals or the earth. Share the information you receive with your family. Talk to them about what you can all do to help animals or the earth.

4. **Use the Process Writing Portfolio.** Look in your portfolio for a list of ideas and writing topics related to this theme.

In the Wild 119

Writing letters of request. Have students work in small groups. Each group can select one or more organizations to write to for information. When responses to the letters are received, have groups reassemble and decide what action they might take to help save the earth. Have groups share their ideas with the class.

Mailbox. Have a volunteer read the letter. Ask, *Have you ever had something stolen from you? Did you think it was "no big deal"?* Have students work in small groups to compose a reply to the letter writer. (See Skills Journal page 119.)

Themework/Teamwork. Have students read the list of suggested projects and select one or more to complete. Students can work independently or collaboratively. Ask students to share completed projects with the class.

SKILLS JOURNAL
PAGES 118-119

Page 118: Expressing opinions; letter writing. Students answer the letter in Mailbox on student book page 118. **Page 119: Science skills.** Students read a car-

---

toon science experiment and draw conclusions. Teaching suggestions are provided in the Skills Journal annotation.

3 ◆ EXTEND

SCIENCE Tracking trash. Encourage students keep a log of the trash they throw away each week. Have them record the information on charts. At the end of the week, ask students to compare their charts and discuss how they can reduce the amount of trash they generate. (CALLA: Grouping)

MATH Measuring trash. Ask students to estimate the amount of trash they throw away each day. Have students use the measure of their daily trash to forecast how much trash they would create in a week, a month, a year, a decade, etc.

ART Creating a poster. Encourage students to create a poster to promote recycling. Display the posters in the hallway for the enjoyment of other classes.

SOCIAL STUDIES Planning a recycling campaign. As a whole class activity, plan a campaign for promoting recycling in their school. Have students divide into interest groups to work on the individual steps of the campaign.

PROCESS WRITING PORTFOLIO See the list of ideas and writing topics related to this theme.

ONGOING ASSESSMENT

PERFORMANCE Oral language. Ask students to tell why they selected a certain project to complete for this lesson.

PORTFOLIO Writing. Save Skills Journal page 118 as an example of independent writing.

PREDICTABLE PROBLEMS

As students work on composing their letters of request, circulate among the groups to help with proper letter and envelope formats.

LESSON 9
HOLISTIC ASSESSMENT

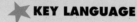 **STUDENT BOOK/SKILLS JOURNAL
PAGES 120–121**

★ **KEY EXPERIENCES**

■ Demonstrating comprehension

■ Summarizing the story

■ Thinking critically

■ Self-assessment

■ Writing about oneself

★ **KEY LANGUAGE**

■ *buddies, cages, grossest, home-less, museum, wildlife*

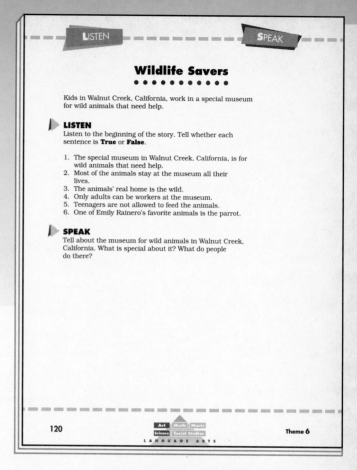

1 ✦ INTRODUCE

These two pages offer a variety of assessment opportunities. The left-hand page consists of listening and speaking activities that follow a taped presentation. In the speaking activity, students are asked to summarize what they have heard. The right-hand page consists of writing and critical thinking activities. These follow a reading passage that completes the listening component. You can use the activities to assess listening, speaking, reading, writing, and critical thinking skills. Have students work as a class or in small groups as you circulate and record observations on the **Anecdotal Record Form,** the **Reading Checklist,** and the **Writing Checklist** in the *All Star Assessment Package.*

Observing and recording student performance. Note the level of participation and the particular abilities of each student. How much do students understand? How well can they express themselves orally? What language structures do they use? What new words and concepts do they use? How actively do they participate? Use the **Anecdotal Record Form** in the *All Star Assessment Package* to record your observations and note areas for further development. Place in students' **portfolios.**

2 ✦ EXPLORE

Previewing. Open to pages 120 and 121 and let the students comment on the illustration. Read the title "Wildlife Savers" or call on a volunteer to do so. Give students time to read the listening questions.

 Listening. Read or play the tape for the first part of "Wildlife Savers." You will find the tapescript in the Appendix. Have students work independently to answer the listening questions. Read or play the tape again for students to check their work.

Speaking. Discuss what students have heard up to this point. Ask multi-level questions such as *Where is the museum? What animals are named? Are all of the workers adults?* If some students are struggling, play the tape again and summarize the story once yourself. Ask questions again. When you are satisfied with this stage, go on to the next.

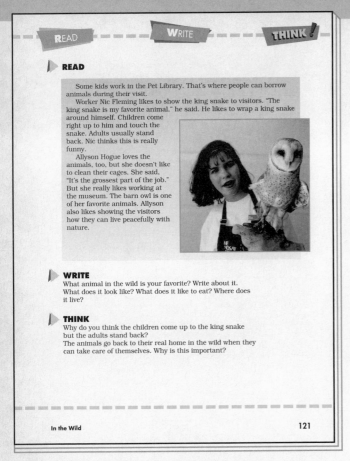

READ — WRITE — THINK!

READ

Some kids work in the Pet Library. That's where people can borrow animals during their visit.

Worker Nic Fleming likes to show the king snake to visitors. "The king snake is my favorite animal," he said. He likes to wrap a king snake around himself. Children come right up to him and touch the snake. Adults usually stand back. Nic thinks this is really funny.

Allyson Hogue loves the animals, too, but she doesn't like to clean their cages. She said, "It's the grossest part of the job." But she really likes working at the museum. The barn owl is one of her favorite animals. Allyson also likes showing the visitors how they can live peacefully with nature.

WRITE
What animal in the wild is your favorite? Write about it. What does it look like? What does it like to eat? Where does it live?

THINK
Why do you think the children come up to the king snake but the adults stand back?
The animals go back to their real home in the wild when they can take care of themselves. Why is this important?

In the Wild   121

3 ◆ EXTEND

ART/SCIENCE *Making a wild animal poster.* With students, discuss what they should do if they find an injured wild animal. If possible, invite in a representative of a state or local wildlife organization to talk with the class. Later students work in small groups to make posters with information describing what to do and what *not* to do if someone finds an injured wild animal.

★ **PREDICTABLE PROBLEM**
To help students understand, you may want to talk about the similarities and differences of a museum and a zoo.

★ **TEACHER TO TEACHER**
If you are able schedule a speaker from a wildlife organization, try to arrange for other classes to join yours.

🔊 **Reading.** Read or play the tape for the story on page 121 as the students listen and follow along in their books. Pause occasionally to ask multilevel questions. Then have the students do partner reading, alternating paragraphs.

Writing. Encourage students to tell you what they have heard and read. Do not look for word-for-word retelling, even from your best students. Have students write their summaries. (CALLA: Summarizing)

Thinking. Ask students questions such as *Do you think the teenagers get paid for working in the museum? Why or why not? Would you like to work there?*

SKILLS JOURNAL
PAGES 120-121
Page 120: Assessment; reinforcing key vocabulary. Students circle the words that do not belong in vocabulary groups. **Page 121: Self-assessment; Home-School connection.** Students check off things they can do and words they know. Teaching suggestions are provided in the Skills Journal annotations.

LESSON 10
LISTEN TO THE WATER

 STUDENT BOOK/SKILLS JOURNAL
PAGE 122

 KEY EXPERIENCES

- Reviewing the theme
- Singing a song
- Writing new verses

 KEY LANGUAGE

- *waterside*

1 ◆ INTRODUCE

Activating prior knowledge: Reviewing the theme.
Have students discuss the selections they read and
activities or projects they completed for this theme.

MULTI-LEVEL TEACHING STRATEGIES

You can include all students by asking questions
appropriate to each student's language level.

Speech Emergence: *What was this theme about?*
Which was your favorite story? Which was
your favorite activity?

Developing Fluency: *What have you learned*
from the selections in this theme?

2 ◆ EXPLORE

Activating prior knowledge. Open to page 122. To
prompt discussion, ask multi-level questions such
as *What is this song about? What might the music*
sound like?

 MUSIC Singing the song. Have volunteers read
aloud the song lyrics. Then ask all students to read
the lyrics chorally. Play the tape of the song, inviting students to sing along when they are ready.

 Creating an original song verse.
Students make up more verses and
motions for the song. Teaching suggestions are provided in the Skills Journal annotation.

3 ◆ EXTEND

Home-School Connection: Sharing the book. Invite
students to take their books home to share with
family and friends. They can read the stories to a
younger sibling, a parent, or a friend. Encourage
students to keep a record of who they read the
story to and their reactions.

MUSIC Writing another song version. Suggest that
students write a new version of the song that tells
a recycling story: beginning verses might describe
the consequences of not recycling (We saw some
_____ by the garbage dump/We saw toxic waste by
the waterside), middle verses could describe recycling efforts, and the ending could be the original
verses. Have students sing their recycling stories
for the class.

 TEACHER TO TEACHER
Students might like to perform their
songs for the enjoyment of other classes.

WRAP UP

ASSESSMENT

You have been collecting assessment data through the ongoing and holistic assessment options (Oral Language Checklist, Reading Checklist, Anecdotal Record Form) in this theme. Following are some additional assessment strategies that will help you evaluate your students' progress as well as adapt your instruction to meet their needs.

Student Self-Assessment. Self-assessment surveys are a means for students to have input into their own learning process. Students can use them to reflect on the work they have done and the learning strategies they have used during this theme. Be sure to check students' self-assessment pages for each theme in the Skills Journal.

Informed Instruction. Evaluate the checklists, anecdotal records, and Process Writing Portfolio collections from this theme as a means of informing your instruction.
- In which areas are students showing confidence and enthusiasm?
- In which areas are they hesitant or confused?
- Should you provide more classroom opportunities for oral language or writing?
- Would certain students (or the whole class) benefit from a focused mini-lesson on a certain area or skill?
- Remember to recycle skills as you teach the next theme and provide students with many opportunities to gain competence.

READING

Don't forget to check on and encourage students' independent reading. Students who weren't ready for independent reading in English at the beginning of this theme may be ready now. Students who continue to read in their first language should be encouraged to do first language book reviews and be an attentive audience for other students' reviews in English.

BOOKBYTES

Have students been able to use the *All Star BookBytes* CD-ROM software? The BookBytes' book list includes the titles on the Theme Booklists for all levels of *All Star English*. BookBytes helps students choose a book to read based on their responses to a short questionnaire, then prompts students to think about and respond to what they've read through writing, drawing, and drama. Students can print out their work and share it with others. They can also choose to see other students' work on-screen in a gallery presentation.

THEME CELEBRATION

If your class is participating as an All Star Team, the end of theme is a good time to review students' accomplishments with the Theme Booklist and Theme Projects. Consider posting a chart in the classroom where students may check off their accomplishments and, if you are using a point system, total their points for the theme. Students should strive to do their best and outdo their *own* scores, not compete with each other. Encourage students to present their All Star projects to the class to allow more oral practice and to sharpen students' presentation skills. You might invite other classes or families to attend the presentations.

In every theme the following material is on tape:

All literature excerpts, photo essays, poems, contemporary fiction and non-fiction selections.

The first two pages of All Star News sections.

Holistic Assessment spreads. The Listening selections on the first page of the spreads are printed below. The second page Reading selections have also been recorded.

All songs.

Theme 1. Page 20.

Meet José Ortiz

You are going to listen to the first part of the story. Listen carefully and take notes. Use your notes to answer the questions. Write your answers in complete sentences on a separate piece of paper.

My name is José Ortiz. I am Carmen's brother. I'm 15 years old. We are from Puerto Rico. Now we live in New York. I like it here very much. I have many friends in New York. I like to play basketball. My friends like to play basketball, too. Every Saturday we play at the park.

My sister Carmen likes to read and she likes to shop at the mall. I like to go to the mall, but not to shop. I hate shopping. I go to the mall with my friends to eat. We eat hot dogs, ice cream, and big, fat pretzels.

Theme 2. Page 40.

Mike's Problem

You are going to listen to the first part of the story. Listen carefully and take notes. Use your notes to answer the questions. Write your answers in complete sentences on a separate piece of paper.

Mike Monson is 13 years old. He likes to skate every day after school. But yesterday he didn't feel well. He had a stomach ache. He called his mother at work. She asked him what was wrong. He said, "Oh, Mom. I don't feel well. My stomach hurts." His mother told him to wait for her at school. She would come and get him.

When Mrs. Monson arrived at school, Mike said, "Mom, I can't be sick. I'm supposed to meet Maria after school to go skating." His mother replied, "Mike, you have the flu. You need to go home and go to bed. I'm sure Maria will understand. You can call her later and explain."

Theme 3. Page 60.

Bonnie Blair, A Champion on Ice

You are going to listen to some information about Bonnie Blair. Listen carefully and take notes. Use your notes to answer the questions. Write your answers in complete sentences on a separate piece of paper.

Bonnie Blair loves to skate. She grew up in Champaign, Illinois, where she learned to skate by the age of three. But Bonnie got serious about skating when she was a teenager.

In school, she was on the student council, and she was a cheerleader. She also competed in skating races and won a lot of them. If she wanted to compete in more and bigger races, she needed to practice more and not do extra things at school. It was a hard decision. Bonnie decided to devote her life to skating.

Theme 4. Page 80.

Martin Luther King, Jr.

You are going to listen to some information about Martin Luther King, Jr. Listen carefully and take notes. Use your notes to answer the questions. Write your answers in complete sentences on a separate piece of paper.

Martin Luther King, Jr., was born in 1929. His father was a black Baptist minister. His mother was a schoolteacher. Young Martin spent a quiet childhood in Atlanta, Georgia. After high school, he went to college and studied to be a minister like his father. Nobody could have guessed the place in history that Martin Luther King, Jr., was to have.

It all started in Montgomery, Alabama, on December 1, 1955. The buses in Montgomery were segregated. African Americans had to sit in the back of the bus, or stand, if the back was full.

One day, an African-American woman, Rosa Parks, was returning home after a hard day's work. She sat in the front of the bus, and then refused to give up her seat to a white passenger who got on the bus after her. Rosa Parks was arrested, and the African-American community of Montgomery was outraged.

Martin Luther King, Jr., led a peaceful protest. He organized a boycott of the bus service. For 381 days, the buses of Montgomery rolled back and forth on their routes, almost empty.

Theme 5. Page 100.

A Bad Day for Abdul.

You are going to listen to the first part of the story. Listen carefully and take notes. Use your notes to answer the questions. Write your answers in complete sentences on a separate piece of paper.

Abdul woke up late one day and missed the school bus. He asked his uncle to drive him to school on his way to work.

When Abdul walked into the classroom, the students were all sitting at their desks. They stopped talking and they all looked at him. No one smiled.

Mrs. Nunez said something to him that he didn't understand. She pointed to a desk in the back, so he walked to the desk and sat down. Mrs. Nunez started talking and wrote some words on the board. He heard her say something about science. He did not understand, but he opened his science book.

Then he heard Mrs. Nunez say his name. What did she want? He didn't know. The boy next to him said something and pointed at his book. But, he didn't understand, so he just smiled at the teacher.

The students laughed and Abdul wanted to cry. He just wanted to go home. He didn't think he would ever learn English.

Theme 6. Page 120.

Wildlife Savers

You are going to listen to some information about Wildlife Savers. Listen carefully and take notes. Use your notes to answer the questions. Write your answers in complete sentences on a separate piece of paper.

Kids in Walnut Creek, California, work in a special museum for wild animals that need help.

<pause>

There is a special museum in Walnut Creek, California, for wild animals that need help . Many of the animals there have been hurt. Some of them are sick. Others are homeless. Most of the animals go back to the wild when they can take care of themselves. The wild is their real home.

At the museum, the adult workers don't do all the work. Young teenagers also work very hard to take care of the animals. They brush the animals, feed them, and clean out their cages.

Emily Rainero loves talking to visitors about the animals. She takes them through the museum. Some days she takes the rabbit out for some grass. One of her favorite animals at the museum is a white rat. She and the white rat are buddies.

GRAMMAR SUMMARY

THEME 1 LOOK AT ME

Letters Review

Aa Bb Cc Dd Ee Ff Gg Hh Ii Jj Kk Ll Mm Nn Oo Pp Qq Rr Ss Tt Uu Vv Ww Xx Yy Zz

Number Review, pages 8-9, 17

Cardinal Numbers

1 = one	11 = eleven	21 = twenty-one
2 = two	12 = twelve	30 = thirty
3 = three	13 = thirteen	40 = forty
4 = four	14 = fourteen	50 = fifty
5 = five	15 = fifteen	60 = sixty
6 = six	16 = sixteen	70 = seventy
7 = seven	17 = seventeen	80 = eighty
8 = eight	18 = eighteen	90 = ninety
9 = nine	19 = nineteen	100 = one hundred
10 = ten	20 = twenty	1,000 = one thousand

Ordinal Numbers

1st = first
2nd = second
3rd = third
4th = fourth
5th = fifth
6th = sixth

Simple Present Tense, pages 4-6

Subject	Verb
I You We They	**live** in New York.
He She It	**lives** in New York.

Present Tense of _be_, pages 4-6, 12-15

Subject	Verb	
I You He She It	am are is is is	a student. an island.
We You They	are	in the United States.

Possessive Adjectives, pages 4-6, 8-9

Subject Pronoun	Possessive Adjectives
I you he she it we you they	my your his her its our your their

THEME 2 YOUR FAMILY, MY FAMILY

Prepositions of Place, pages 28-29
Prepositions of place tell where something is. These are common prepositions of place.

in	on	under
beside	between	

The ring is **in** the box.
The ball is **between** a chair and a table.

Present Progressive, pages 32-33
Use the present progressive to talk about an action that is happening now (as you are speaking).

Subject	_be_	Base Form of Verb + _-ing_
I	am	
You	are	
He She It	is	eating.
We You They	are	

THEME 3 GETTING ALONG TOGETHER

Regular Present Verbs: -s and -es, pages 48-49
Add -s to form the third person singular of most verbs.

She plays soccer.

Add -es to words that end in *ch, s, sh, x,* or *z.*

She teaches at a daycare center.

Here are some regular present verbs.

eat	eats	teach	teaches
play	plays	go	goes
walk	walks	watch	watches
ride	rides	practice	practices
pick	picks	wash	washes
clean	cleans	write	writes
help	helps	wake	wakes

Days of the Week Review, pages 48-49
Sunday
Monday
Tuesday
Wednesday
Thursday
Friday
Saturday

Compound Words, pages 44-46
A word or word group with two or more parts that act as a unit.

Here are some compound words from Themes 1, 2, and 3.

baseball	tryouts	workshop	weekend
rain forest	sunlight	basketball	lighthouse
dog house	fireplace	drugstore	hairdresser

THEME 4 HOPES AND DREAMS

Regular Past Tense, pages 68-69
Use the simple past tense to talk about an event that happened in the past.

Subject	Base Form of Verb + -*ed*, -*d*, -*ied*
I	
You	
He	
She	cook**ed.**
It	arriv**ed.**
We	cr**ied.**
You	
They	

There are three ways to pronounce past endings: /-t/, /-d/, and /-id/
Here are some examples:

/t/	/d/	/id/
laughed	played	wanted
missed	skied	attended
wished	snowed	rested

Irregular Past Tense, pages 64-67
Here are some irregular past verbs.

come	came	ride	rode
get	got	sing	sang
go	went	speak	spoke
grow	grew	wake	woke
hold	held	write	wrote
kneel	knelt		

THEME 5 NEW FACES, NEW PLACES

Modals, pages 84-85
Modals are words that come before verbs. They can change the meanings of
the verbs in some way. For example, modals can express ability or possibility.
Here are some examples.

He **can** swim but he **can't** dive.
Ten years ago she **couldn't** use a computer. Now she **can.**

Pronouns, pages 90-91
Pronouns take the place of people or things in a sentence. Here are some
common pronouns.

I	we/us	our/ours	myself
her/him	you	yours	yourself
he/she/it	they/them	his/hers	himself/herself

THEME 6, IN THE WILD

Future Tense: *be/going to,* pages 108-109

Subject	Be	Going to	
I	am		
You	are		
He	is		
She	is	going to	school tomorrow.
You	are		
We	are		
They	are		
It	is		rain tomorrow.

INDEX

(continued)